HONDA 1972-1977

WORKSHOP MANUAL

350F & 400F FOUR CYLINDER

**A Floyd Clymer Publication
This edition published in 2023 by
www.VelocePress.com**

**All rights reserved. this work may
not be reproduced or transmitted
in any form without the express
written consent of the publisher.**

INTRODUCTION

Welcome to the world of digital publishing ~ the book you now hold in your hand was printed using the latest state of the art digital technology. The advent of print-on-demand has forever changed the publishing process, never has information been so accessible and it is our hope that this book serves your informational needs for years to come. If this is your first exposure to digital publishing, we hope that you are pleased with the results. Many more titles of interest to the classic automobile and motorcycle enthusiast, collector and restorer are available via our website at www.VelocePress.com. We hope that you find this title as interesting as we do.

NOTE FROM THE PUBLISHER

The information presented is true and complete to the best of our knowledge. All recommendations are made without any guarantees on the part of the author or the publisher, who also disclaim all liability incurred with the use of this information.

TRADEMARKS

We recognize that some words, model names and designations, for example, mentioned herein are the property of the trademark holder. We use them for identification purposes only. This is not an official publication.

INFORMATION ON THE USE OF THIS PUBLICATION

This manual is an invaluable resource for those interested in performing their own maintenance. However, in today's information age we are constantly subject to changes in common practice, new technology, availability of improved materials and increased awareness of chemical toxicity. As such, it is advised that the user consult with an experienced professional prior to undertaking any procedure described herein. While every care has been taken to ensure correctness of information, it is obviously not possible to guarantee complete freedom from errors or omissions or to accept liability arising from such errors or omissions. Therefore, any individual that uses the information contained within, or elects to perform or participate in do-it-yourself repairs or modifications acknowledges that there is a risk factor involved and that the publisher or its associates cannot be held responsible for personal injury or property damage resulting from the use of the information or the outcome of such procedures.

WARNING!

One final word of advice, this publication is intended to be used as a reference guide, and when in doubt the reader should consult with a qualified technician.

PREFACE

This SERVICE MANUAL has been prepared as a service guide for the mechanic responsible for the upkeep of the HONDA CB 350 F and CB 400 F.

It is compiled into various functional groups and summarizes procedures for disassembling, inspecting and reassembling the machine components.

Strict adherence to the instructions will result in better, safer service work.

Modified information and operation procedures for the CB 400 F are given separately.

HONDA MOTOR CO., LTD.
Service Publications Office

CONTENTS

I. 8 RULES FOR EFFECTIVE SERVICEWORK 3
II. INSPECTION AND ADJUSTMENT 4
   1. Tappet 4
   2. Breaker point gap and ignition timing 5
   3. Carburetor 6
   4. Clutch 8
   5. Cam chain 8
   6. Engine oil 8
   7. Front brake 9
   8. Rear brake 9
   9. Air cleaner 10
   10. Drive chain 10
   11. Front forks 10
III. ENGINE 11
   1. On-vehicle servicing 11
   2. Engine removal and installation 11
   3. Cylinder head · Camshaft · Cylinder · Piston .. 12
   4. Oil pump · Oil filter 18
   5. Clutch 20
   6. Kick starter 22
   7. Gear shift mechanism 23
   8. Transmission 26
   9. Primary shaft 28
   10. Cam chain tensioner 30
   11. Crankshaft · Connecting rod 31
   12. Crankcase 34
   13. Carburetor 35
IV. FRAME 39
   1. Front wheel 39
   2. Front disc brake 42
   3. Rear wheel · Rear brake 45
   4. Steering handlebar 47
   5. Steering stem 49
   6. Front suspension 50
   7. Rear suspension 52
   8. Frame body 53
V. ELECTRICAL SYSTEM 57
   1. General description 57
   2. Ignition system 58
   3. Charging system 61
   4. Starting system 65
   5. Electrical equipment 69
VI. SERVICE DATA 72
   1. Special tools 72
   2. Maintenance schedule 74
   3. Torque specification 75
   4. Service data 76
   5. Trouble shooting 79
   6. Wiring diagram 84
   7. Specifications 85

CB 400 F SUPPLEMENT
I. TECHNICAL FEATURES 87
II. INSPECTION AND ADJUSTMENT 88
   1. Clutch 88
   2. Rear brake 88
   3. Wheel 88
   4. Spark plug 89
   5. Fuel filter 89
   6. Air cleaner 90
   7. Front suspension 90
   8. Rear suspension 91
   9. Side stand 92
III. ENGINE 93
   1. Piston rings 93
   2. Clutch 93
   3. Gearshift mechanism 94
   4. Carburetor 95
IV. FRAME 96
   1. Front suspension 96
   2. Rear suspension 98
   3. Frame body 98
V. ELECTRICAL SYSTEM 100
   1. Charging system 100
   2. Starting system 100
   3. Electrical equipment 101
VI. SERVICE DATA 103
   1. Special tools 103
   2. Maintenance schedule 104
   3. Torque specifications 105
   4. Service data 106
   5. Wiring diagram 109
   6. Routing 110
   7. Specifications 111
VII. CB 400 F '77 SUPPLEMENT 113

I. 8 RULES FOR EFFECTIVE SERVICE WORK

1. Use new packings, gaskets, O-rings and cotter pins when reassembling.
2. When tightening bolts or nuts where no sequence is specified, begin with center or larger diameter bolts and tighten them in a criss-cross pattern to the specified torque.
3. Use genuine HONDA parts and lubricants or their equivalent.
4. Use special tools where specified.
5. Clean engine parts in or with solvent after disassemling. Apply lubricant to their sliding surfaces when reassembling.
6. Coat or fill parts with grease where specified.
7. When assembling, check every part for proper installation and movement or operation.

Precautions for Readers
1. The reassembly procedures for engine and frame parts are not described. Follow the reverse order of the disassembly procedures.
2. The service data for each component is compiled on the pages 76 and 106.

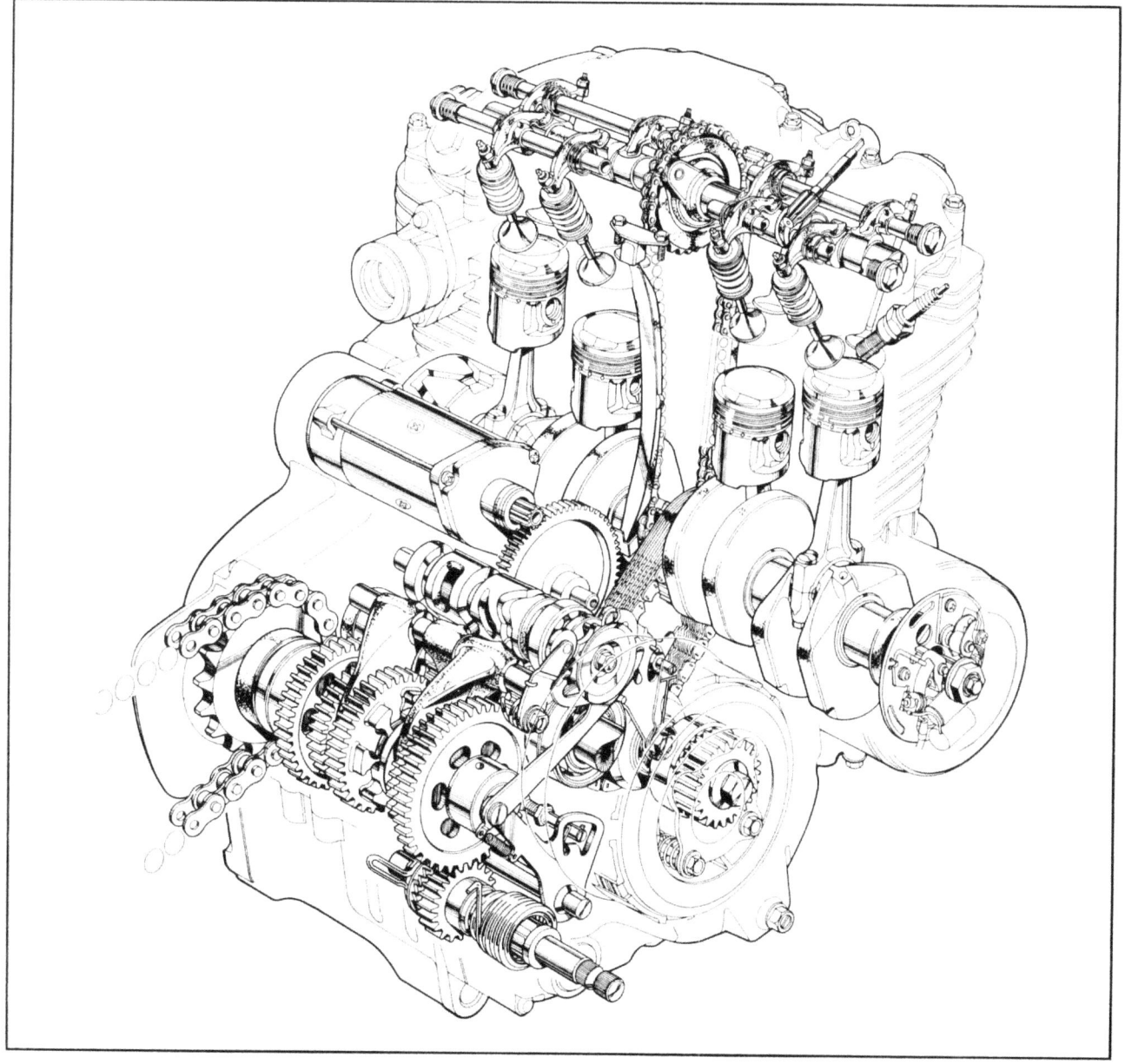

II. INSPECTION AND ADJUSTMENT

This section describes inspection and adjustment procedures for periodical maintenance of the HONDA CB350F and CB400F. Refer to the MAINTENANCE SCHEDULE on page 74. For items other than those described in this section, refer to "Inspection" of each part in this manual.

Fig. 2-1　① Special nut　③ Matching mark
　　　　 ② Mark "T" 1.4

Fig. 2-2　Cylinder No

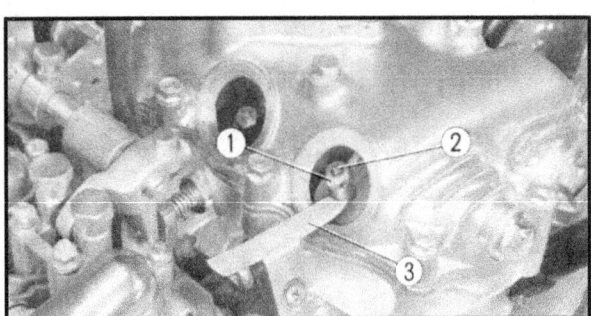

Fig. 2-3　① Lock nut　③ Feeler gauge
　　　　 ② Adjusting screw

1. TAPPET

Inspection and adjustment of tappet clearance should be made when the engine is cold.
1. Remove the fuel tank.
2. Remove the eight tappet hole caps and the point cover.
3. Rotate the crankshaft clockwise at the special nut to align the "T" mark 1.4 with the matching mark.
4. Make sure the No. 1 piston is at the TDC position on the compression stroke. If it isn't, rotate the crankshaft a full turn clockwise to it.
5. Check and adjust the tappet clearance of the "O" valves. (See table below).
To adjust, loosen the lock nut and turn the adjusting screw.

Tappet clearance	Intake valve 0.05 mm (0.002 in.)
	Exhaust valve 0.05 mm (0.002 in.)

Cylinder	No. 1	No. 2	No. 3	No. 4
Intake valve	O	×	O	×
Exhaust valve	O	O	×	×

6. Rotate the crankshaft a full turn clockwise to align the "T" mark 1.4 with the matching mark (in this position, the No. 4 piston is at TDC of the compression stroke) and check the "×" valves for correct tappet clearance.
7. After inspecting and adjusting the tappet clearance, install the tappet hole caps and point cover.
8. Install the fuel tank. Check fuel tube for proper connection.

II. INSPECTION AND ADJUSTMENT

2. BREAKER POINT GAP AND IGNITION TIMING

Breaker point gap

1. Remove the point cover.
2. Rotate the crankshaft clockwise at the special nut. Check the maximum gap of the points 1.4.
   Maximum gap: **0.3~0.4 mm (0.012~0.016 in.)**
   To adjust loosen screw "a" and move the breaker base 1.4.
3. Check the point gap of the points 2.3 in the same manner as for the points 1.4.
   To adjust, loosen screw "b" and move the breaker base 2.3.

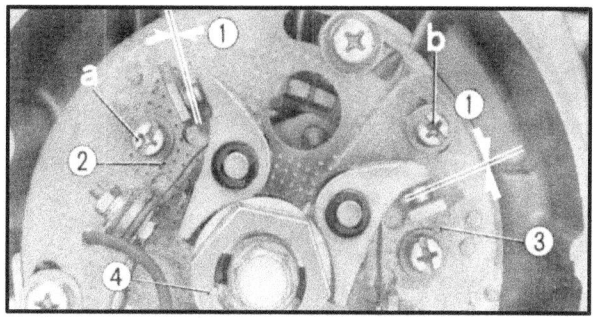

Fig. 2-4 ① Point gap ③ Breaker base 2.3
② Breaker base 1.4 ④ Special nut

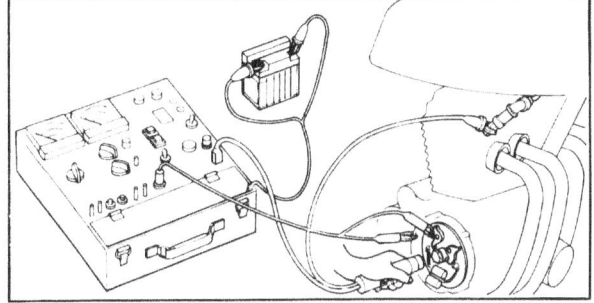

Fig. 2-5 Checking ignition timing

Ignition timing

Test and adjust ignition timing with a stroboscopic timing light (Service Tester SRH 500, Tool No. 07171-99900).

1. Make the connection for the service tester, following tester manufacturer's instructions.
   Connect the timing light cord to the spark plug of the No. 1 or 4 cylinder.
2. Start the engine and set the idle speed to 1,200 rpm. Illuminate the matching mark with the timing light and check if the "F" mark 1.4 is aligned with the matching mark. If it is not, loosen the three screws "c" and move the breaker base plate "e" in either direction.
   Moving the plate to the right will advance the ignition timing and to the left will retard the timing.
3. Increase the engine speed to 2,500 rpm and check the matching mark. If the mark remains within the advance marks, the timing is correct.
4. Connect the timing light cord to the spark plug of the No. 2 or 3 cylinder. Idling the engine, check if the mark "F" 2.3 is aligned with the matching mark. If it is not, loosen the two screws "d" and move the breaker base plate "f" in either direction.

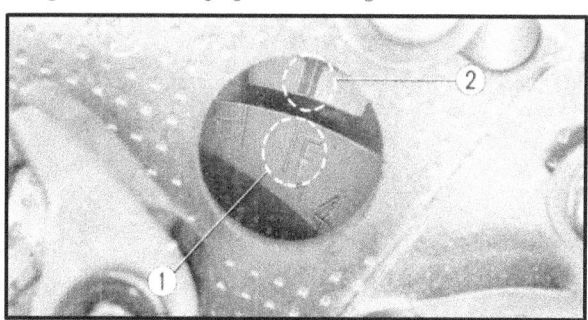

Fig. 2-6 ① Mark "F" 1.4
② Matching mark

Fig. 2-7 ① Breaker base plate "e"
② Breaker base plate "f"

5. Increase the engine speed to 2,500 rpm and check if the "F" mark 2.3 remains within the two advance marks.

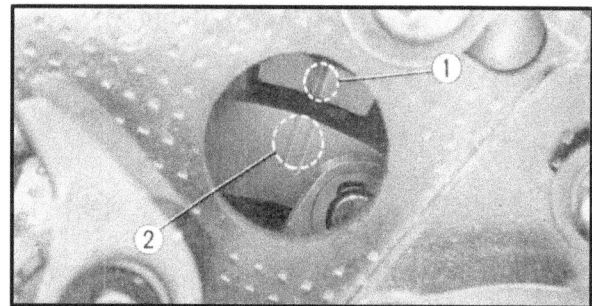

Fig. 2-8 ① Matching mark
② Advance marks

II. INSPECTION AND ADJUSTMENT

Fig. 2-9 ① Throttle stop screw

3. CARBURETOR

The carburetor should be serviced after the engine is warm.

Checking idle engine speed

1. To set the engine speed to 1,200 rpm, turn the throttle stop screw. Turning the screw clockwise (in direction "A") will increase the engine idle speed, and turning counterclockwise (in direction "B") will decrease engine idle speed.

Checking synchronization

1. Remove the four screws from the intake manifolds of the carburetors. Install attachment A (Tool No. 07510-3000100) and B (Tool No. 07510-3000200) and install the vacuum gauges (Tool No. 07504-3000100).
2. Start the engine and read each gauge.
   Specified value: **16~24 cmHg**
   NOTE:
   All the gauges should register the same value within the specification.

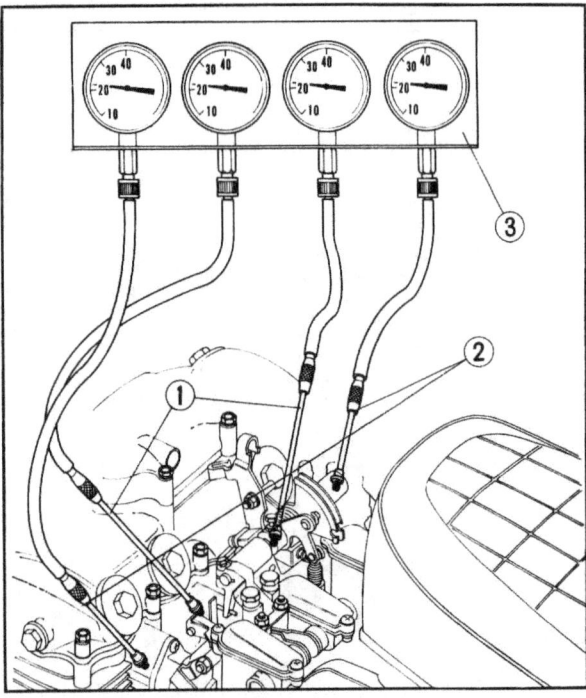

Fig. 2-10 ① Adaptor A ③ Vacuum gauge
② Adaptor B

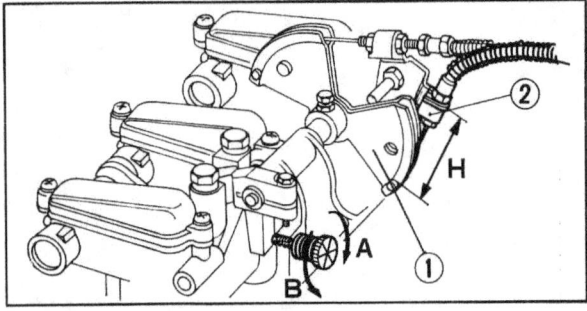

Fig. 2-11 ① Throttle lever
② Stay

Adjusting synchronization

1. Remove the fuel tank. Connect the fuel tube of the carburetor to the tank.
2. Turn the throttle stop screw to adjust the distance (H) between the throttle lever and stay to **56 mm (2.205 in.)**. Turning the screw clockwise (direction "A") will increase the distance (H), and turning it counterclockwise (direction "B") will decrease the distance.
3. Start the engine and check that the value is within the specification. If out of specification, loosen the lock nut and turn the adjusting screw. Turning the screw in direction "B" will increase the vacuum pressure, and turning it in direction "A" will decrease the pressure.

NOTE:
After adjustment, tighten the lock nut securely and snap the throttle grip three or four times to check synchronization.

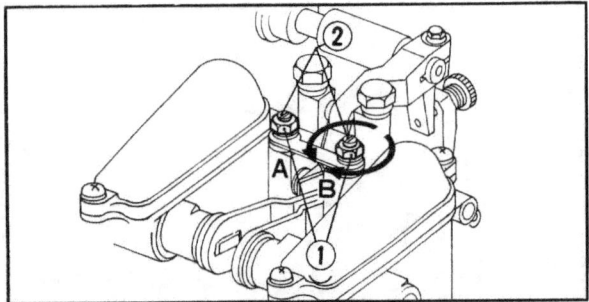

Fig. 2-12 ① Lock nut
② Adjusting screw

II. INSPECTION AND ADJUSTMENT

Adjusting fast idle speed

The adjustment should be made after the engine is warmed-up after synchronizing the carburetors.

1. Place the choke lever in the fully open position and check the clearance (ℓ) between the link plate and adjusting screw.
   Specified clearance: **0~0.3 mm (0~0.012 in.)**
   To adjust the clearance, loosen the lock nut and turn the adjusting screw. Turning the screw clockwise (in direction "A") will decrease the clearance and turning it counterclockwise (in direction "B") will increase the clearance.

2. Start the engine. Slowly operate the choke lever up and down to find the maximum engine rpm.
   If within **3,500~4,500 rpm**, the fast idle speed is satisfactory. If it is not, adjust with the adjusting screw. Turning the screw clockwise (direction "A") will increase the engine rpm, and turning it counterclockwise (direction "B") will decrease the rpm.

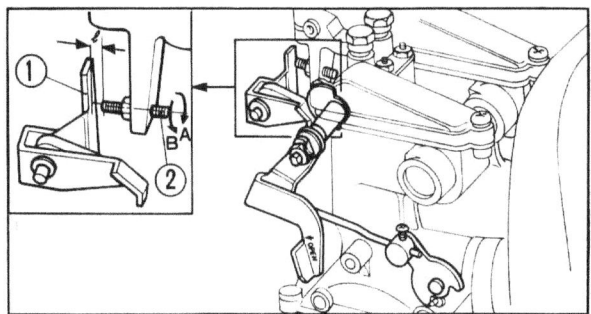

Fig. 2-13 ① Link plate
② Adjusting screw

Fig. 2-14 ① Choke lever

Adjusting overtravel stopper

1. Return the throttle grip to the closed position. Loosen the lock nut and turn the link pin to adjust the clearance (H).
   Specified clearance: **2.0~2.1 mm (0.079~0.083 in.)**

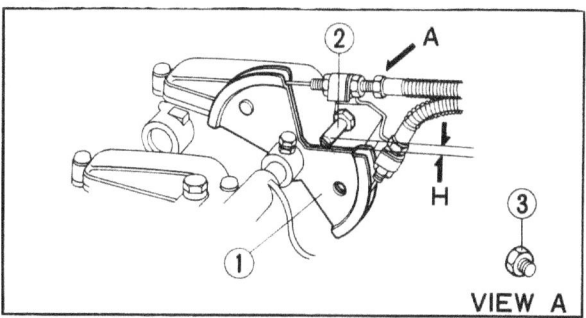

Fig. 2-15 ① Throttle lever ③ Lock nut
② Link pin

Adjusting throttle cable

1. Check the throttle grip free play.
   Specified play: approximately 10° around the grip
   To adjust free play, loosen the lock nuts and turn the adjusting nut. Turning the nut clockwise (direction "A") will increase the play, and turning it counterclockwise (direction "B") will decrease play.

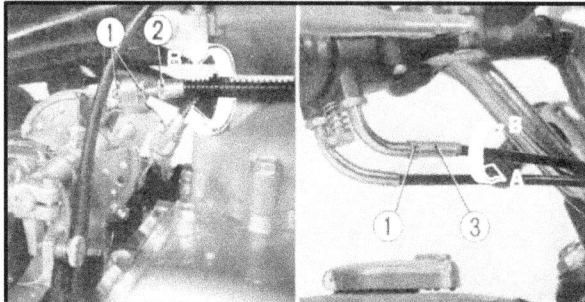

Fig. 2-16 ① Lock nut ③ Cable adjuster
② Adjusting nut

2. For fine adjustment, loosen the cable lock nut and turn the cable adjuster. Turning the adjuster clockwise (direction "A") will decrease the play, and turning it counterclockwise (direction "B") will increase the play.

3. With the throttle grip in the fully closed position, check that the throttle lever contacts the link pin. Replace the throttle return cable if the lever does not contact the pin.

Fig. 2-17 ① Throttle lever
② Link pin

II. INSPECTION AND ADJUSTMENT

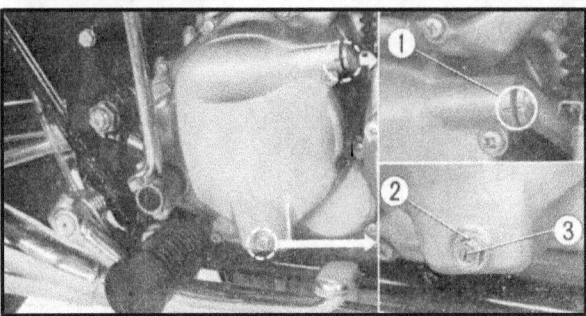

Fig. 2-18　① Matching mark　③ Clutch adjuster
　　　　　② Lock nut

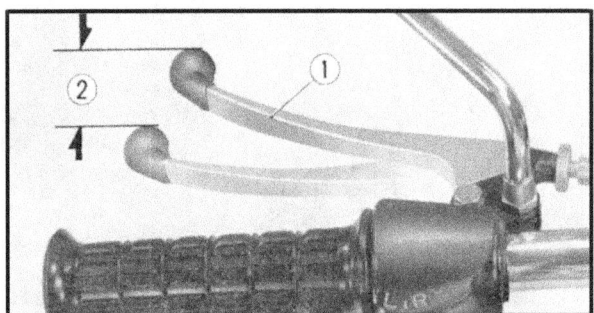

Fig. 2-19　① Clutch lever　② Clutch lever free play

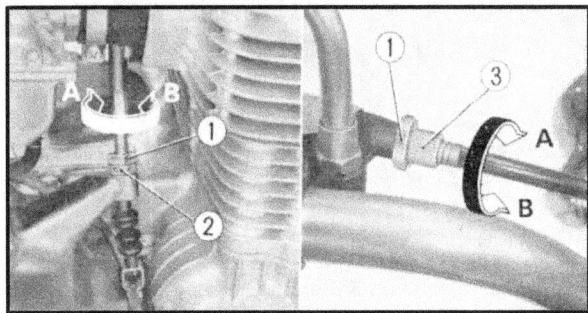

Fig. 2-20　① Lock nut
　　　　　② Clutch cable lower adjuster
　　　　　③ Clutch cable upper adjuster

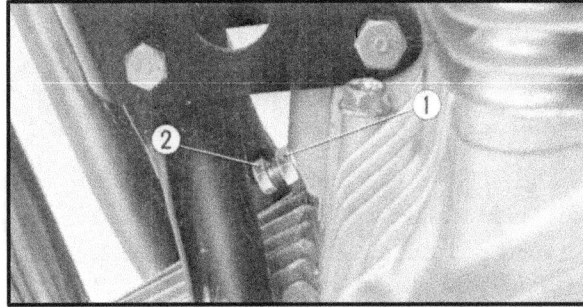

Fig. 2-21　① Lock nut　② Adjusting bolt

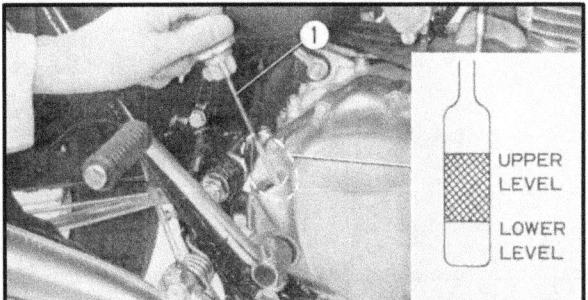

Fig. 2-22　① Oil level gauge

4. CLUTCH

1. Align the matching mark on the clutch lever with the mark on the right crankcase cover and loosen the lock nut. Turn the clutch adjuster counterclockwise all the way and back off about 1/4 turn. Tighten the lock nut.

2. Check the clutch lever tip free play.
   Specified play: **10~20 mm (0.4~0.8 in.)**
3. To adjust free play, loosen the lock nut. Turning the lower adjuster clockwise (direction "A") will increase the play, and turning counterclockwise (direction "B") will decrease the play.

4. Fine adjustment is made with the upper adjuster of the clutch cable. When adjusting, loosen the lock nut.
5. After adjustment, check for proper clutch operation.

5. CAM CHAIN

1. Start the engine.
2. Set the engine idle speed to 1,200 rpm. Loosen the lock nut and tensioner adjusting bolt with the box wrench contained in the tool kit.
3. Retighten the adjusting bolt and secure the lock nut.

NOTE:
Do not pull or push the tensioner push bar, as it is self-adjusting.

6. ENGINE OIL

Checking oil level

1. Lower the main stand and support the machine on a level surface. Insert the oil level gauge into the engine case to check the oil level. Oil should be at the upper level on the gauge.

II. INSPECTION AND ADJUSTMENT

Changing oil

1. Loosen the drain bolt and remove the oil filter by loosening its center bolt. Drain the oil from the crankcase.
2. Retighten the drain bolt and reinstall the oil filter.
3. Fill with recommended oil through the oil filler opening.
   Capacity: **3.5 ℓ (3.7 US qt., 3.1 Imp. qt.)**
   Recommended oil: **SAE 10 W-40 (All weather)**
   SAE 20 W-50 (Above 59°F or 15°C)

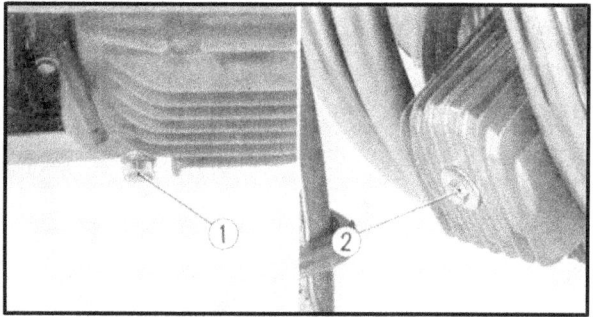

Fig. 2-23 ① Drain bolt
② Oil filter center bolt

7. FRONT BRAKE

Checking fluid level

1. Remove the fluid cup cap of the master cylinder.
2. Check to see if the brake fluid level is at the level line inside the cup. If the level is low, add **SAE DOT 3** brake fluid.

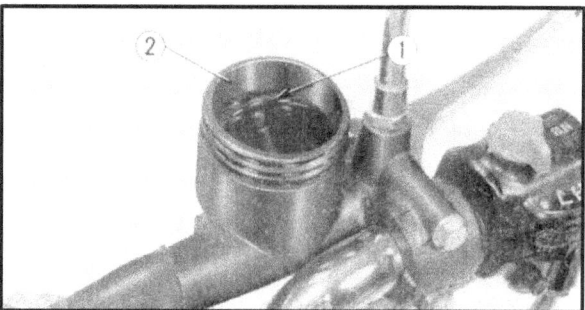

Fig. 2-24 ① Level line
② Fluid cup

Adjusting calipers

1. Loosen the lock nut and turn the adjusting bolt counterclockwise until pad B contacts the disc.
2. Turn the bolt clockwise 1/3 to 1/2 turn and tighten the lock nut.

Bleeding

1. Fill the fluid cup with brake fluid to the fluid level line.
2. Remove the bleeder cap and connect a vinyl hose to the bleeder valve.
3. As shown in Fig. 2-26, attach a piece of rubber about 15mm thick to the end of the handle grip to decrease the stroke as measured at the handle lever tip.
4. Operate the brake lever several times until resistance is felt. Loosen the bleeder valve about 1/4 turn with a spanner to bleed air. Retighten the bleeder valve and do not operate the brake lever. Repeat this procedure until no bubbles are in the fluid coming out of the valve.

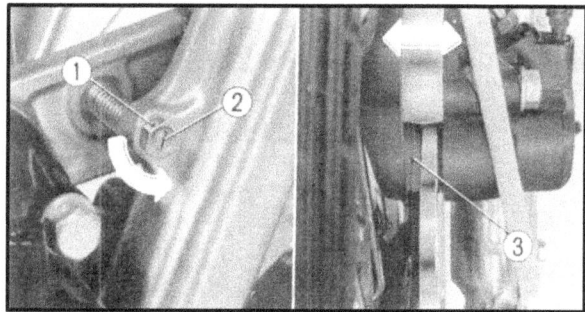

Fig. 2-25 ① Lock nut   ③ Pad B
② Adjusting bolt

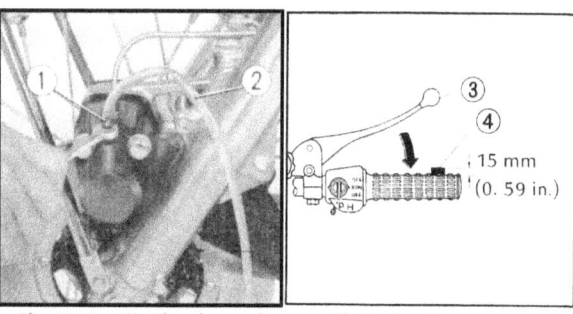

Fig. 2-26 ① Bleeder valve   ③ Brake lever
② Vinyl hose   ④ Rubber

NOTE:
Keep the fluid cup properly filled during the bleeding operation.

8. REAR BRAKE

1. To adjust the rear brake pedal height, loosen the lock nut and turn the adjusting bolt. Turning the bolt clockwise (direction "A") will decrease the height, and turning it counterclockwise (direction "B") the height will increase.

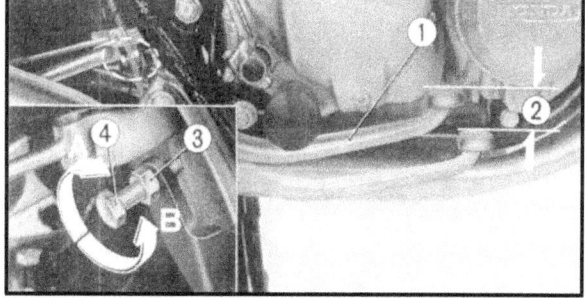

Fig. 2-27 ① Rear brake pedal   ③ Lock nut
② Free travel   ④ Adjusting bolt

II. INSPECTION AND ADJUSTMENT

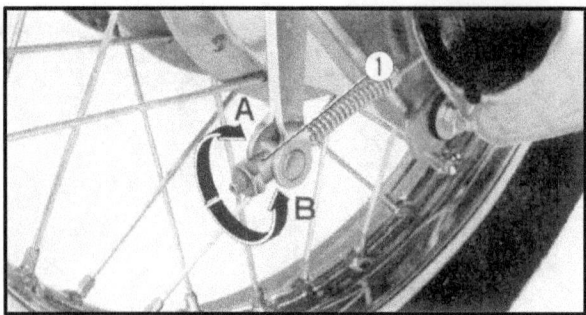

Fig. 2-28 ① Adjusting nut

2. To adjust the free travel at the pedal tip, turn the adjusting nut. Turning the nut clockwise (direction "A") will decrease the free travel, and turning it counterclockwise (direction "B") will increase it.
Specified free travel: **20~30 mm (0.8~1.2 in.)**

9. AIR CLEANER

1. Open the seat.
2. Remove the tool tray and air cleaner cover.
3. Remove the set spring to remove the air cleaner element.
4. Lightly tap the element and apply compressed air from inside.
5. Check the hole at the bottom of the air cleaner case for clogs.

Fig. 2-29 ① Air cleaner case ③ Air cleaner
② Set spring

10. DRIVE CHAIN

Checking drive chain tension

1. Check the chain tension by depressing it at a point halfway between the sprockets, measuring the slack.
Specified slack **20 mm (3/4 in.)**

Fig. 2-30 Checking drive chain sag

2. To adjust, remove the cotter pin, loosen the axle nut and lock nut, and turn the adjusting nut in either direction.
After adjusting, align the index marks on the right and left drive chain adjusters with the same notches in the side scales. Tighten the axle nut and install the cotter pin.

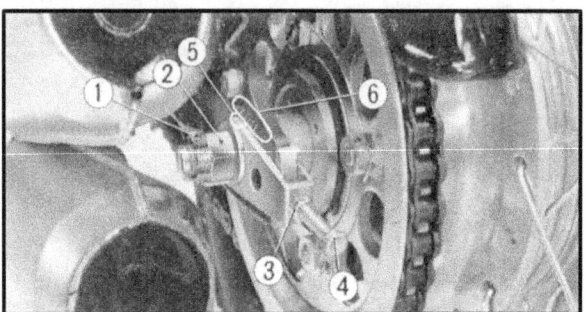

Fig. 2-31 ① Cotter pin ④ Adjusting nut
② Axle nut ⑤ Index mark
③ Lock nut ⑥ Side scale

11. FRONT FORK

Changing fork oil

1. Loosen the front fork bolts and drain bolts. Drain oil from the fork cylinders.
2. Retighten the drain bolts and fill the front fork cylinders with automatic transmission fluid.
Capacity: **105 cc (3.6 ozs.) per cylinder**
NOTE:
* **125 cc (4.2 ozs.) ATF is required to fill one fork upon disassembly.**
* **Torque the front fork bolt to specification.**

Fig. 2-32 ① Front fork bolts
② Drain bolt

III. ENGINE

1. ON-VEHICLE SERVICING

Parts to be serviced	Ref pages
Cylinder head and camshaft	12
Cylinder and pistons	12
Oil Pump and oil filter	18
Clutch	20
Kick starter	22
Gear shift mechanism	23
Cam chain tensioner	30
Carburetor	35
Electrical system (generator and contact points)	—

2. ENGINE REMOVAL AND INSTALLATION

The preliminary items for engine removal are shown in the diagram below. Proceed in the numerical order shown. To install, reverse the removal order.

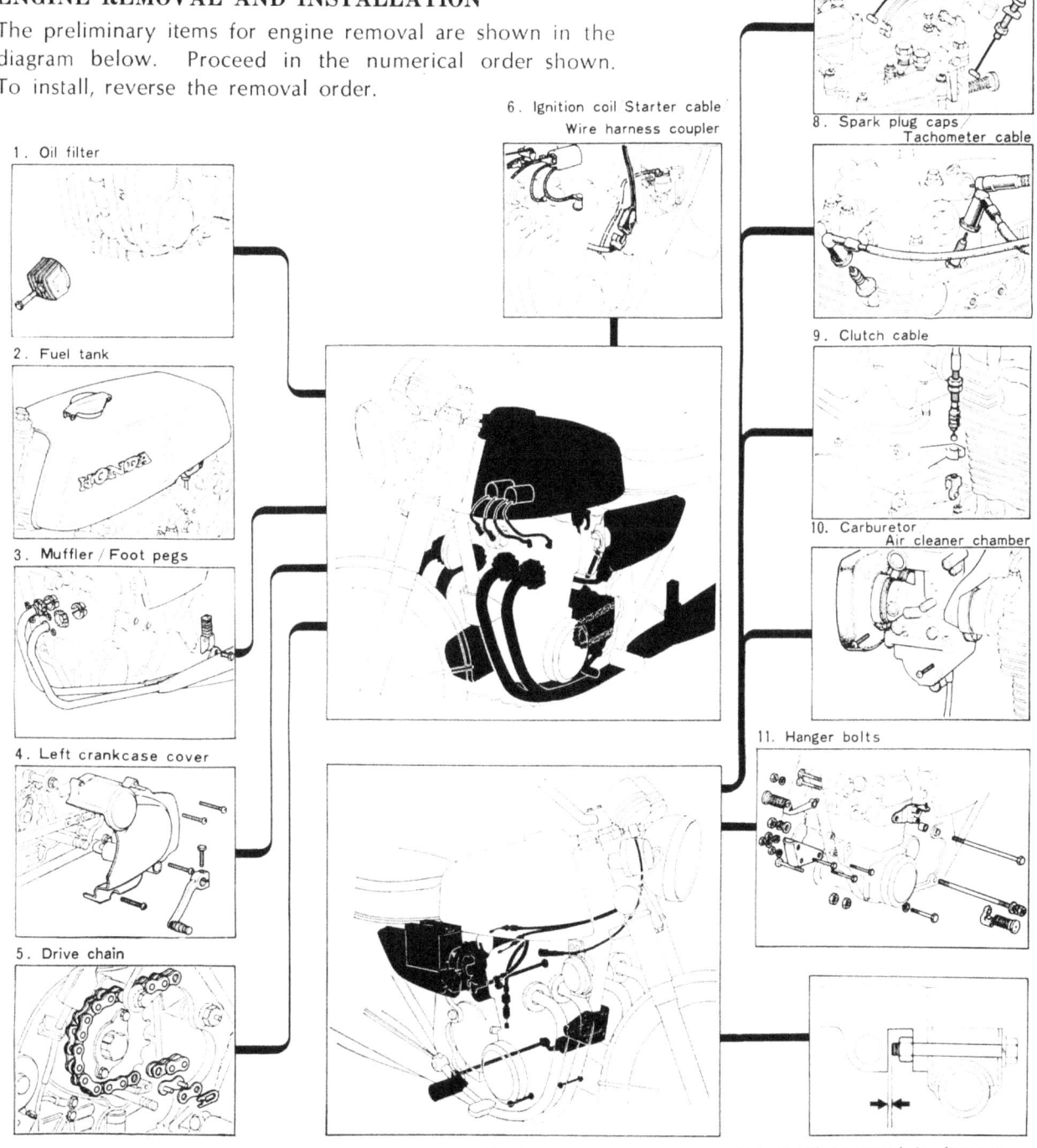

1. Oil filter
2. Fuel tank
3. Muffler / Foot pegs
4. Left crankcase cover
5. Drive chain
6. Ignition coil Starter cable Wire harness coupler
7. Throttle cable
8. Spark plug caps Tachometer cable
9. Clutch cable
10. Carburetor Air cleaner chamber
11. Hanger bolts

Fig. 3 1

Use specified hanger bolts (10x75mm) at lower crankcase front. Be sure to install spring washer.

3. CYLINDER HEAD, CAMSHAFT, CYLINDER AND PISTONS

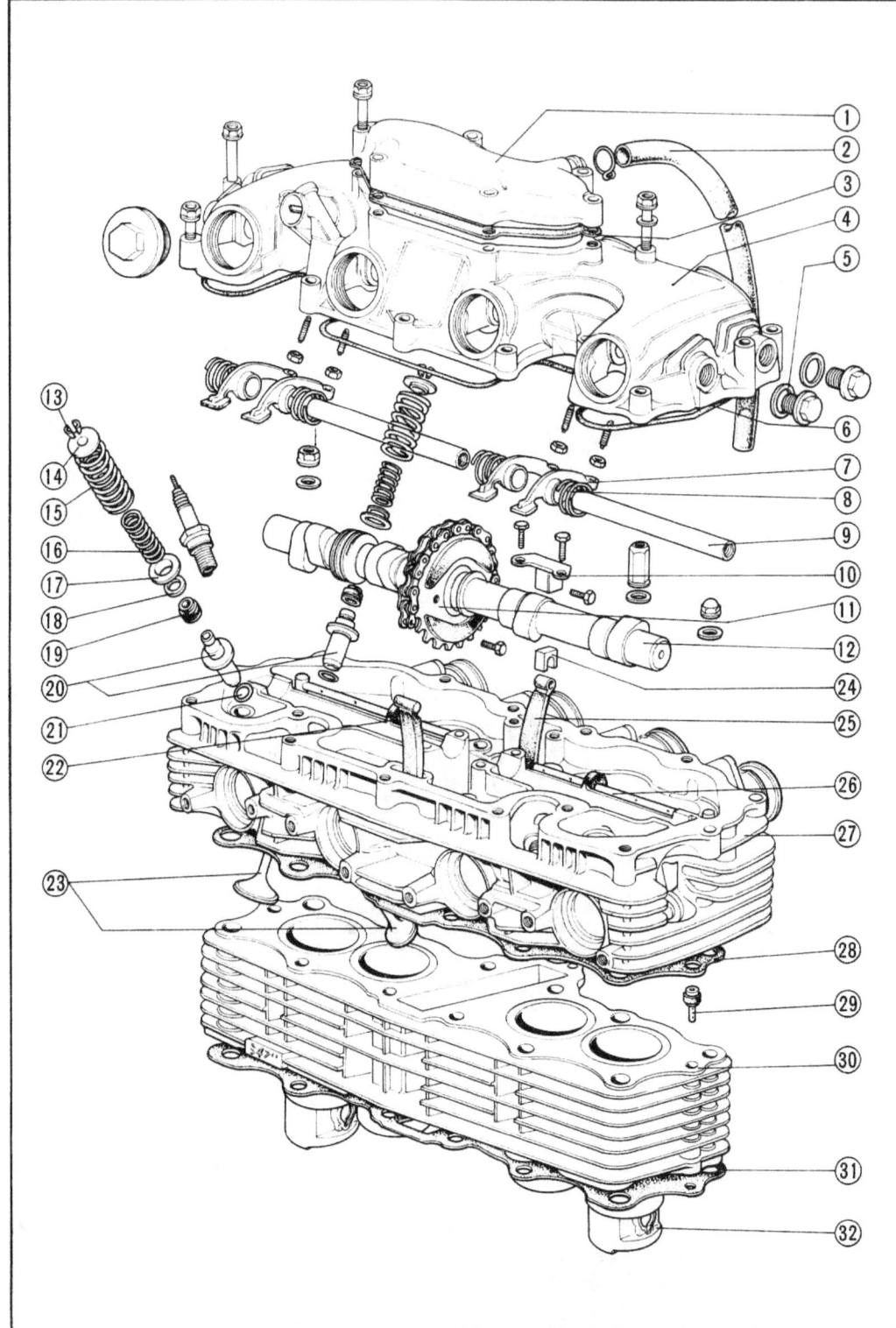

① Breather cover
② Breather tube
③ Breather cover packing
④ Cylinder head cover
⑤ Sealing bolts (four)
⑥ Cylinder head cover packing
⑦ Valve rocker arms (8)
⑧ Rocker arm side springs (8)
⑨ Rocker arm shafts (4)
⑩ Cam chain tensioner holder
⑪ Cam sprocket
⑫ Camshaft
⑬ Valve cotters (16)
⑭ Valve spring retainers (8)
⑮ Outer valve springs (8)
⑯ Inner valve springs (8)
⑰ Outer seats (8)
⑱ Inner seats (8)
⑲ Valve stem seals (8)
⑳ Intake and exhaust valve guides (4 each)
㉑ O-rings (8), 10×1.6
㉒ Cam chain guide
㉓ Intake and exhaust valves (4 each)
㉔ Tensioner dampers (2)
㉕ Tensioner slipper
㉖ Oil pipes (2)
㉗ Cylinder head
㉘ Cylinder head gasket
㉙ Oil control orifice valves (2)
㉚ Cylinder
㉛ Cylinder packing
㉜ Pistons (4)

Fig. 3-2

III. ENGINE

Disassembly

1. Open the seat. Remove the fuel tank.
2. Remove the ignition coils.
3. Remove the breather cover.
4. Disconnect the tachometer cable.
5. Remove the eight tappet hole caps and loosen the rocker arm adjusting screws. Remove the cylinder head cover. To remove the rocker arm shaft, remove the cap nut and screw a 10 mm (pitch 1.25 mm) bolt in the shaft.

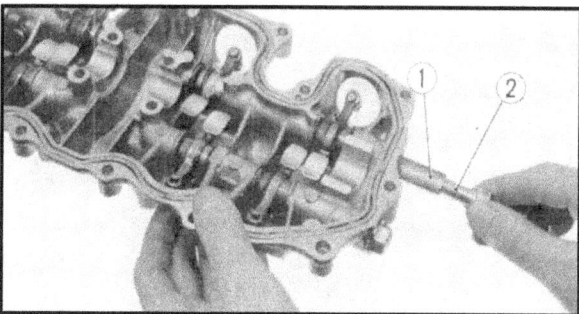

Fig. 3-3 ① Rocker arm shaft
② 10 mm (pitch 1.25 mm) bolt

6. Remove the muffler.
7. Remove the four spark plug caps and Nos. 2 and 3 spark plugs.
8. Remove the cam chain tensioner holder and the cam chain tensioner slipper.

Fig. 3-4 ① Cam chain tensioner holder
② 6×20 bolts

9. Remove the point cover.
10. Hand-rotate the crankshaft at the special nut until one of the cam sprocket knock bolts comes up. Remove the bolt. Further rotate the crankshaft a full turn to remove each bolt.

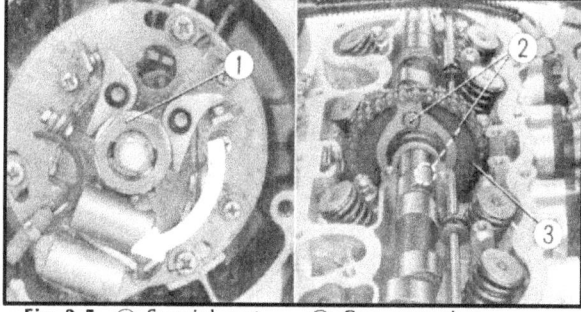

Fig. 3-5 ① Special nut ③ Cam sprocket
② Knock bolts

11. Remove the cam sprocket from the camshaft and remove the cam chain.
12. Pull the camshaft out from the right side.
NOTE:
Hold the cam chain with wire to prevent the chain from falling in the crankcase.

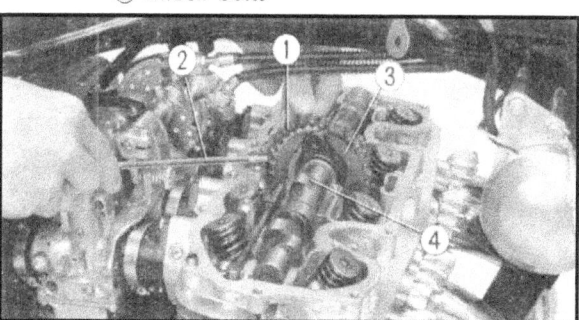

Fig. 3-6 ① Cam chain ③ Cam sprocket
② Screwdriver ④ Camshaft

13. Remove the air cleaner element and loosen the air cleaner chamber retaining screw.

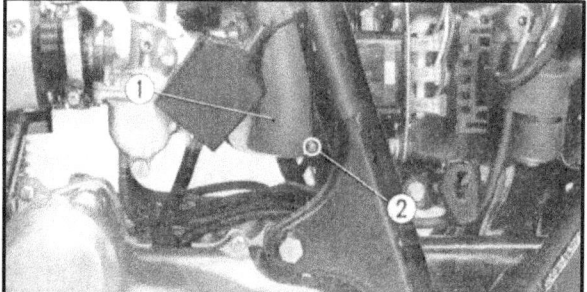

Fig. 3-7 ① Air cleaner chamber
② Retaining screw

III. ENGINE

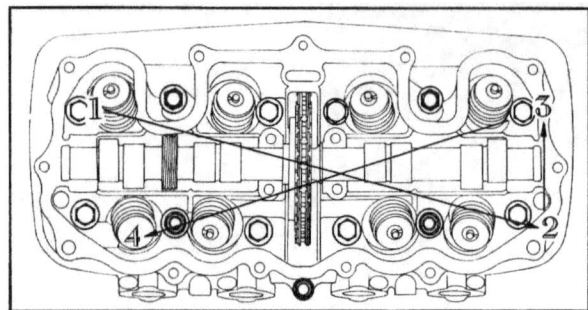

Fig. 3-8 Removal sequence of cylinder head securing bolts

14. Remove the carburetors.
15. Loosen the cylinder head securing bolts in a crisscross pattern, as shown in Fig. 3-8.
16. Remove the cam chain guide and the cylinder head.

Fig. 3-9 ① Valve lifter

1) Use valve lifter (Tool No. 07957-3290000) to compress the valve spring and remove the valve cotters. Remove the valve and valve spring.

Fig. 3-10 ① Valve guide remover

2) Replacing valve guide
   Use valve guide remover (Tool No. 07942-3290200) to remove the valve guide.
17. Remove the cylinder.

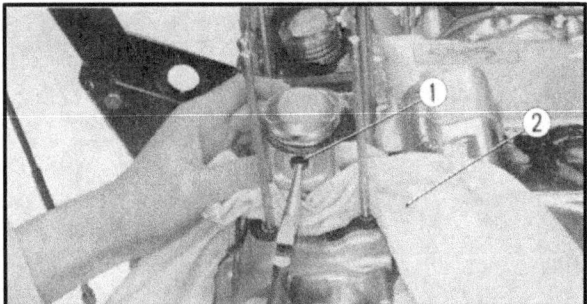

Fig. 3-11 ① Piston pin clip
② Cloth

18. Remove the piston pin clips to pull the piston pin out. Remove the piston.

NOTE:
1. **Put a cloth under the piston to prevent pin clips from falling into the crankcase.**
2. **Do not damage the piston when removing the piston rings.**

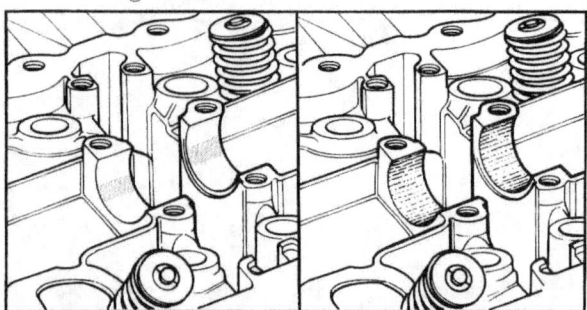

Fig. 3-12 Good   No good

Inspection
Camshaft and cylinder head
1. Check the rocker arm-to-rocker arm shaft clearance.
2. Check the cylinder head camshaft bearing surfaces for scratches and excessive wear.

3. Measure the cam height.
4. Check the camshaft center journal for deflection.
5. Measure the valve seat width.
   Apply a thin coat of prussian blue to the valve seat. Hold the valve against the seat and rotate it one turn. If the prussian blue shows uniform width all the way around both seat and valve, the valve contact is proper. If the contact is improper, lap the valve and recheck. If still defective, reface the valve seat.

CAUTION:
Use the valve seat grinder (Tool No. 07782-0020000, A set) to correct the valve seat width and contact from the following serial number:
ENo. CB350FE—1034532~
Read the valve seat grinder instructions carefully.

6. Measure the outside diameter of the valve stem.
7. Check the valve-to-valve guide clearance.
8. Measure the free length of the valve spring.
9. Check the cylinder head surface for flatness.

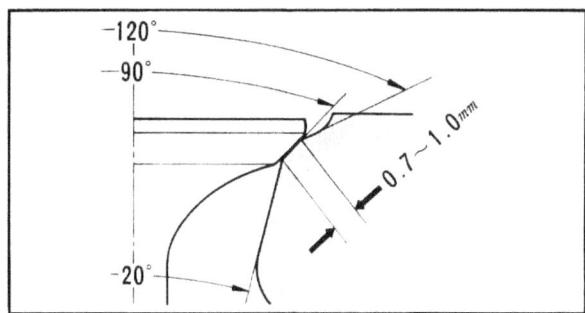

Fig. 3-13 Valve seat contact

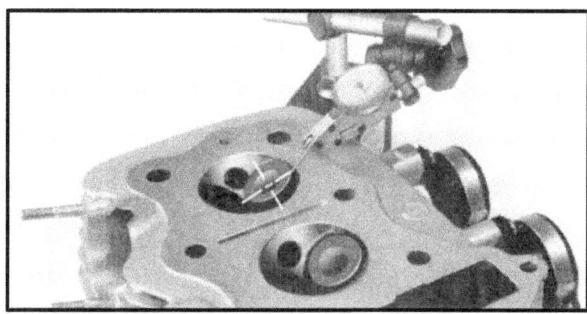

Fig. 3-14 Checking valve-to-valve guide clearance

Cylinder and pistons

1. Measure the inside diameter of each cylinder.
   Measure the cylinder inside diameter with a cylinder gauge at the top, center and bottom, in parallel (X) with, and at right angles (Y) to, the center line of the cylinder.
2. Measure the outside diameter of the piston at its skirt.
3. Measure the inside diameter of the piston pin hole.
4. Measure the outside diameter of the piston pin.
5. Check the piston ring-to-piston pin groove clearance.
6. Check the piston ring end gap.
   Insert the cylinder skirt to measure the gap with a thickness gauge.

Fig. 3-15 Checking inside diameter of cylinder

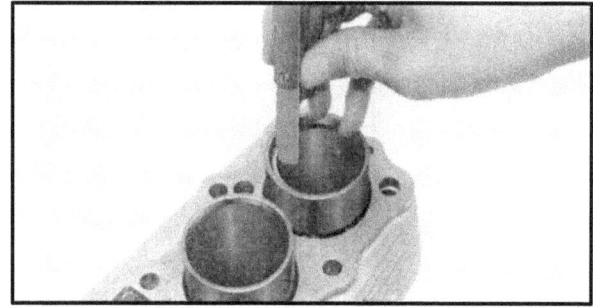

Fig. 3-16 Checking piston ring end gap

Reassembly

Piston rings

1. Use the piston rings of the same manufacturer in a set. Install the rings to the piston with their markings facing up.

Marking	Manufacturer
N	NIHON PISTON RING
R	RIKEN PISTON RING
T	TEIKOKU PISTON RING

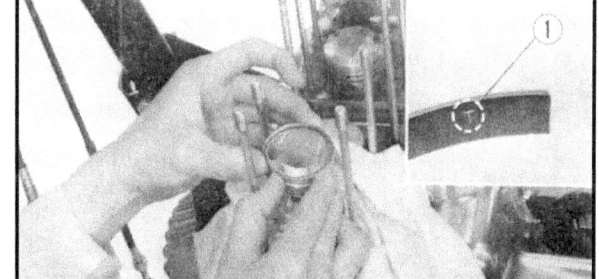

Fig. 3-17 (1) Marking

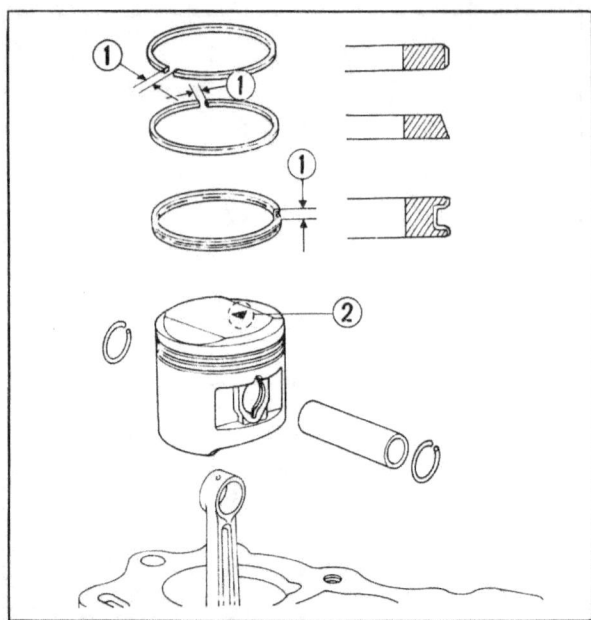

Fig. 3-18 ① Piston ring gap
② Piston mark

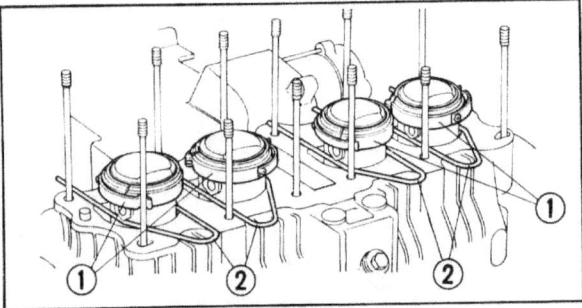

Fig. 3-19 ① Piston ring compressors
② Piston bases

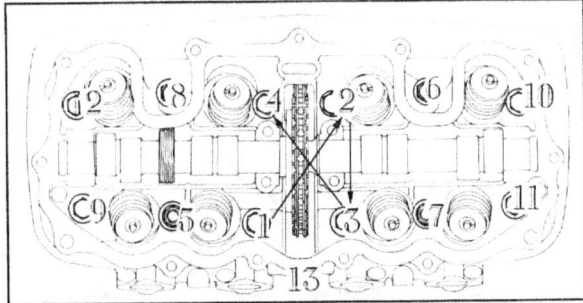

Fig. 3-20 Cylinder head nuts tightening sequence

Fig. 3-21 ① "T" 1.4 mark
② Matching mark

2. When replacing with a new ring, check for proper fit in the piston ring groove.
3. Position the rings so that their gaps of the top, second and oil rings are staggered 120° apart at right angles to the piston pin.

Pistons

Install the piston with the arrow mark on the piston head facing the front (exhaust side) and the "IN" mark facing the rear (intake side) of the engine.

Cylinder

1. Rotate the crankshaft so that all four pistons rise. Install the piston bases (Tool No. 07958-3330000) to the pistons. Set the base in the groove below the piston boss. Install the piston compressors (Tool No. 07955-3330000) on the piston rings. Gradually lower the cylinder until all the piston rings enter the cylinder bores. Remove the piston bases and piston compressors.

NOTE:
Apply a coat of engine oil to the piston rings before installing the pistons into the cylinder.

2. Check the oil control orifice valve for clogging before installation.

Cylinder head

1. When installing a new valve guide, insert it with a valve guide driver (Tool No. 07942-3290200) and ream with reamer (Tool No. 07984-200000).
2. Apply a coat of engine oil to the threads of the nut and tighten the nuts in a criss-cross pattern, as shown in Fig. 3-20.
   Torque specification:
   200 kg-cm (14.5 ft-lbs)

Valve timing

1. Rotate the crankshaft and align the "T" mark 1.4 on the spark advancer with the matching mark as shown in Fig. 3-21.

2. Install the cam chain to the cam sprocket so that the matching lines on the sprocket will be aligned with the upper surface of the cylinder head.
3. Install the cam sprocket to the camshaft with two knock bolts.

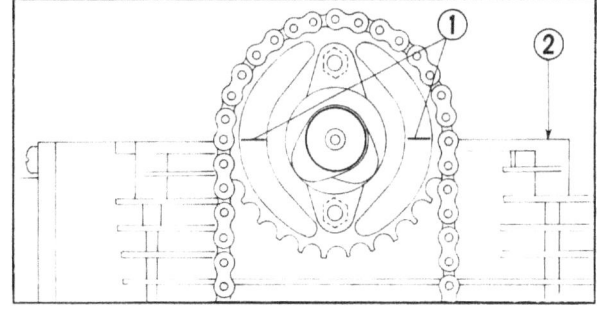

Fig. 3-22 ① Cam sprocket matching lines
② Cylinder head upper surface

Cylinder head cover

1. Apply a liquid packing to the cylinder head cover packing groove. Install the packing.
Replace packing if damaged.

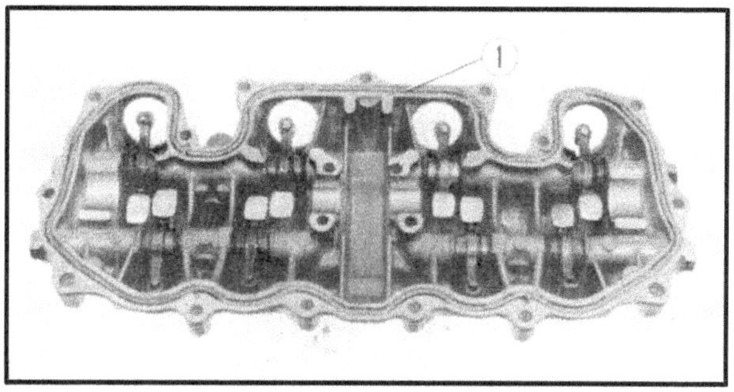

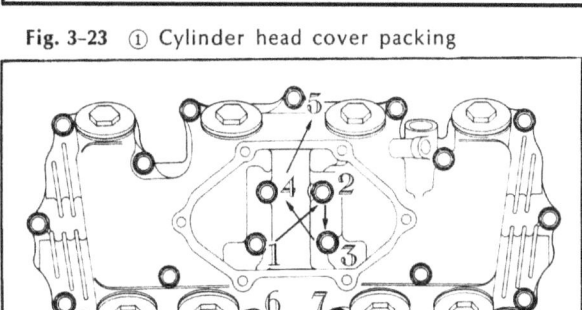

Fig. 3-23 ① Cylinder head cover packing

2. Tighten the bolts securing the cylinder head cover in the sequence shown in Fig. 3-24.
Torque specification:
 70~110 kg-cm (5.1~8.0 lbs-ft)
NOTE:
The torque difference of each bolt should be within 20 kg-cm (1.5 lbs-ft).

Fig. 3-24 Tightening sequence of cylinder head cover bolts

4. OIL PUMP AND OIL FILTERS

- The oil pump is a double trochoid pump driven by the primary shaft.
- One oil filter utilizes a screen and a paper element to provide two-stage filtering.

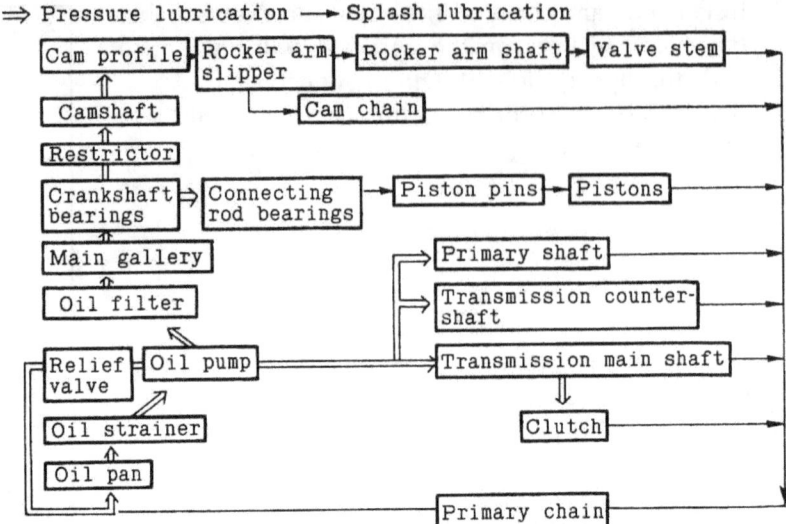

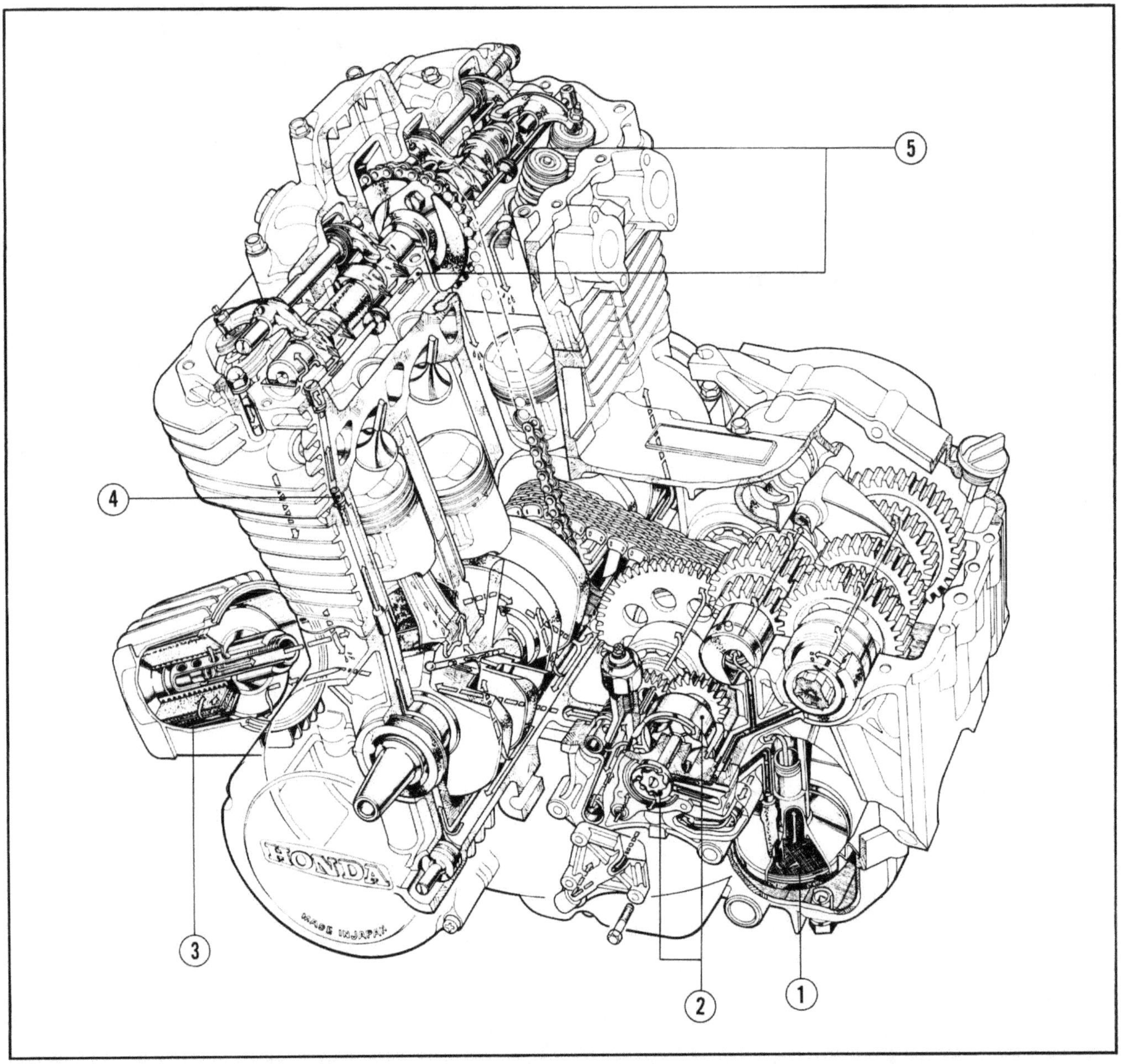

Fig. 3-25 Lubricating oil circuits

① Oil strainer ② Oil pump ③ Oil filter ④ Oil control orifice valve ⑤ Oil pipe

Disassembly

Oil pump
1. Remove the gear change pedal and left foot peg.
2. Remove the left crankcase cover.
3. Disconnect the oil pressure switch cord.
4. Remove the oil pump.

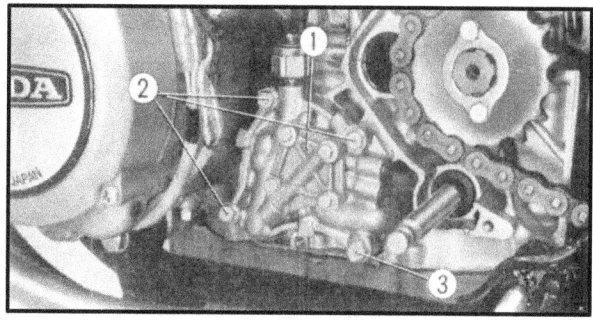

Fig. 3-26 ① Oil pump ③ 8mm bolt
② 6mm bolts

Oil screen filter
1. Drain the crankcase.
2. Remove the oil pan.
3. Remove the oil screen filter.

Fig. 3-27 ① Oil screen filter

Oil filter
1. Loosen the oil filter center bolt to remove the oil filter.

Inspection

Oil pump
1. Check the outer rotor-to-pump body clearance.
2. Check the inner rotor-to-outer rotor clearance.
3. Check the relief valve for dust entry and operation.

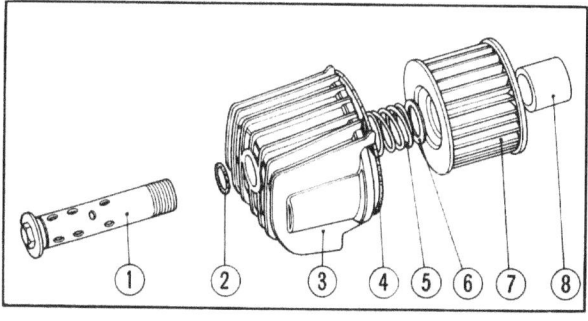

Fig. 3-28 ① Oil filter center bolt
② O-ring, 15×2.5
③ Oil filter case
④ O-ring, 89×4.5
⑤ Set spring
⑥ Spring seat
⑦ Oil filter element
⑧ Oil filter bolt collar

Reassembly
1. Be sure to install O-rings as shown in Fig. 3-29.
2. Check the oil level in the crankcase and add oil if necessary.
3. Make sure the oil filter is properly assembled. (See Fig. 3-28)

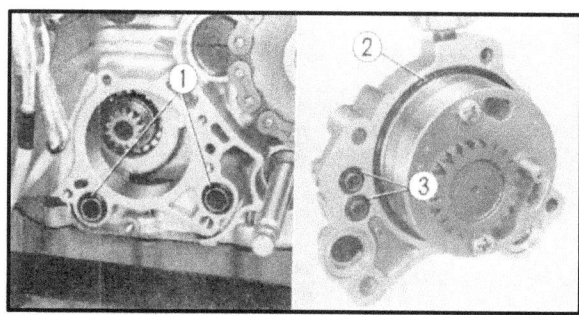

Fig. 3-29 ① O-ring, 15×2.5
② O-ring, 63×2.5
③ O-ring, 9.9×1.5

5. CLUTCH

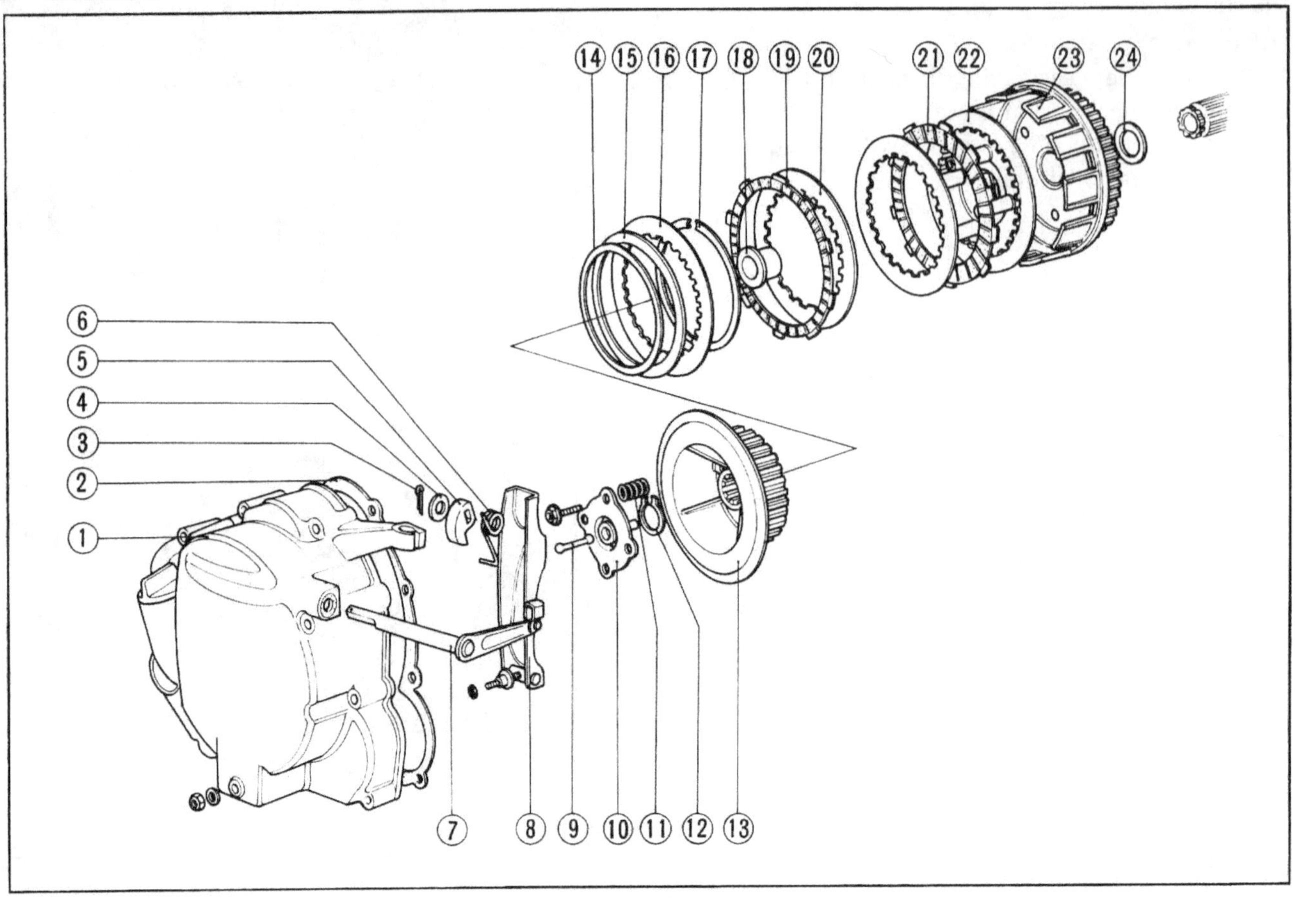

Fig. 3-30

① Crankcase cover, R
② Cover packing
③ Cotter pin, 2.0×15
④ Washer, 10mm
⑤ Clutch lifter cam
⑥ Clutch lever return spring
⑦ Clutch lever
⑧ Clutch adjusting lever
⑨ Clutch lifter rod
⑩ Clutch lifter plate
⑪ Clutch springs (four)
⑫ Snap ring, 25mm
⑬ Clutch center
⑭ Disc spring seat
⑮ Clutch disc spring
⑯ Clutch plate B
⑰ Special set ring, 92mm
⑱ Collar, 25mm
⑲ Clutch friction disc
⑳ Clutch plates (six)
㉑ Clutch friction discs (six)
㉒ Clutch pressure plate
㉓ Clutch outer
㉔ Thrust washer, 25mm

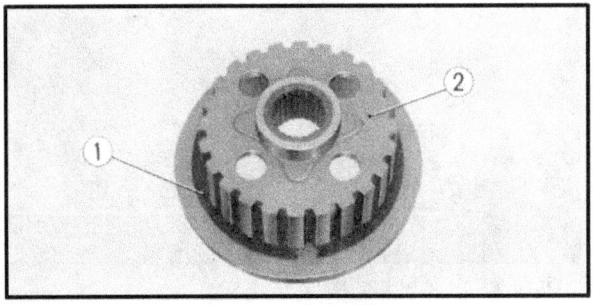

Fig. 3-31 ① 25mm snap ring
② Clutch assembly

Fig. 3-32 ① 92mm special set ring
② Clutch center

Disassembly

1. Drain oil from the crankcase.
2. Remove the right foot peg and kick starter pedal.
3. Remove the right crankcase cover.
4. Remove the clutch pressure plate.
5. Remove the 25mm snap ring and remove the clutch assembly.
6. Remove the 92mm special set ring from the clutch center. Disassemble clutch plate B, the clutch disc spring and disc spring seat.
7. Remove the clutch lever and clutch adjuster lever from the right crankcase cover.

Inspection

1. Measure the friction disc thickness.
2. Check the clutch plate for distortion.
3. Measure the clutch spring free length.
4. Check the clutch center-to-clutch plate B clearance (ℓ), and if beyond specified limit, replace clutch plate B.

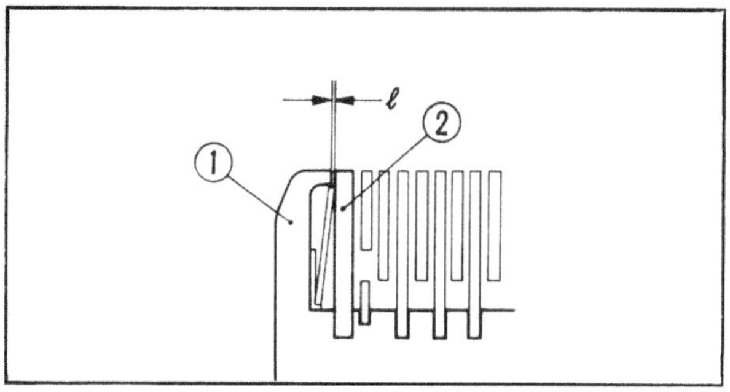

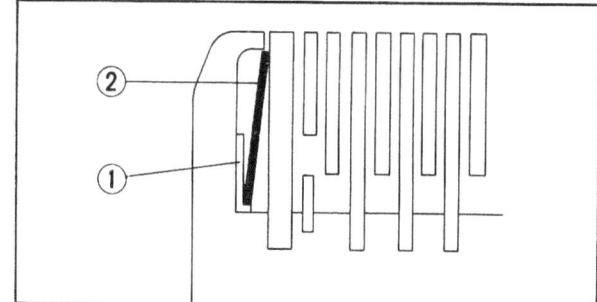

Fig. 3-33 ① Clutch center
② Clutch plate B

Reassembly

1. Install the disc spring seat and clutch disc spring as shown in Fig. 3-34.

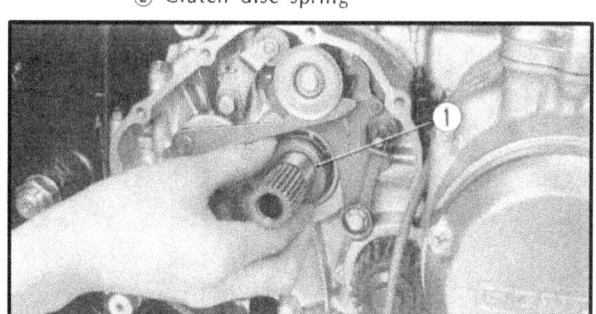

Fig. 3-34 ① Disc spring seat
② Clutch disc spring

2. Be sure to install the 25 mm thrust washer.
3. Alternately install the friction discs and clutch plates to the clutch outer, and install the 8 mm friction disc (see ⑲, Fig. 3-30).

Fig. 3-35 ① 25 mm thrust washer

MEMO

6. KICK STARTER

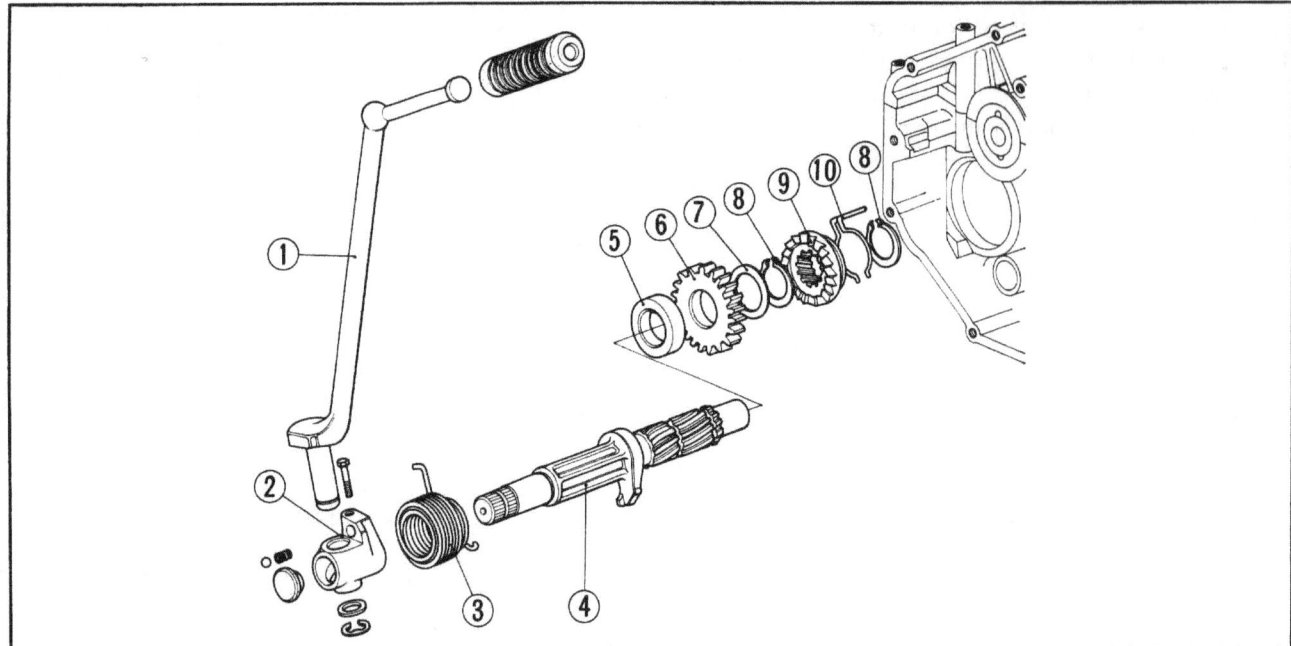

Fig. 3-36

① Kick starter arm
② Kick arm joint
③ Kick starter spring
④ Kick starter spindle
⑤ Collar
⑥ Kick starter pinion
⑦ Thrust washer, 20 mm
⑧ Set rings (two) 20 mm
⑨ Starter drive ratchet
⑩ Starter pinion friction spring

Fig. 3-37 ① Kick starter spring
② Kick starter spindle

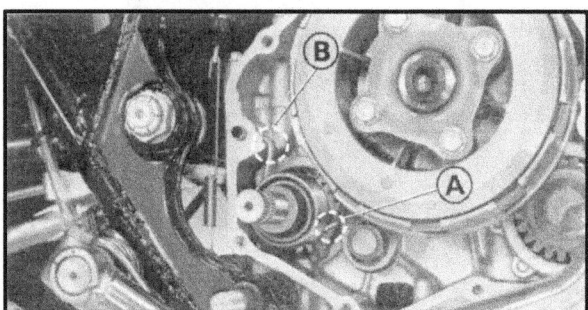

Fig. 3-38 Installing kick starter spring

Disassembly

1. Drain oil from the crankcase.
2. Remove the right foot peg and kick starter pedal.
3. Remove the right crankcase cover.
4. Remove the kick starter spring and remove the kick starter assembly.

Inspection

1. Check the starter drive ratchet for smooth and proper operation.
2. Check the kick starter pinion-to-kick starter spindle clearance.

Reassembly

1. Insert the hair pin section of the starter pinion friction spring into the crankcase stopper groove.
2. Hook the end Ⓐ of the kick starter spring as shown in Fig. 3-37, and install the kick starter assembly. Install the other end Ⓑ of the spring to the crankcase rib as shown in Fig. 3-38.
3. Check to be sure the starter pinion gear is properly meshed with the low gear.

III. ENGINE

7. GEAR SHIFT MECHANISM

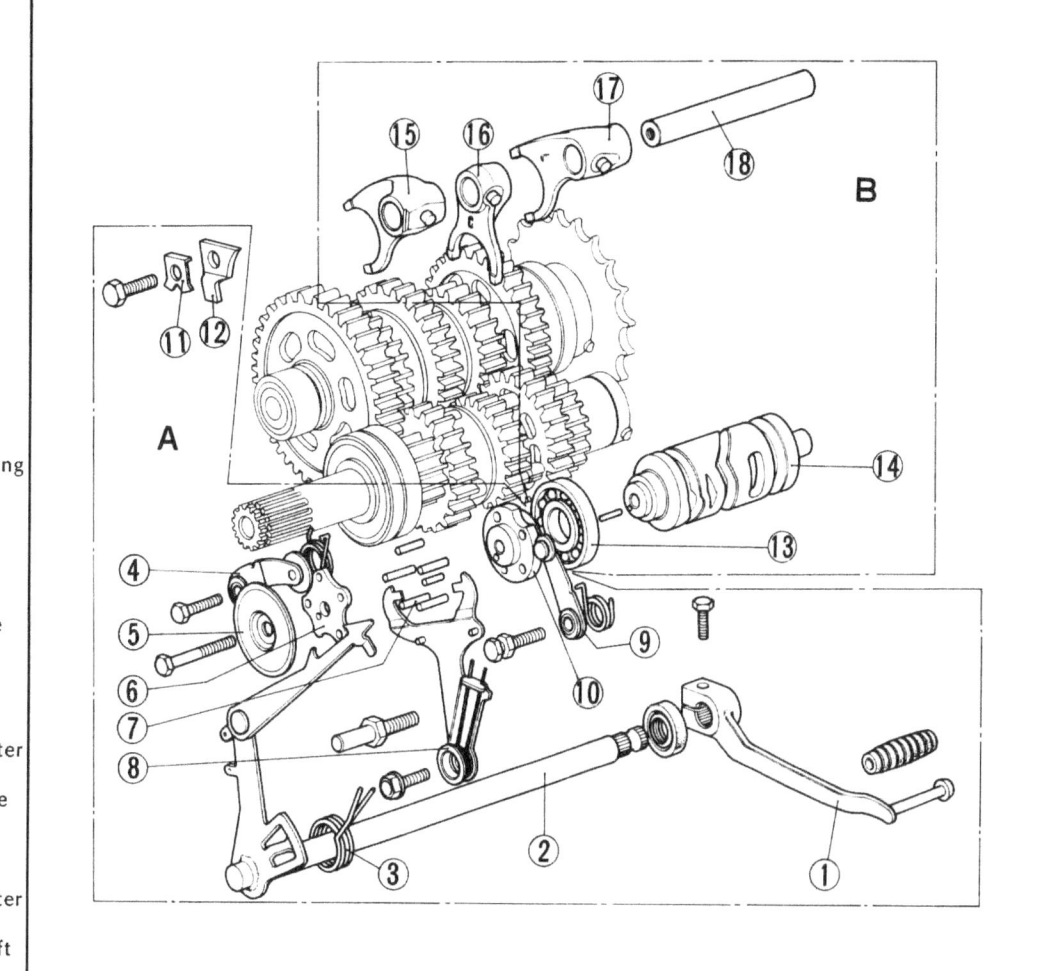

Group A
On-vehicle servicing

Group B
On-work stand servicing

① Gear change pedal
② Gear shift spindle
③ Return spring
④ Gear shift drum stopper
⑤ Gear shift side plate
⑥ Drum stopper plate
⑦ Rollers (six)
⑧ Rositive stopper
⑨ Neutral stopper arm
⑩ Gear shift drum center
⑪ Lock washer, 8 mm
⑫ Guide shaft set plate
⑬ 16004 ball bearing
⑭ Gear shift drum
⑮ Gear shift fork, R
⑯ Gear shift fork, center
⑰ Gear shift fork, L
⑱ Shift fork guide shaft

Disassembly

Group A

1. Drain oil from the crankcase.
2. Remove the right foot peg and kick starter pedal.
3. Remove the gear change pedal.
4. Remove the right crankcase cover.
5. Remove the gear shift spindle.
6. Disassemble the positive stopper, gear shift drum stopper and neutral stopper arm. Fig. 3-41 shows the transmission gears in neutral.

Fig. 3-40 ① Gear shift spindle

Fig. 3-41 ① Positive stopper
② Gear shift drum stopper
③ Neutral stopper arm

III. ENGINE

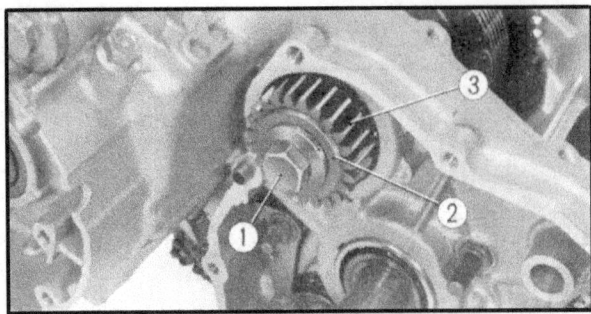

Fig. 3-42　① 12 mm bolt
　　　　　② Primary shaft lock washer
　　　　　③ Secondary drive gear

Fig. 3-43　① Primary shaft

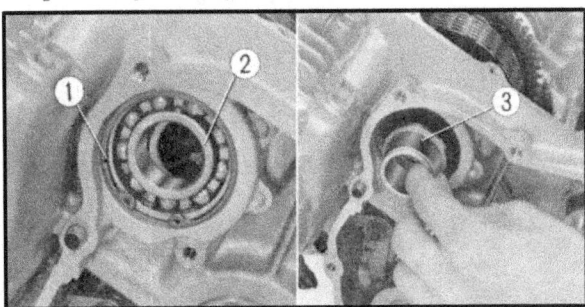

Fig. 3-44　① 52 mm internal circlip
　　　　　② 6205 ball bearing
　　　　　③ 25 mm collar

Fig. 3-45　① Main shaft
　　　　　② Countershaft

Fig. 3-46　① Shift fork guide shaft
　　　　　② Gear shift drum

7. Remove the contact breaker base and spark advancer.
8. Remove the oil pump.
9. Remove the secondary drive gear from the primary shaft by removing the 12 mm bolt.

Group B

1. Dismount the engine from the machine and follow steps 1 through 9 above.
2. Pull the primary shaft out to the right.

3. Remove the 52 mm internal circlip, and disassemble the 6205 ball bearing and 25 mm collar.
4. Loosen the bolts securing the upper and lower crankcases to remove the lower crankcase.

5. Remove the transmission main shaft and the countershaft at the same time.

6. Remove the gear shift set plate, and pull the shift fork guide shaft and gear shift drum out.

III. ENGINE

Inspection
1. Measure the gear shift fork finger width.
2. Measure the outside diameter of the shift fork guide shaft.
3. Measure the inside diameter of the gear shift fork.
4. Check the gear shift fork guide-to-gear shift drum groove clearance.

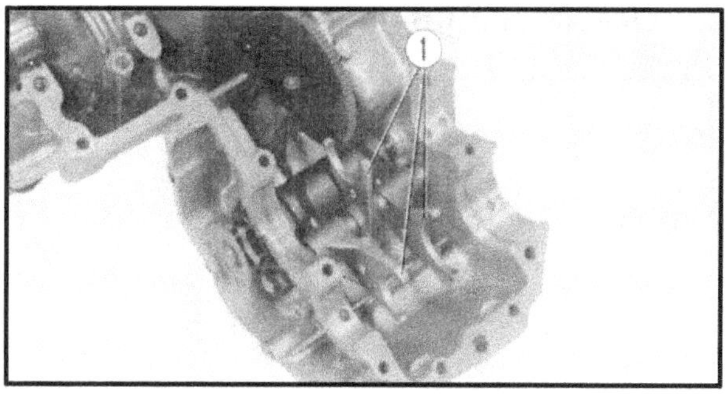

Fig. 3-47 ① Gear shift forks

Reassembly
1. Install the gear shift drum and gears in the neutral position.
2. Install the guide set plate, and bend the lug of the lock washer against the flat of the 8 mm bolt.
3. Install the gear shift forks properly in their respective positions. They are identified by marks "R", "C" and "L".
4. Check that the gear shift drum stopper, neutral stopper arm and positive stopper are in their respective positions. Check them for operation.
5. Move the gear shift spindle to check each related part for smooth operation.
6. Refer to pages 26~27 for transmission installation.
7. Refer to page 34 for upper and lower crankcase installation.

Fig. 3-48 ① Guide set plate
② Lock washer
③ 8 mm bolt

MEMO

III. ENGINE

8. TRANSMISSION

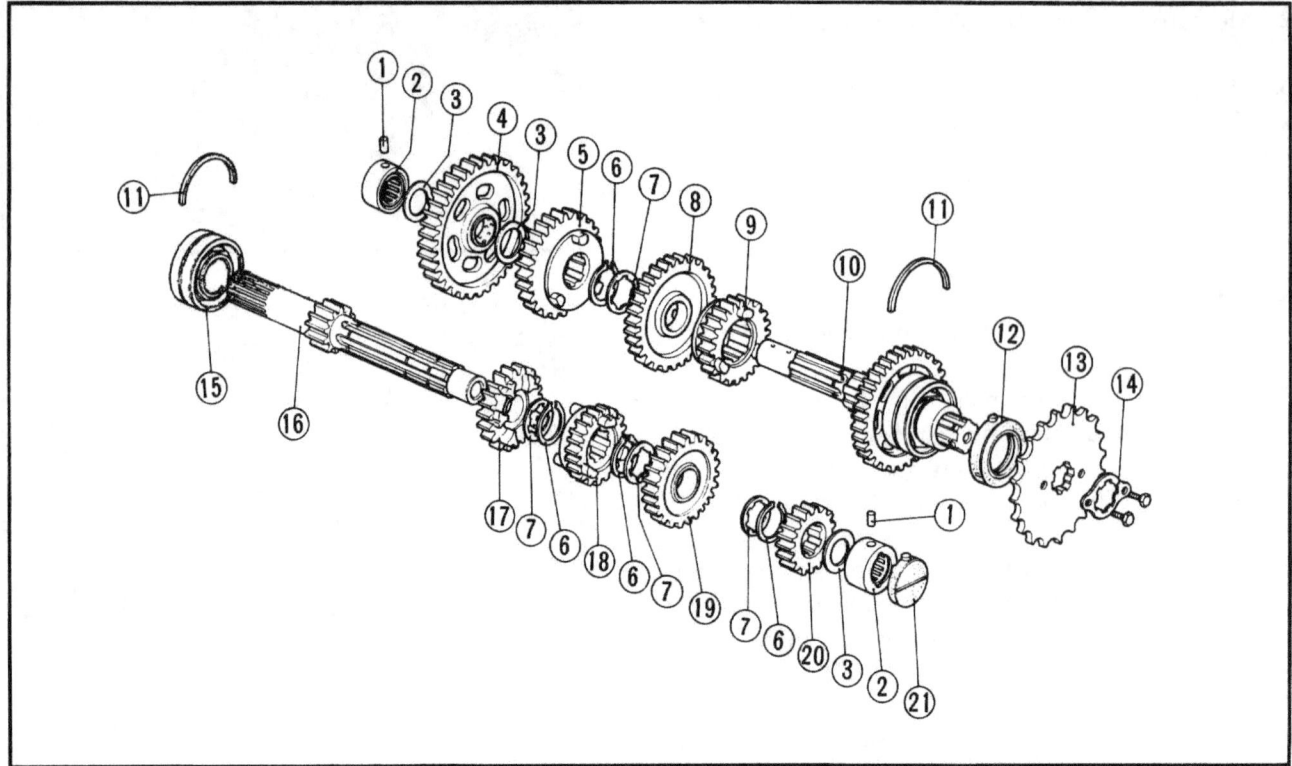

Fig. 3-49

① Gear shift fork guide pins (two), 6 mm
② Needle bearings (two), 20 mm
③ Thrust washers (three), 20 mm
④ Countershaft low gear, 41 T
⑤ Countershaft fourth gear, 31 T
⑥ Circlips (four), 25 mm
⑦ Thrust washers (four)
⑧ Countershaft third gear, 34 T
⑨ Countershaft top gear, 28 T
⑩ Countershaft, 37 T
⑪ Bearing set rings (two), 52 mm
⑫ Oil seal
⑬ Drive sprocket, 17 T
⑭ Drive sprocket fixing plate
⑮ Ball bearing, 5205 HS
⑯ Main shaft
⑰ Main shaft fourth gear, 27 T
⑱ Main shaft third gear, 24 T
⑲ Main shaft top gear, 29 T
⑳ Main shaft second gear, 20 T
㉑ Oil seal

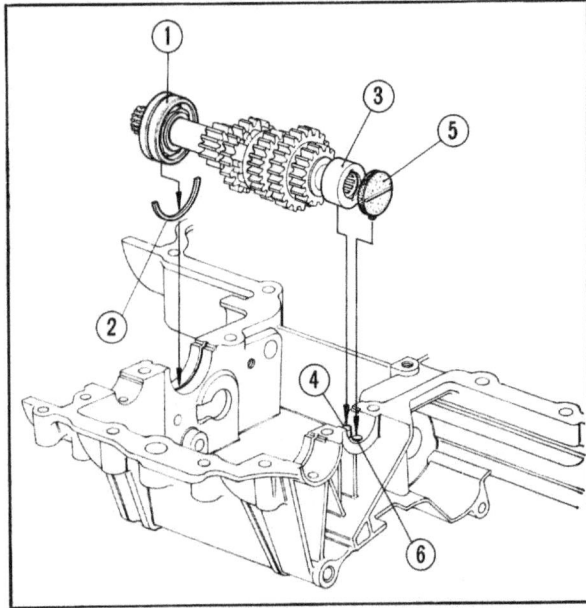

Fig. 3-50
① 5205 HS ball bearing
② 52 mm bearing set ring
③ 20 mm needle bearing
④ 6 mm guide pin
⑤ Oil seal
⑥ Pin hole

Disassembly
1. Remove the main shaft and countershaft from the upper crankcase. (See page 24)

Inspection
1. Check the gears for backlash.
2. Replace any gear if its lugs are excessively worn or damaged. Check the gears for smooth sliding on the shaft splines.
3. Check each gear to its mounting shaft clearance.

Reassembly
Main Shaft
1. Install the 5205 HS ball bearing with its groove fitted with the 52 mm bearing set ring in place.
2. Install the 20 mm needle bearing with its pin hole fitted with the 6 mm guide pin.
3. Install the oil seal with its dowel fitted into the pin hole in the upper crankcase.

Countershaft

1. Install the 20mm needle bearing with its pin hole fitted with the 6mm guide pin in the upper crankcase.
2. Install the 5205 ball bearing with its ring groove fitted with the 50mm bearing set ring installed in the upper crankcase.
3. Install the oil seal with its dowel fitted into the pin hole in the upper crankcase.

Rotate the crankshaft to check each gear for smooth operation.

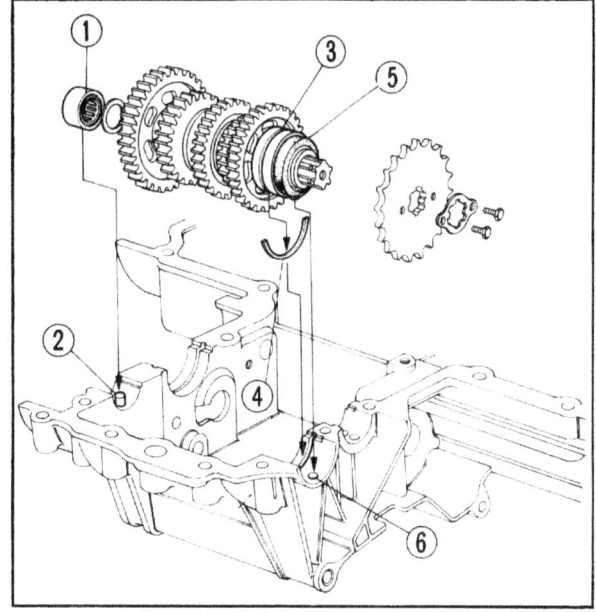

Fig. 3-51
① 20 mm needle bearing
② 6 mm guide pin
③ 5205 ball bearing
④ 50 mm bearing set ring
⑤ Oil seal
⑥ Pin hole

MEMO

9. PRIMARY SHAFT

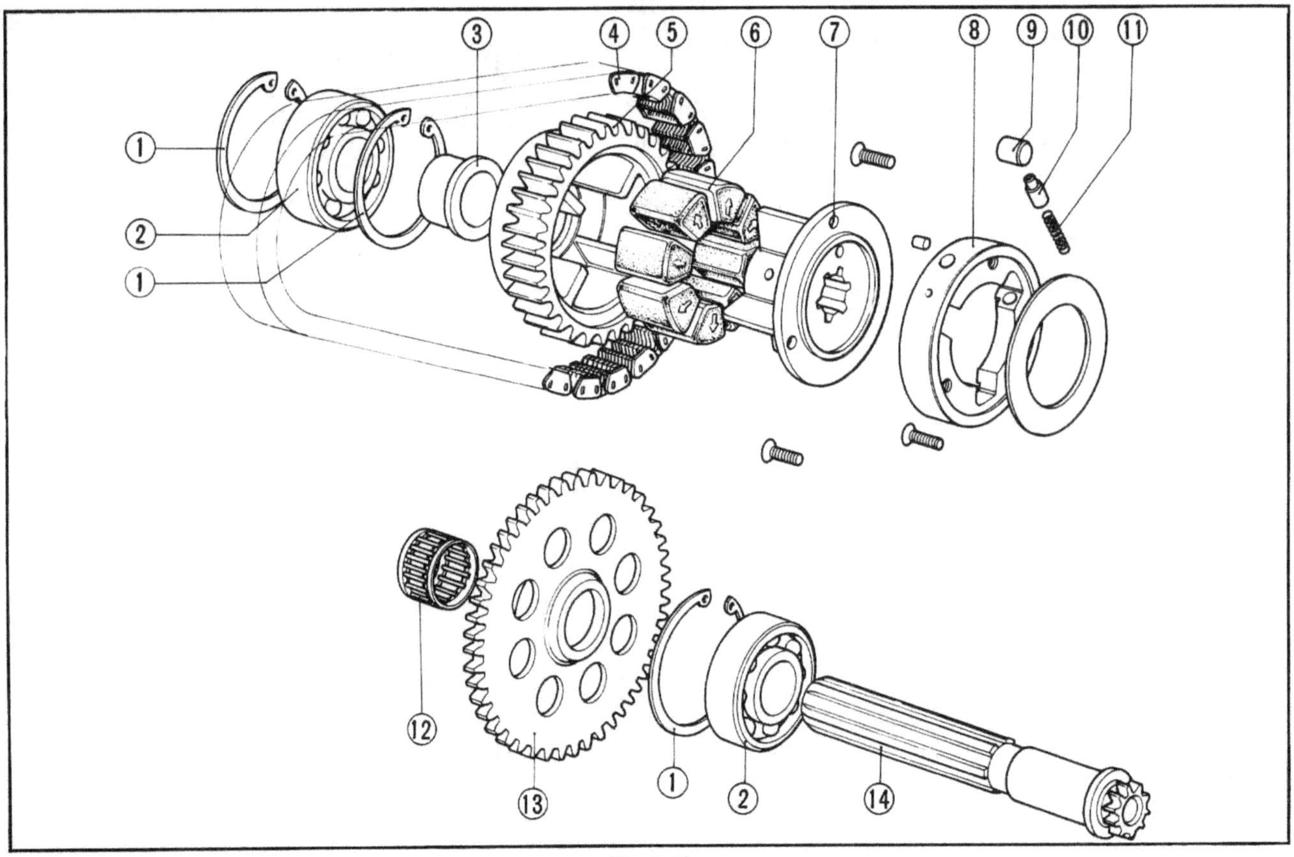

Fig. 3-52

① Internal circlips (three), 52 mm
② Ball bearings (two), 6205
③ Collar, 25×21.8
④ Primary drive chain
⑤ Primary driven sprocket
⑥ Rubber dampers (eight)
⑦ Driven sprocket hub
⑧ Clutch outer
⑨ Rollers (three), 10.2×9.5
⑩ Caps (three)
⑪ Springs (three)
⑫ Needle bearing
⑬ Starter driven gear
⑭ Primary shaft

Fig. 3-53 ① Primary driven sprocket
② Starter driven gear

Disassembly

1. Pull the primary shaft out. (See page 24)
2. Remove the primary driven sprocket and starter driven gear.

3. Remove the driven sprocket hub from the primary driven sprocket.
4. Remove the rubber dampers.

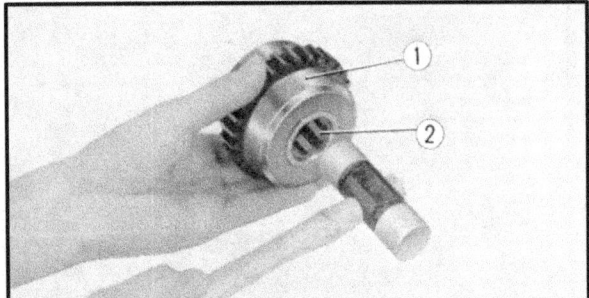

Fig. 3-54 ① Primary driven sprocket
② Driven sprocket hub

Inspection

1. Check the starting clutch and its related parts for wear or other damage. Also check the rollers for smooth operation.
2. Check the starter driven gear needle bearing for damage.

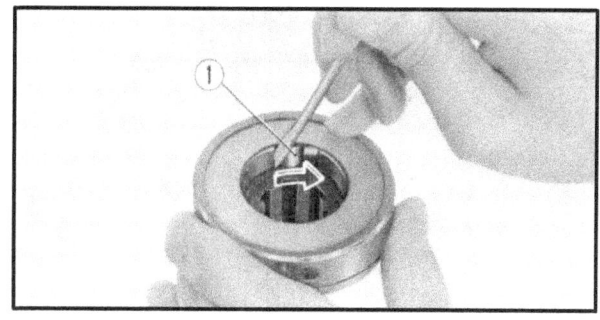

Fig. 3-55 ① Starting clutch roller

Reassembly

1. When the clutch outer body has been disassembled, tighten the three 6 mm flat screws to secure the driven sprocket hub to the clutch outer body, and stake each screw head in two positions as shown in Fig. 3-56.

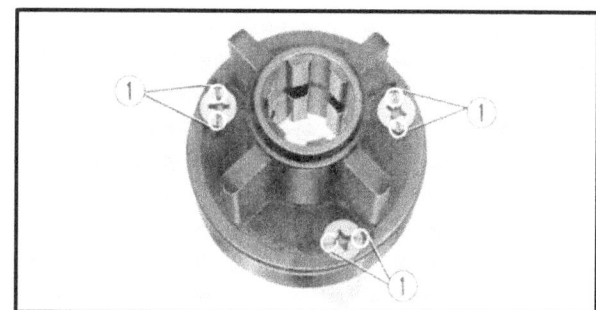

Fig. 3-56 ① Stake

2. After assembling the upper and lower crankcases, insert the primary shaft into the crankcase from the right side. Install the collar.

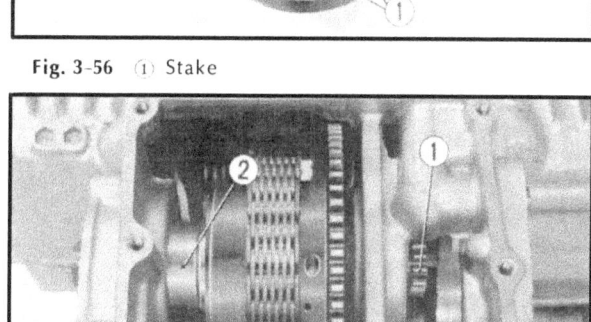

Fig. 3-57 ① Primary shaft
② 25 mm collar

3. Drive the 6205 ball bearing into the primary shaft, and secure with the 25 mm internal circlip.
4. Tighten the crankcases with securing bolts. (See page 34)

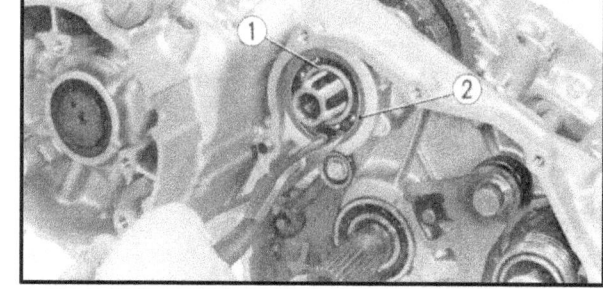

Fig. 3-58 ① 6205 ball bearing
② 52 mm internal circlip

5. Install the primary shaft lock washer with the "OUTSIDE" mark facing out.

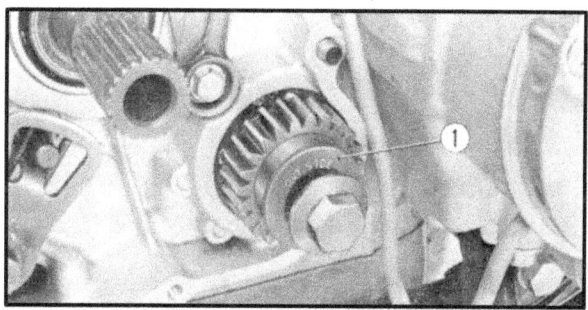

Fig. 3-59 ① Lock washer

10. CAM CHAIN TENSIONER

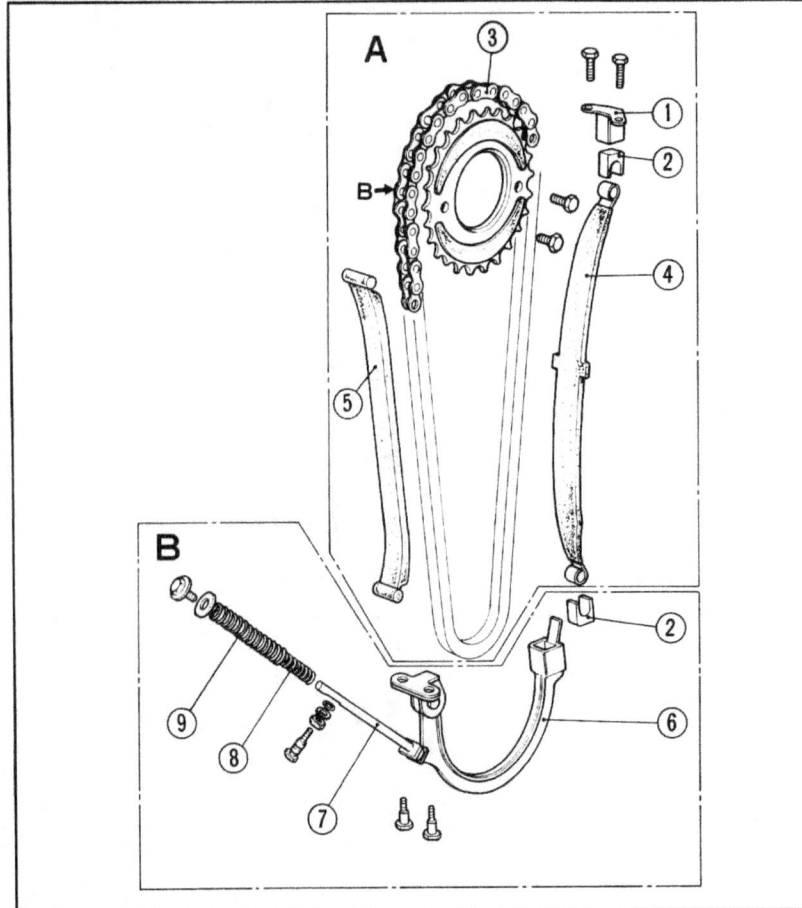

Fig. 3-60

| Group A | On-vehicle servicing |
| Group B | On-work stand servicing |

① Cam chain tensioner holder
② Tensioner dampers (two)
③ Cam chain
④ Tensioner slipper
⑤ Cam chain guide
⑥ Cam chain tensioner arm
⑦ Push bar
⑧ Tensioner inner spring
⑨ Tensioner outer spring

Fig. 3-61 ① Tensioner arm
② Push bar

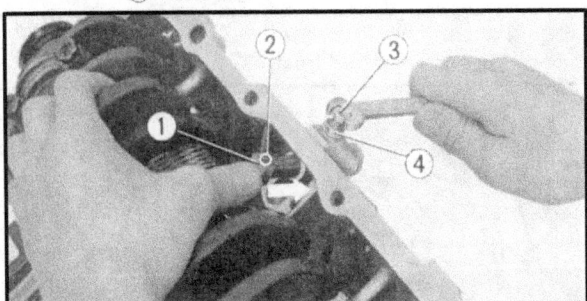

Fig. 3-62 ① Push bar
② Mark
③ Tensioner adjusting bolt
④ Lock nut

Disassembly

Group A

1. Remove the cam chain guide and tensioner slipper. (See pages 12–14)

Group B

1. Remove the lower crankcase. (See pages 23–24)
2. Remove the tensioner arm and tensioner push bar.

Inspection

1. Check the cam chain guide and tensioner slipper for wear.

Reassembly

1. Install the tensioner push bar with the mark facing up as shown in Fig. 3-62.
   Depress the push bar and secure it with the tensioner adjusting bolt and lock nut.

III. ENGINE

11. CRANKSHAFT AND CONNECTING RODS

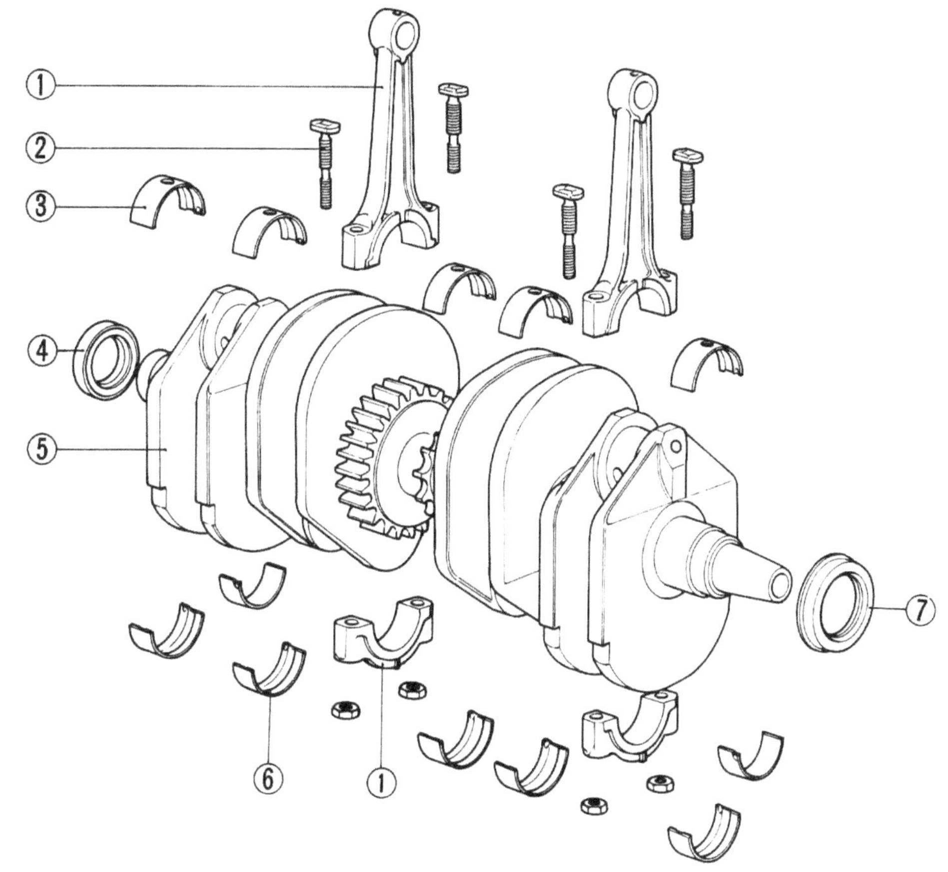

Fig. 3-63
1. Connecting rods (four)
2. Connecting rod bolts (eight)
3. Crankshaft bearings (ten)
4. Oil seal, 30×42×8
5. Crankshaft
6. Connecting rod bearings (eight)
7. Oil seal, 30×45×8

Disassembly

1. Remove the cylinder head, cylinder and pistons. (See pages 12-14)
2. Pull the A-C generator rotor out using the rotor puller (Tool No. 07933-3330000).
3. Separate the lower crankcase from the upper one. (See pages 23-24)

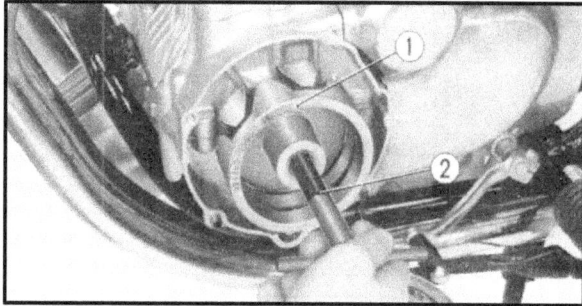

Fig. 3-64
1. A-C generator rotor
2. Rotor remover

4. Remove the cam chain tensioner arm. (See page 30)
5. Remove the crankshaft.

Fig. 3-65 1. Crankshaft

III. ENGINE

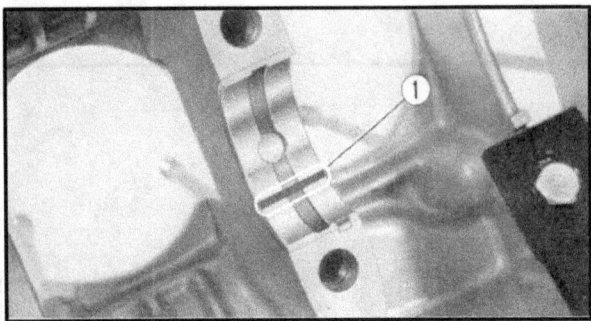

Fig. 3-66 ① Plastigauge

Fig. 3-67 Checking bearing seat inside diameter

Inspection

1. Check the crankshaft center journal for runout.
2. Check the crankshaft-to-crankshaft bearing clearance as follows:
   1) Place a piece of plastigauge on the bearing as shown in Fig. 3-66 and install the crankshaft on it.
   2) Assemble the upper and lower crankcases by torquing the securing bolts to specification.
   3) Remove the upper crankcase and measure the clearance by the plastigauge. If beyond specified limit, replace crankshaft bearing with a new one.
3. Select the crankshaft bearings in a set as follows:
   1) Remove the crankshaft bearings and tighten the upper and lower crankcases to the specified torque. Check the inside diameter of each bearing seat as shown in Fig. 3-67.
   2) Measure the outside diameter of the crankshaft journals.
   3) Select bearings according to the readings taken in steps 1) and 2) above.
      The bearings can be identified by a daub of color print on the side or a letter stamped on the rear side.

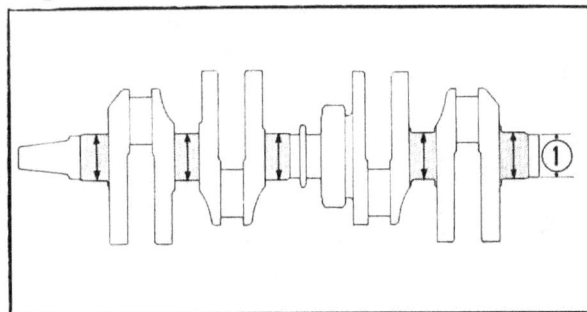

Fig. 3-68 ① Crankshaft journal outside diameter

Unit: mm (in.)

Crankcase bearing I.D. \ Crankshaft journal O.D.	31.99–32.00 (1.2594–1.2598)	31.98–31.99 (1.2590–1.2594)	31.97–31.98 (1.2586–1.2590)
35.000–35.008 (1.3780–1.3783)	D (yellow)	C (green)	B (brown)
35.008–35.016 (1.3783–1.3786)	C (green)	B (brown)	A (black)
35.016–35.024 (1.3786–1.3789)	B (brown)	A (black)	AA (blue)

4. Measure the inside diameter of the connecting rod small end.
5. Check the side clearance of the connecting rod big end.
6. Check the connecting rod big end-to-crankshaft journal clearance as follows:
   1) Remove the connecting rod bearing cap and place a piece of plastigauge on the bearing surface. Torque the bearing cap bolts to specification.
   2) Remove the cap and measure the clearance by the plastigauge. If beyond the specified limit, replace bearing with a new one.

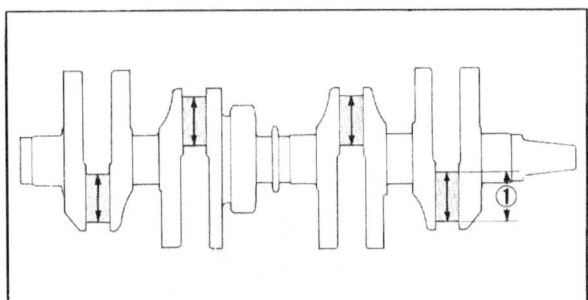

Fig. 3-69 ① Crankshaft pin outside diameter

III. ENGINE

7. Select the connecting rod bearings in a set as follows:
   1) Measure the outside diameter of the crankshaft pin.
   2) Check to make sure the code number (1, 2 and 3) stamped on the connecting rod big end side is properly matched as shown.
   3) After following steps 1) and 2) above, select the bearings according to the table below.

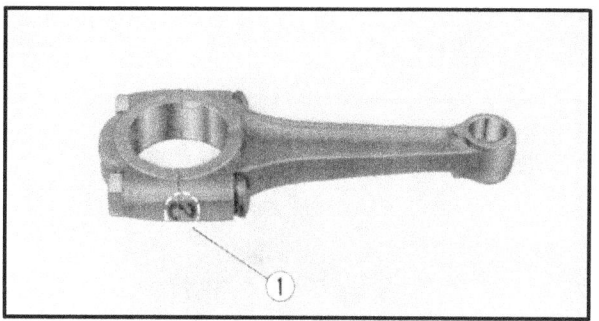

Fig. 3-70　① Code No.

Unit: mm (in.)

Crankshaft pin O.D. Connecting rod code no.	31.99-32.00 (1.594-1.2598)	31.98-31.99 (1.2590-1.2594)	31.97-31.98 (1.2586-1.2590)
1	E (red)	D (yellow)	C (green)
2	D (yellow)	C (green)	B (brown)
3	C (green)	B (brown)	A (black)

NOTE:
The bearings must be installed with the tang facing the front (exhaust side).

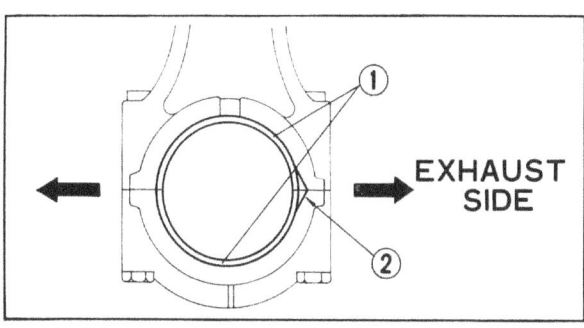

Fig. 3-71　① Bearing　② Tang

8. Select the connecting rods
   When replacing a connecting rod matching the letter stamped on the connecting rod big end side as shown in Fig. 3-72.

NOTE:
The connecting rod weight does not include the bearings weight.

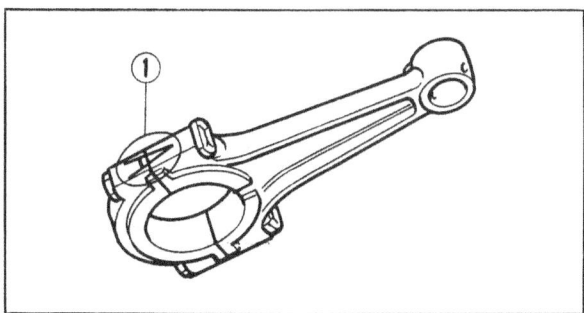

Fig. 3-72　① Code mark

Reassembly

1. Apply liquid packing to the mating surfaces of the crankcases and install the bearings after the packing dries.
2. Apply molybdenum disulfide compound or engine oil to the bearing surfaces.

Fig. 3-73　① Bearings

12. CRANKCASE

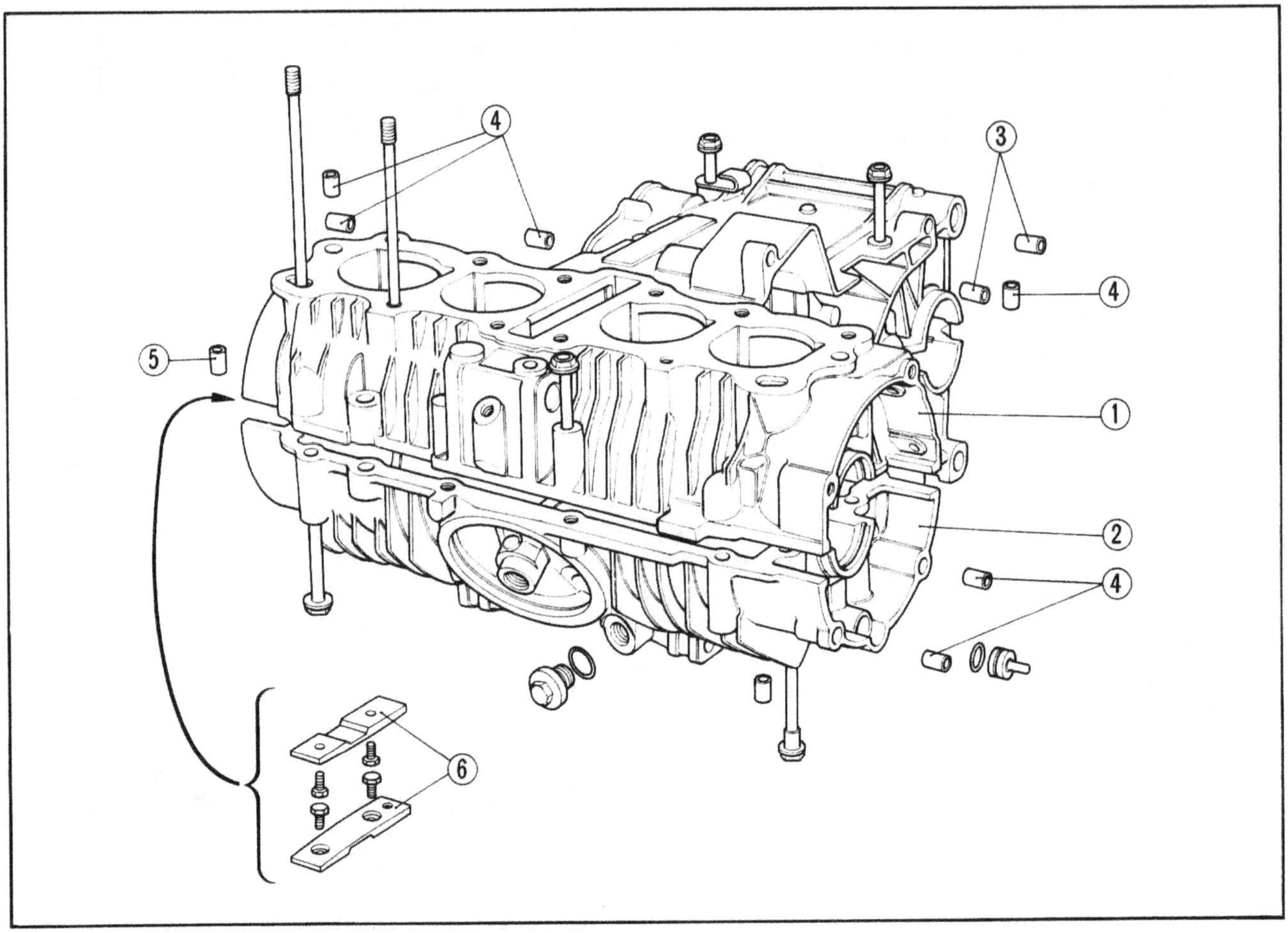

Fig. 3-74
① Upper crankcase
② Lower crankcase
③ Dowel pins (two), 8×10
④ Dowel pins (six), 8×14
⑤ Dowel pins (two), 10×14
⑥ Primary chain guides (two)

Fig. 3-75 ① Primary chain guide
② Recessed mark

Disassembly
1. Separate the upper and lower crankcases. (See pages 23-24)

Inspection
1. Check the crankcase oil passage for clogs.
2. Check the primary chain guides for wear.

Fig. 3-76 Tightening sequence

Reassembly
1. Install the primary chain guide with its recessed mark facing the transmission.
2. Apply a coat of liquid packing to the crankcase mating surfaces.
3. Make sure all dowel pins are properly installed.
4. Tighten the ten UBS bolts on the crankcase in the sequence shown in Fig. 3-76.

III. ENGINE

13. CARBURETOR

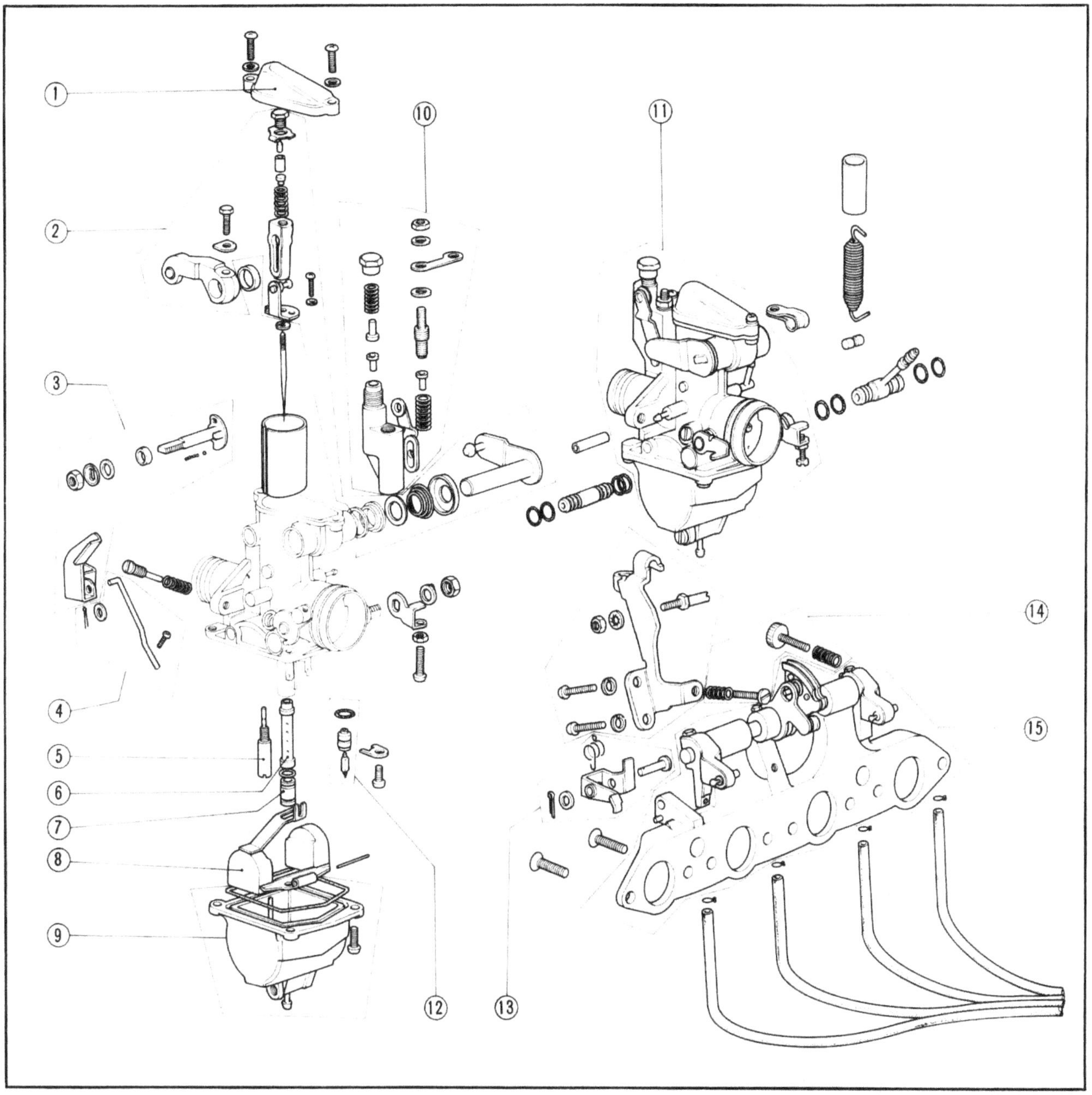

Fig. 3-77
① Top set
② Link arm set A
③ Link set
④ Choke rod set
⑤ Slow set
⑥ Jet needle set
⑦ Main jet set
⑧ Float set
⑨ Float chamber set A
⑩ Adjust holder set A
⑪ Carburetor assembly
⑫ Float valve set
⑬ Link set
⑭ Screw set B
⑮ Stay plate set

● Carburetor Component Parts

The carburetor component parts are available in a set as shown in Fig. 3-77. It is recommended that each part be replaced as a set to maintain a satisfactory carburetor performance.

Disassembly

1. Remove the carburetor assembly. (See page 11)

Stay plate and carburetor body

2. Remove the throttle return spring from the link lever.

Fig. 3-78 ① Throttle return spring

Fig. 3-79 ① Hex. nuts ③ Cap nuts
② Dust plate B

3. Remove the dust plate B by loosening hex. nuts. Loosen the cap nuts.

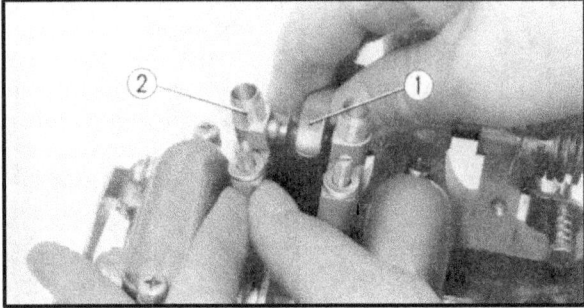

Fig. 3-80 ① Link arm
② Adjuster holder

4. Remove the link arm from the adjuster holders.
5. Loosen the eight 6 mm flat screws and remove the four carburetors from the stay plate.

Fig. 3-81 ① Lock washers ③ 6 mm bolt
③ 4 mm bolt

Throttle valves and jet needles

6. Remove the carburetor top.
7. Straighten the lugs of the lock washers to remove the 4 mm and 6 mm bolts.

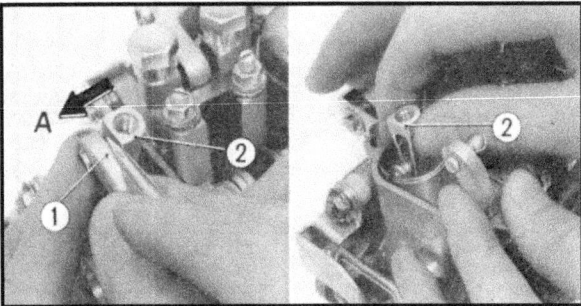

Fig. 3-82 ① Link arm ② Throttle shaft

8. Pry the link arm out from the throttle shaft in direction (A) with a screwdriver.

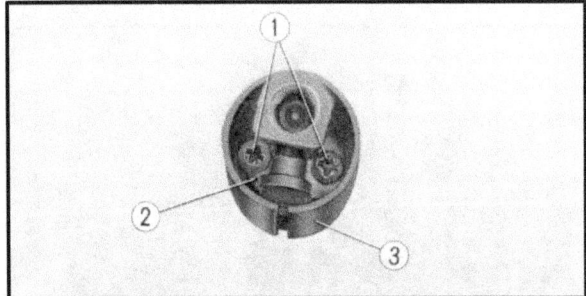

Fig. 3-83 ① 3 mm screws ③ Throttle valve
② Valve plate

9. Loosen the two 3 mm screws and remove the valve plate from the throttle valve by turning the plate 90°.
10. Remove the jet needle from the throttle valve.

Adjuster holders

1. Remove the carburetor from the plate. (Refer to steps 1 through 5 on page 35-37).
2. Remove the adjusting screw from the adjuster holder. Remove the holder from the lever.

Fig. 3-84　① Adjusting screw　② Adjuster holder

Float, main jet and slow jet

1. Remove the float chamber.
2. Remove the leaf spring, main jet and slow jet.

Fig. 3-85　① Leaf spring　③ Slow jet
　　　　　② Main jet

3. Pull the float arm pin out and remove the float.

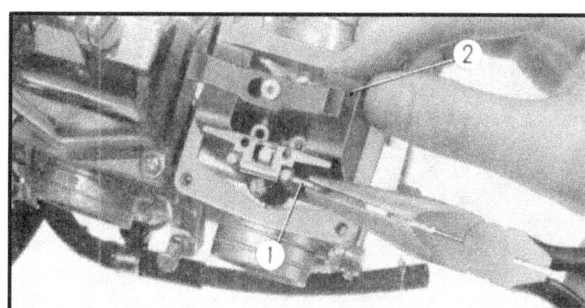

Fig. 3-86　① Float arm pin　② Float

4. Remove the clip plate and the valve seat.

Fig. 3-87　① Clip plate　② Valve seat

Inspection

1. Check the main and slow jets for clogging.
2. Adjusting fuel level
   Move the float so that the float arm comes in contact with the tip of the float valve. Check the float height with a float level gauge as shown in Fig. 3-88. If out of specification, adjust by bending the float arm.

Fig. 3-88　① Float
　　　　　② Float level gauge

Reassembly

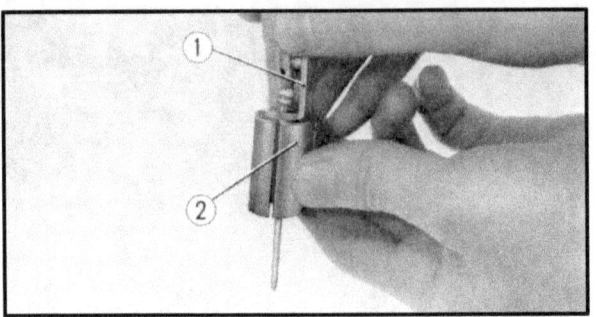

Fig. 3-89 ① Valve plate
② Throttle valve

1. Place the two 3 mm screws with the spring washers on the valve plate, and press the plate down in the throttle valve. Align the protrusion of the valve plate with the slot of the throttle valve. Turn the plate 90° toward the link arm side and tighten with the 3 mm screws.

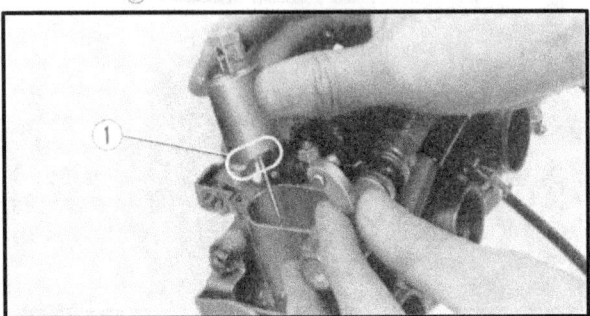

Fig. 3-90 ① Cutaway part

2. Install the throttle valve to the carburetor body by aligning the carburetor protrusion with the throttle valve slot. Check to make sure the cutaway part of the throttle valve is facing the choke valve side.

Fig. 3-91 ① Fuel tube (2.5×16) ③ Fuel tube
② Fuel joint ④ Fuel tube (3.5×600)

3. Install the fuel tubes and fuel joint to the carburetor.

Fig. 3-92 ① Fuel tube ③ Clips
② Fuel tube (3.5×600)

4. Install and route each carburetor tube as shown in Fig. 3-92.

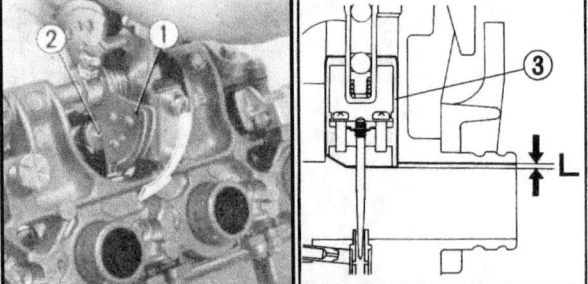

Fig. 3-93 ① Throttle lever ③ Throttle valve
② Adjusting screw

5. Move the throttle lever until it contacts the adjusting screw, and check the throttle valve-to-throttle bore clearance (L). If out of specification (**0~1.0 mm/0~0.04 in.**), adjust the clearance with the adjusting screw.

IV. FRAME

1. FRONT WHEEL

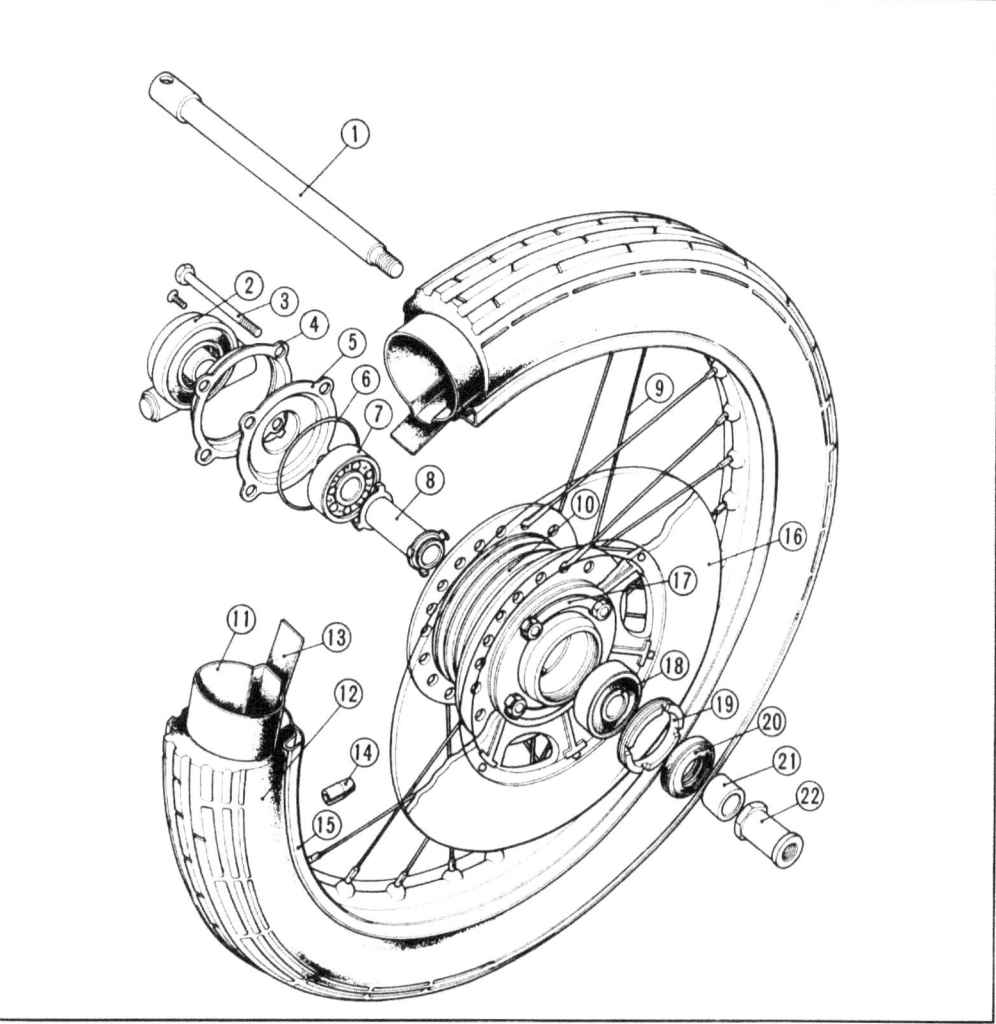

Fig. 4-1
1. Front wheel axle
2. Speedometer gear box
3. Bolts (4) 8×90
4. Gear box retainer cover
5. Gear box retainer
6. Retainer O-ring
7. 6302U radial ball bearing
8. Front axle distance collar
9. Spokes (36)
10. Front wheel hub
11. Front wheel tube
12. Front wheel tire
13. Front tire flap
14. Wheel balance weight
15. Front wheel rim
16. Front brake disc
17. 8 mm lock washer (2)
18. 6302U radial ball bearing
19. Front wheel bearing retainer
20. Dust-seal 22×36×8
21. Wheel side collar
22. Front wheel axle nut

Disassembly

1. Using a jack, raise the front wheel off the ground.
2. Remove the speedometer cable.
3. Loosen the axle holder retaining nuts and remove the front wheel from the front forks.

NOTE:

Do not operate the front brake lever with the front wheel removed.

4. Loosen the front wheel axle nut and remove the front wheel axle.
5. Straighten the lugs of the lock washers and remove the front brake disc.
   1) When the brake disc has been removed, the gear box retainer cover can be removed as an assembly.

Fig. 4-2 ① Jack   ③ Axle holder
② Speedometer cable

Fig. 4-3 ① Lock washer   ② Brake disc

IV. FRAME

Fig. 4-4 ① Bearing retainer wrench

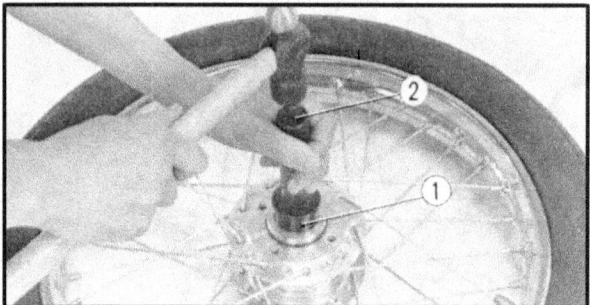

Fig. 4-5 ① Outer bearing driver attachment
② Driver handle

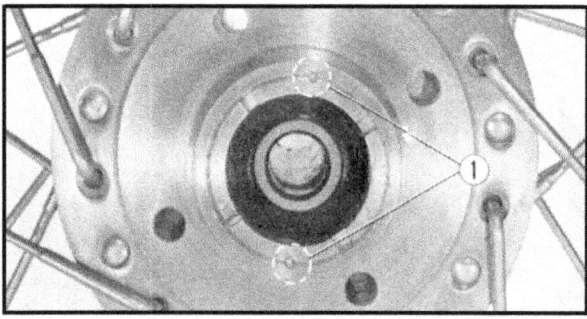

Fig. 4-6 ① Stake

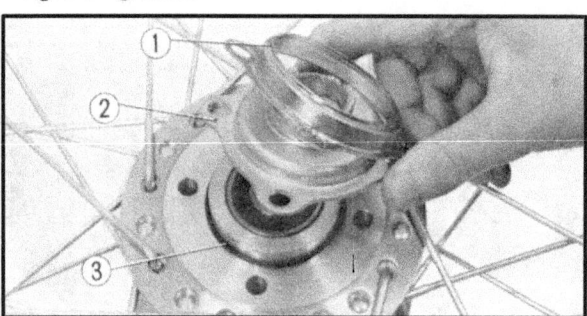

Fig. 4-7 ① Gear box retainer cover
② Gear box retainer
③ Retainer O-ring

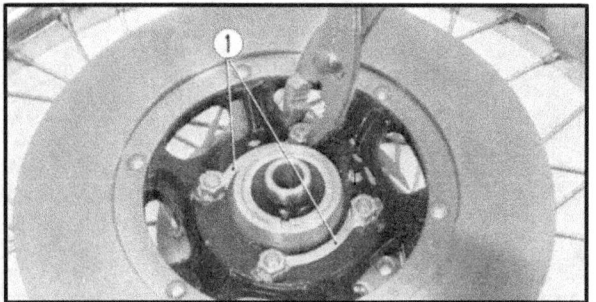

Fig. 4-8 ① Lock washers

6. Remove the dust seal and remove the bearing retainer with bearing retainer wrench (Tool No. 07088-32301).

Inspection

1. Check the front axle for bending.
2. Check the front wheel rim for face runout.
3. Check the spokes for looseness, bending or other damage.
   Spoke torque specifications: **25~30 kg/cm (1.9~2.2 lbs-ft)**.
4. Check the tire for cracks, excessive wear or other damage.
5. Check the tube valve for air leaks.
6. Check the tire pressure.
   Tire pressure specification: **1.8 kg/cm^2 (26 psi)**

Reassembly

1. Fill the ball bearings and the front wheel hub with grease. Drive the bearings in the hub.
   1) Use the outer bearing driver attachment (Tool No. 07945-3330200) and ball bearing driver handle (Tool No. 07949-6110000) for the bearing installation.
   2) Be sure to install the distance collar.
2. Stake the bearing retainer at two places as shown in Fig. 4-6.
3. Make sure the retainer O-ring is properly installed. Install the gear box retainer and retainer cover with the 8 mm bolts. Place the brake disc on the opposite side of the wheel hub.

4. Install the brake disc to the wheel hub with the nuts.

NOTE:
Replace the lock washers. Bend the lugs of the washers properly after tightening the nuts.

5. Install the speedometer gear box to the gear box retainer.

Fig. 4-9 ① Gear box retainer
② Speedometer gear box

6. Install the front wheel to the front forks.
Tighten the axle holder at the left side (brake disc side) first and then tighten the axle holder at the right side.
To prevent misalignment, tighten the front axle holder nut first, then tighten the rear nut until the axle is secure.

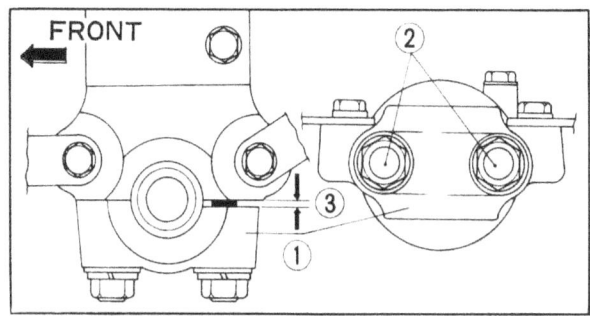

Fig. 4-10 ① Axle holder
② Axle holder nuts
③ Gap at rear

Wheel balancing

1. Jack up the machine to clear the wheel off the ground.
Mark the side of the tire and lightly spin the wheel several times.
2. If the mark comes to rest at the same point each time, it is an indication that the wheel is out of balance.

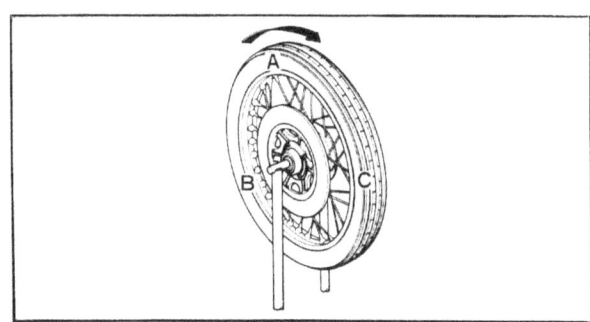

Fig. 4-11 Wheel balancing

3. Install a balance weight to the nipple end of the spoke at the top of the wheel directly opposite the heaviest point (the bottom of the wheel).
Balance weights are available in four weights: **5, 10, 15** and **20 gr**.
4. Repeat several times. If the wheel does not stop at the same place each time, it is balanced.
5. Wheel balancing should be made with the brake disc installed.

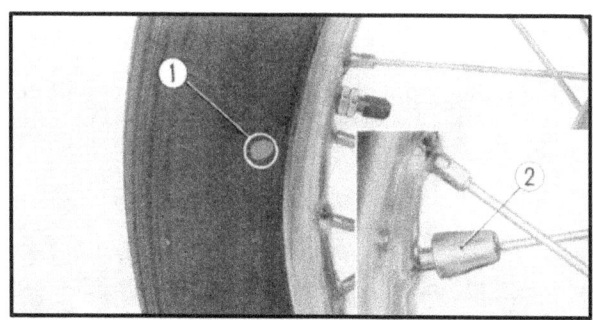

Fig. 4-12 ① Balance marking
② Balance weight

2. FRONT DISC BRAKE

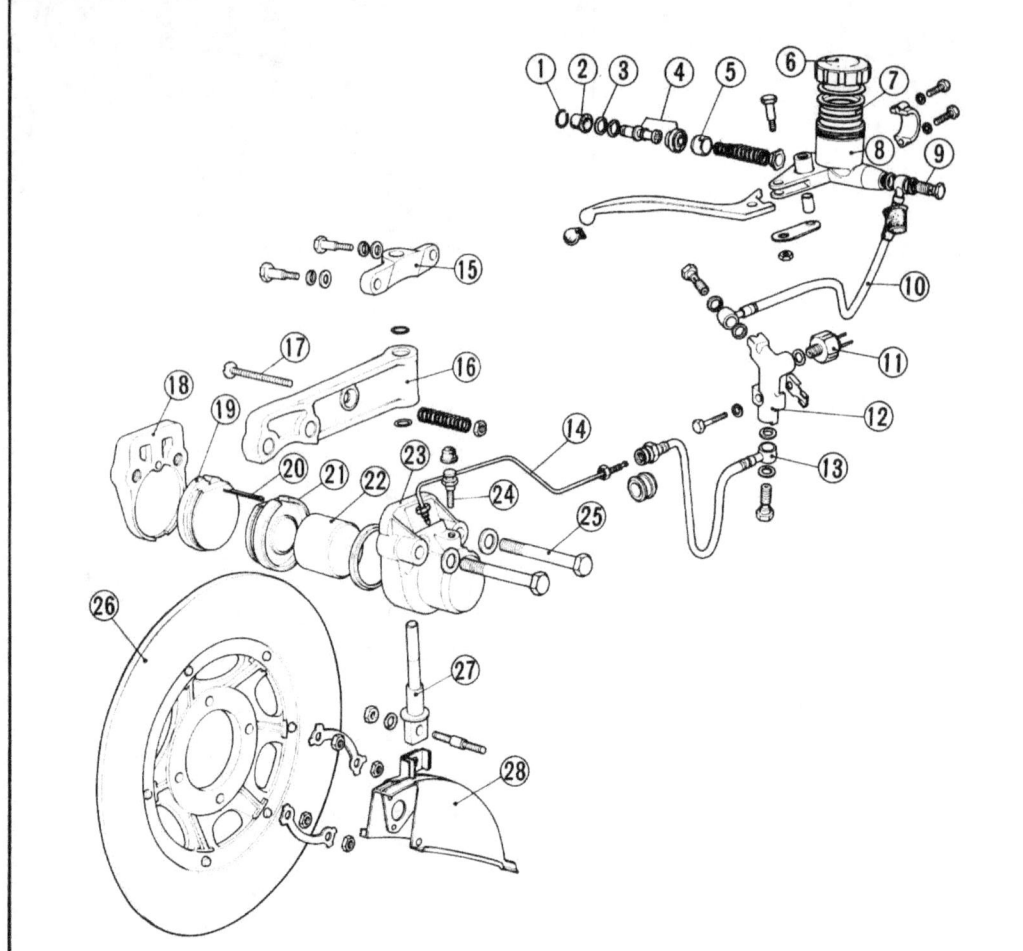

Fig. 4-13
① Clip
② Boot
③ 18 mm internal circlip
④ Piston
⑤ Primary cup
⑥ Oil cup cap
⑦ Diaphragm
⑧ Master cylinder
⑨ Oil bolt
⑩ Front brake hose B
⑪ Stop switch
⑫ 3 way joint
⑬ Front brake hose A
⑭ Front brake pipe
⑮ Caliper holder joint
⑯ Caliper holder
⑰ Caliper adjust bolt
⑱ Caliper B
⑲ Pad B
⑳ Cotton pin 1.6×22
㉑ Pad A
㉒ Piston
㉓ Caliper A
㉔ Bleeder valve
㉕ Caliper securing bolts (two)
㉖ Front brake disc
㉗ Caliper holder
㉘ Disc cover

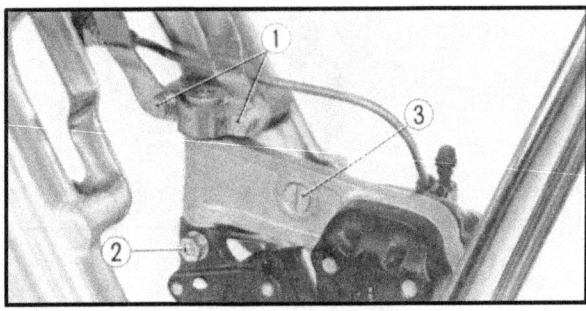

Fig. 4-14 ① 6 mm bolts ③ Caliper adjusting bolt
② 8 mm nut

Disassembly

Front brake disc

1. Drain the brake fluid.
2. Disconnect the front brake pipe from the caliper.
3. Remove the front fender.
4. Loosen the caliper adjusting bolt and 8 mm nut to remove the disc cover and caliper assembly.
5. Loosen the two caliper securing bolts to separate calipers A and B.

Fig. 4-15 ① Caliper securing bolts

IV. FRAME

6. Pull the cotter pin out to remove pad B from caliper B.

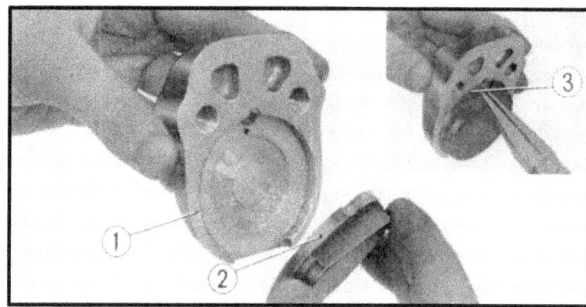

Fig. 4-16 ① Caliper B
② Pad B
③ Cotter pin

7. Remove pad A from caliper A by lightly tapping the caliper head.

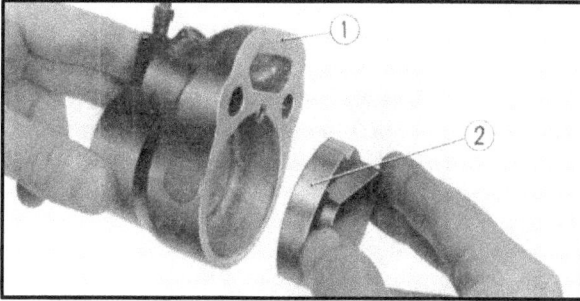

Fig. 4-17 ① Caliper A
② Pad A

Master cylinder

1. Remove the master cylinder.
   1) Remove the master cylinder boots and loosen the oil bolt.
   2) Loosen the hex. bolts to remove the master cylinder holder.
   3) Loosen the brake lever pivot bolt to remove the brake lever.

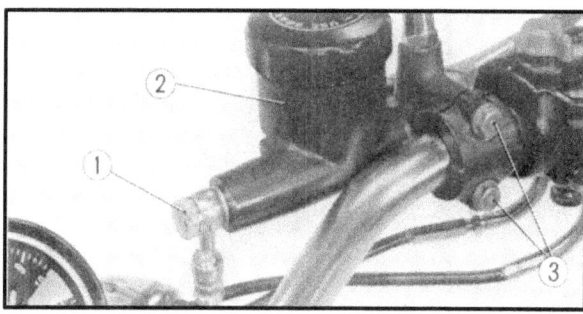

Fig. 4-18 ① Oil bolt
② Master cylinder
③ Hex. bolts

2. Remove the boot from the cylinder, being careful not to damage it. Remove the circlip using snap ring pliers (Tool No. 07914-3230000).

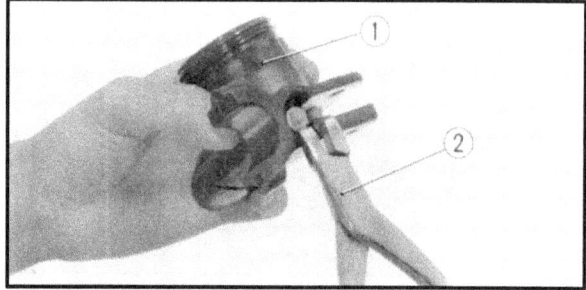

Fig. 4-19 ① Master cylinder
② Snap ring pliers

3. Remove the piston, primary cup, spring and check valve from the master cylinder in that order.

NOTE:
1. Apply 2~3 kg/cm² (28~43 psi) of air pressure to the brake hose joint to remove the primary cup.
2. Do not damage the check valve when removing it.

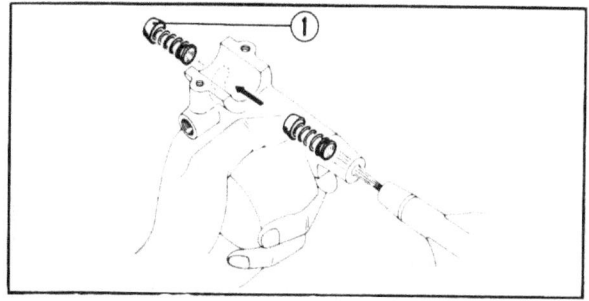

Fig. 4-20 ① Primary cup

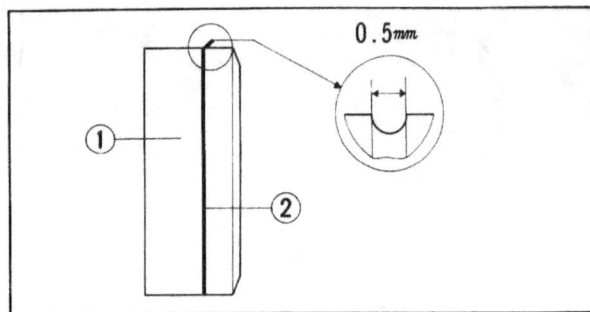

Fig. 4-21　① Pad
　　　　　② Wear limit line

Inspection

1. Check pads A and B for excessive wear. Replace the pad if it is worn to the wear limit line.
2. Measure the inside diameter of the caliper cylinder and the outside diameter of the piston.
3. Measure the inside diameter of the master cylinder and the outside diameter of the piston.

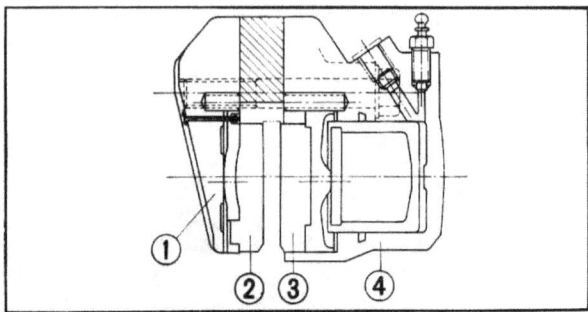

Fig. 4-22　① Caliper B　　③ Pad A
　　　　　② Pad B　　　　④ Caliper A

Reassembly

Caliper assembly

1. Apply a coat of silicone sealing grease to the sliding surface of the calipers when installing pads A and B.

NOTE:
1. Do not lubricate the friction surfaces of the pads.
2. Prevent foreign material from entering the caliper assembly during reassembly.

Master cylinder

1. Apply a coat of brake fluid to the inside surface of the cylinder.
2. Install the check valve with the return spring to the cylinder.

NOTE:
Check that the valve is properly installed in the cylinder.

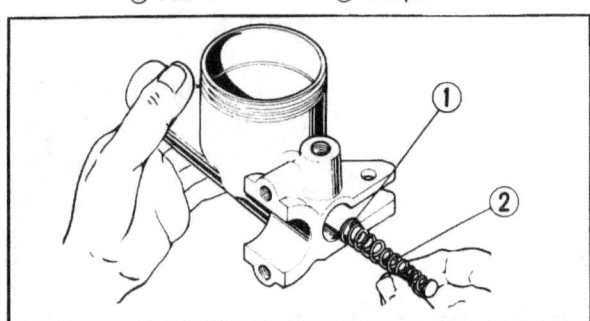

Fig. 4-23　① Check valve　　② Return spring

3. Apply a thin coat of brake fluid around the primary cup, and properly install it to the cylinder.

NOTE:
1. Do not damage the primary cup during installation.
2. Be sure to replace primary cup when it is disassembled.

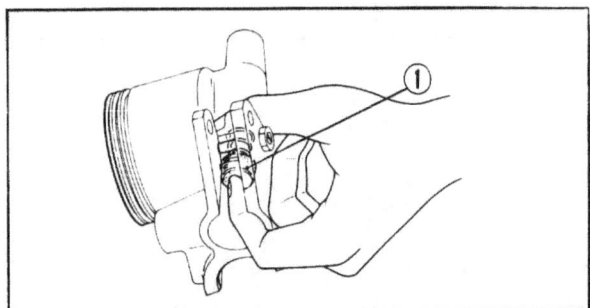

Fig. 4-24　① Primary cup

4. Install the 18 mm circlip. Make sure the circlip is properly installed.
5. Bleed the brake line and fill the master cylinder fluid cup with **SAE DOT3 brake fluid**.

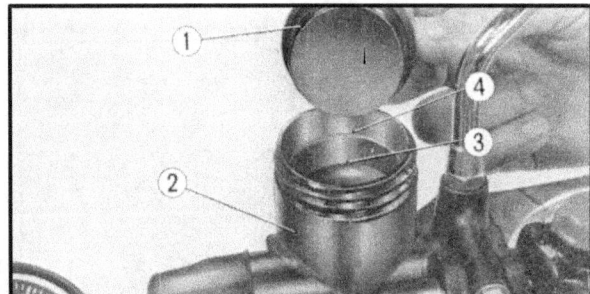

Fig. 4-25　① Diaphragm　　　　③ Brake fluid
　　　　　② Master cylinder　　④ Level line

IV. FRAME

3. REAR WHEEL AND REAR BRAKE

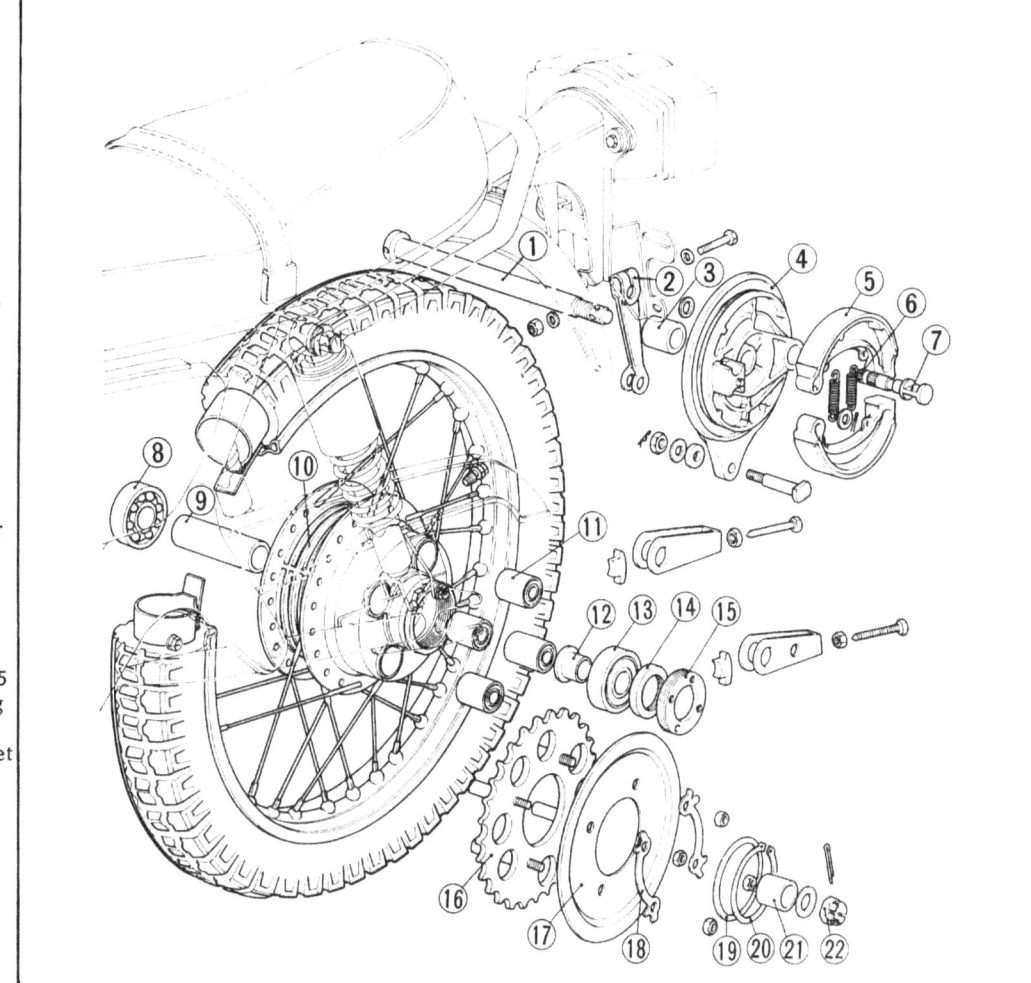

Fig. 4-26
① Rear wheel axle
② Rear brake arm
③ Rear brake panel side collar
④ Rear brake panel
⑤ Rear brake shoe (2)
⑥ Rear brake shoe spring (2)
⑦ Rear brake cam
⑧ 6303 radial ball bearing
⑨ Rear axle distance collar A
⑩ Rear wheel hub
⑪ Rear wheel damper bush (4)
⑫ Rear axle distance collar B
⑬ 6304 radial ball bearing
⑭ Dust-seal 30×45×9.5
⑮ Rear wheel bearing retainer
⑯ Final driven sprocket
⑰ Sprocket side plate
⑱ 10 mm lock washer (2)
⑲ Washer 70 mm
⑳ External circlip 69 mm
㉑ Rear wheel side collar
㉒ Castle nut 16 mm

Disassembly

1. Remove the muffler at each side.
2. Remove the rear brake rod and rear brake stopper arm.
3. Loosen the drive chain adjusting bolt and lock nut on each side. Remove the cotter pin and loosen the axle nut.
4. Remove the drive chain from the final driven sprocket. Remove the rear wheel with the chain adjuster stopper and rear wheel axle.
5. Remove the 69 mm external circlip and remove the final driven sprocket. The lock washers need not be removed.

NOTE:
1. When replacing the final driven sprocket, also replace the fixing bolts.
2. When the lock washer has been removed, replace it with a new one after reassembly.

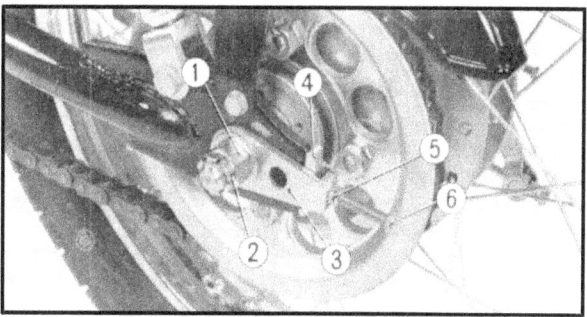

Fig. 4-27
① Axle nut
② Cotter pin
③ Drive chain adjuster
④ Chain adjuster stopper
⑤ Lock nut
⑥ Chain adjusting bolt

Fig. 4-28 ① Final driven sprocket ② Wood block

IV. FRAME

Fig. 4-29 ① Bearing retainer wrench

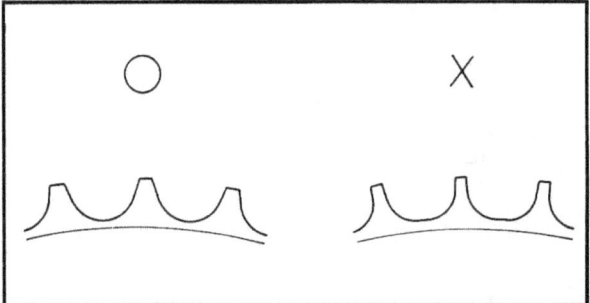

Fig. 4-30 Final driven sprocket wear

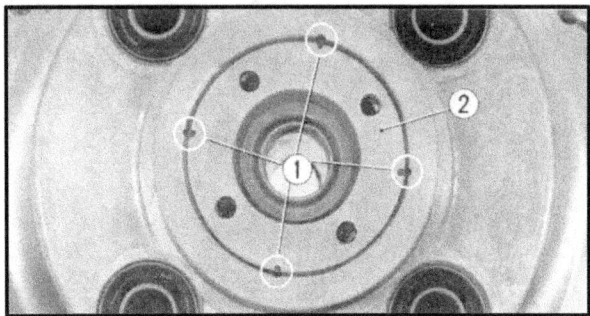

Fig. 4-31 ① Stake
② Bearing retainer

Fig. 4-32 Install the driven sprocket

Fig. 4-33 ① Brake shoes
② Anchor pin
③ Brake shoe springs
④ Brake shoe cam

6. Remove the rear wheel bearing retainer with the bearing retainer wrench (Tool No. 07910-3290000).

Inspection

1. Check the rear wheel axle for bending.
2. Check the ball bearings for excessive play.
3. Check the rim for face runout.
4. Check the spokes for looseness, bending, or other damage.
   Spoke torque specification: **20~30 kg-cm (1.5~1.9 lbs-ft)**.
5. Check the final driven sprocket for wear or other damage.
6. Check the drive chain for excessive wear, elongation or other damage.
7. Check the tire for cracks, excessive wear or other damage.
8. Check the tire pressure.
   Tire pressure specification: **2.0 kg/cm² (28 psi)**.
9. Check the brake lining for excessive wear.
10. Check the brake panel for cracks or other damage.
11. Check the brake drum for excessive wear.

Reassembly

1. Fill the ball bearings and the wheel hub with grease. Insert the distance collar into the hub and drive in the bearing using bearing driver handle (Tool No. 07949-6110000) and driver attachment (Tool No. 07945-3330200).
2. Install the bearing retainer using retainer wrench (Tool No. 07910-3290000). Stake the bearing retainer at four places as shown in Fig. 4-31.
3. Install the driven sprocket to the pivot bushing of the wheel hub and secure it with the 69 mm cir-clip.
4. Lubricate the anchor pin before installing the brake shoes.

NOTE:
The brake shoe lining must be free from any grease or oil.

5. After completing reassembly, check the drive chain tension and adjust properly.
   Also check the rear brake pedal height and free play and adjust properly if necessary.

4. STEERING HANDLEBAR

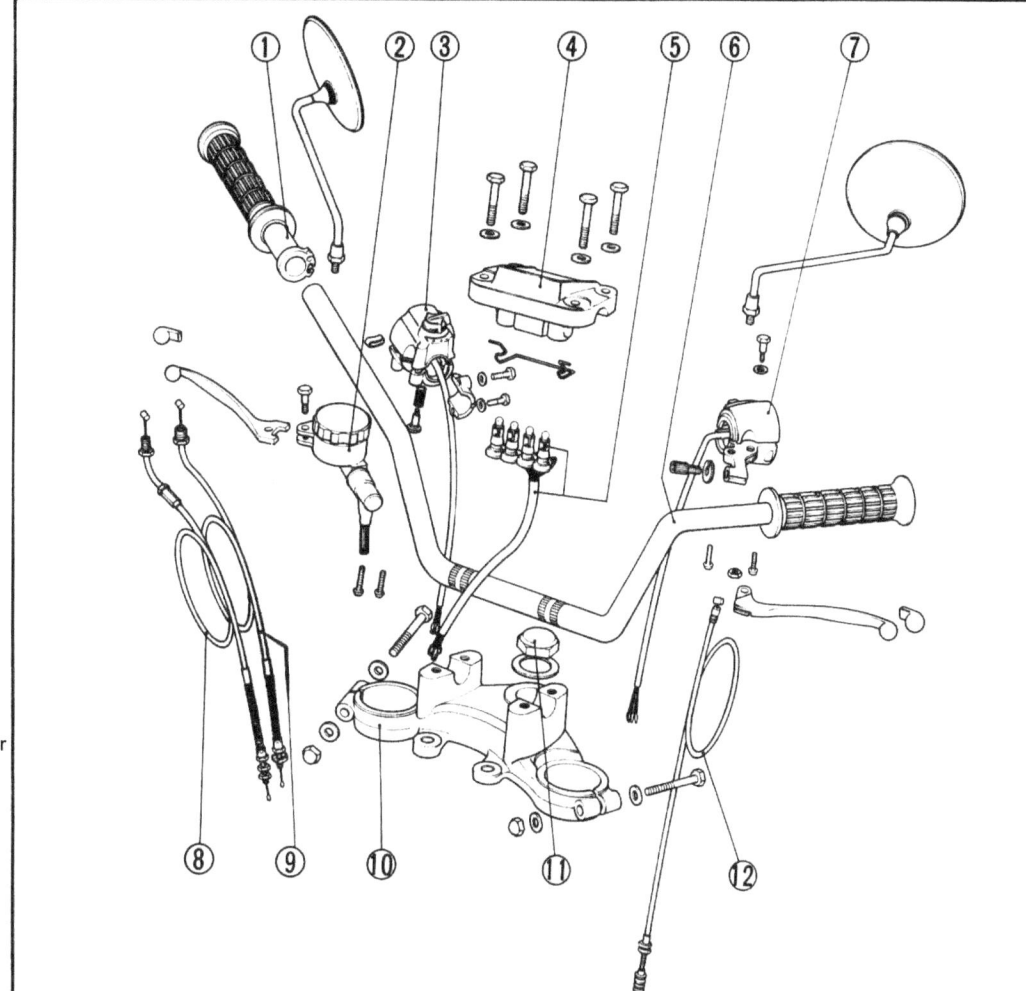

Fig. 4-34
1. Throttle grip pipe
2. Master cylinder
3. Starter, headlight, emergency switch
4. Upper handle holder
5. Pilot lamp
6. Steering handlebar
7. Turn signal, horn switch
8. Throttle cable A
9. Throttle cable B
10. Fork top bridge
11. Steering stem nut
12. Clutch cable

Disassembly

1. Remove the master cylinder, being careful not to spill brake fluid.
2. Disconnect the clutch cable at the lever.
3. Disconnect throttle cables A and B from the carburetor throttle cable stay.

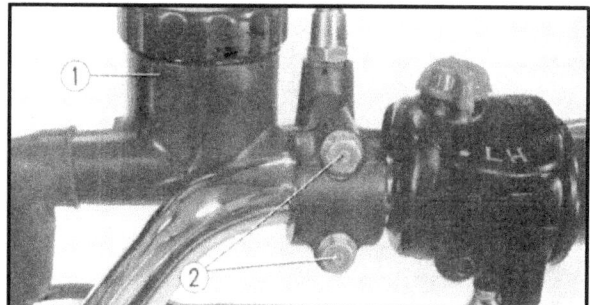

Fig. 4-35 ① Master cylinder
② 6mm hex bolts

4. Remove the headlight unit from the case and disconnect the wiring at the harness in the case.
5. Remove the upper handle holder and the steering handlebar.

Fig. 4-36 ① Upper handle holder
② Steering handlebar

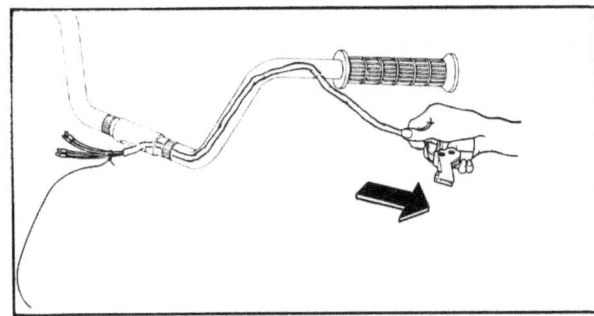

Fig. 4-37

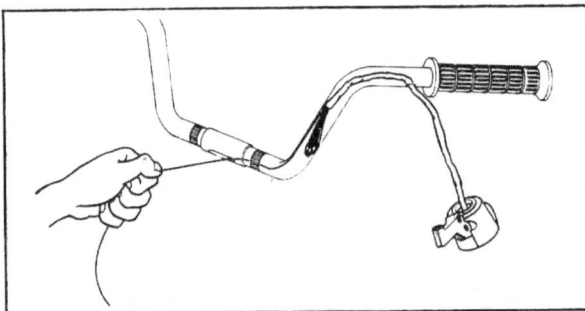

Fig. 4-38

6. Carefully pull the lighting switch assembly and turn signal switch assembly out from the steering handlebar.

Inspection

1. Check the steering handlebar for twisting or other damage.
2. Check each wire for breakage or other damage.
3. Check each cable for damage.

Reassembly

1. Install the lighting switch assembly and turn signal switch assembly to the steering handlebar. Use a wire to tie the ends of the wirings so that they can be pulled through the pipe without binding or kinking.

Fig. 4-39   ① Punch marks

2. Install the steering handlebar, aligning the punch marks on the handlebar with the mating edges of the holder and fork top bridge.

NOTE:
1. **When tightening the upper holder to the fork top bridge, tighten the hex. bolts at the front first and then the ones at the rear.**
2. **Do not bind or kink the wirings.**

Fig. 4-40   ① Clutch cable   ③ Speedometer cable
            ② Tachometer cable ④ Throttle cables

3. Check to be sure each wiring and cable is free from binding or kinking when turning the steering handlebar fully in either direction.

Fig. 4-41   ①② Clutch cable
            ③ Throttle cables

IV. FRAME

5. STEERING STEM

Disassembly

1. Remove the front wheel and caliper assembly.
2. Remove the steering handlebar.
3. Remove the headlight unit from the headlight case and disconnect the wiring at the harness in the case. Remove the case from the steering stem.
4. Disconnect the brake hose at the three-way joint at the steering stem.
5. Remove the speedometer and tachometer. Disconnect the meter cables at the engine and front wheel sides.

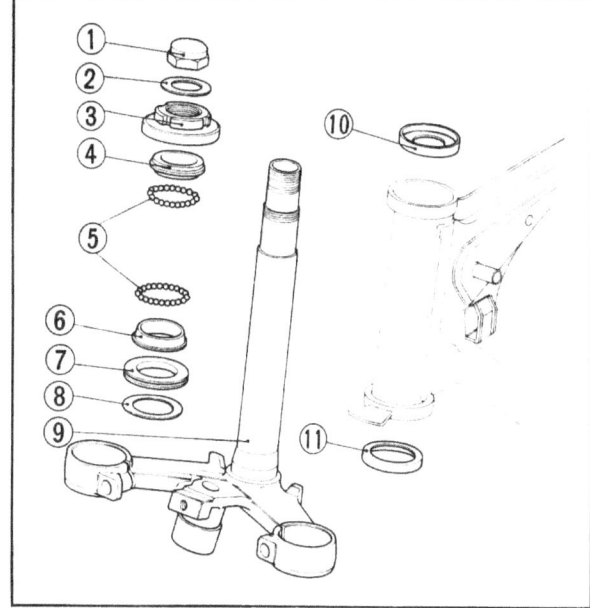

Fig. 4-42
① Steering stem nut
② Steering stem nut washer
③ Steering top thread
④ Steering top cone race
⑤ #5 steel balls (thirty seven)
⑥ Steering bottom cone race
⑦ Steering head dust seal
⑧ Dust seal washer
⑨ Steering stem
⑩ Steering top ball race
⑪ Steering bottom ball race

6. Loosen the front fork bolt at the steering stem bottom bridge, and loosen the bolts securing the forks at the fork top bridge. Pull the front fork assembly out.
7. Loosen the steering stem nut on top of the stem, and remove the fork top bridge.

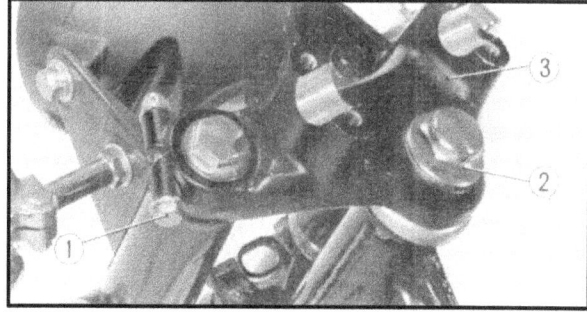

Fig. 4-43
① Front fork bolts
② Steering stem nut
③ Fork top bridge

8. Loosen the steering head top thread to remove the steering stem.

NOTE:
Do not lose the steel balls (Upper: 19; Lower: 18)

Inspection

1. Check the steering stem for bending or other damage.
2. Check the steering top and bottom cone races for excessive wear or other damage.
3. Check the steering head dust seal for excessive wear.

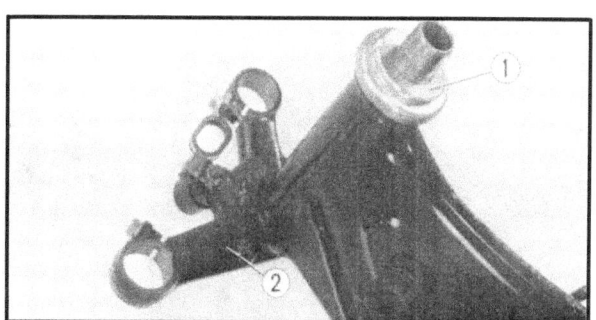

Fig. 4-44
① Steering head top thread
② Steering stem

IV. FRAME

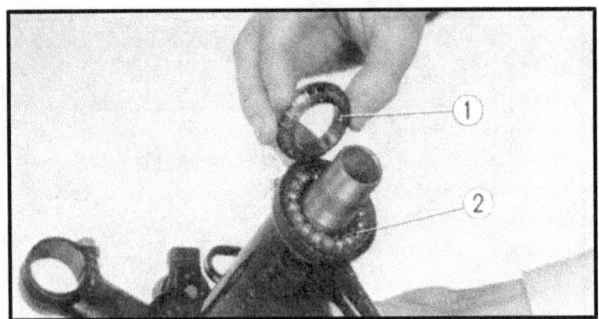

Fig. 4-45　① Top cone race
　　　　　② #8 steel balls

Reassembly

1. Install #8 steel balls (upper: **19** and lower: **18**) to each race properly. Fully tighten the steering head top thread and turn it so that the stem rotates easily without rattling when turned to either side.

NOTE:
Be sure to clean the cone races, ball races and steel balls in solvent, and apply a coat of grease before reassembly.

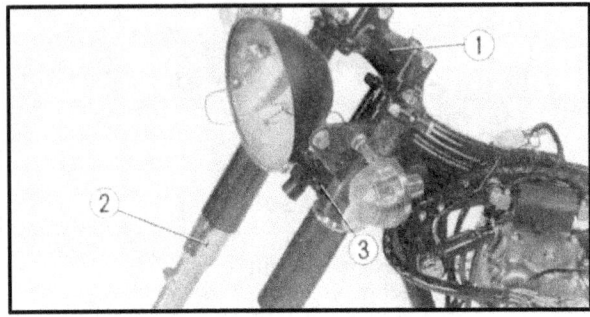

Fig. 4-46　① Fork top bridge
　　　　　② Front fork assembly
　　　　　③ Steering stem

2. The fork top bridge should be installed before securely tightening the steering stem.

6. FRONT SUSPENSION

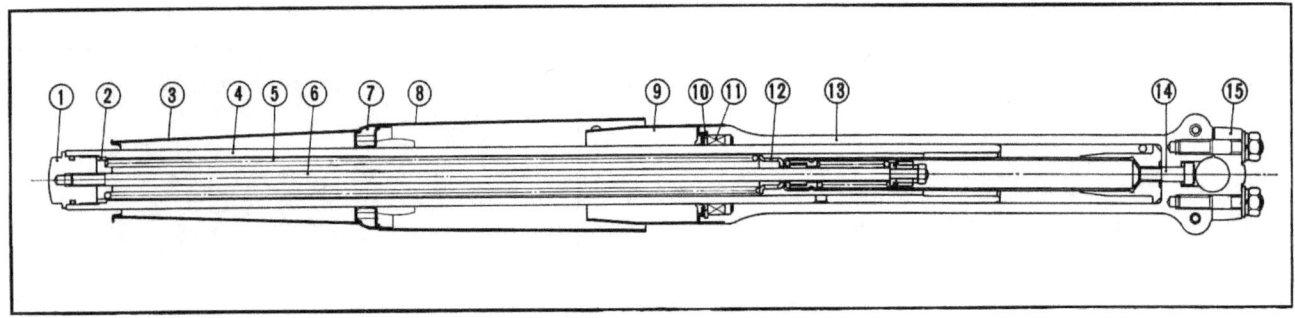

Fig. 4-47

① Front fork bolt
② Lock nut
③ Front fork cover
④ Front fork pipe
⑤ Front cushion spring
⑥ Damper
⑦ Front fork rib
⑧ Front fork under cover
⑨ Bottom case cover
⑩ 47 mm internal circlip
⑪ Oil seal 33×46×10.5
⑫ Cushion spring seat
⑬ Front fork bottom case
⑭ Socket bolt 8 mm
⑮ Axle holder

Fig. 4-48　① 8 mm bolt at fork top bridge
　　　　　② 8 mm bolt at steering stem bottom bridge

Disassembly

1. Remove the front wheel.
2. Remove the caliper assembly and front fender.
3. Loosen the 8 mm bolts that secure the front fork assembly at the steering stem bottom bridge and at the fork top bridge. Pull the assembly out.

NOTE:
Before loosening the 8 mm bolts, loosen the front fork bolts.

4. Drain the front suspension oil.

IV. FRAME

5. Remove any rust on the front fork pipe, an emery cloth.
6. Loosen the 8 mm socket bolt at the bottom of the fork bottom case with a hollow wrench (Tool No. 07917-3230000).
   The front fork pipe with the damper unit can be removed from the bottom case as shown in Fig. 4-50 Ⓐ.

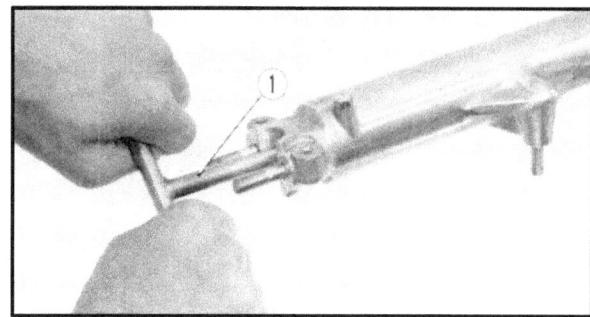

Fig. 4-49 ① Hollow wrench

7. Remove the front fork bolt on top of the fork pipe to remove the front cushion spring and spring seat.
8. To remove the oil seal, remove the bottom case cover and the circlip.

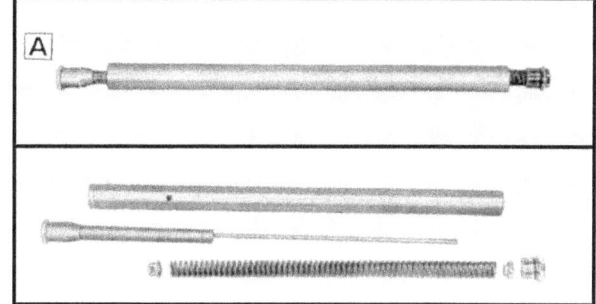

Fig. 4-50

Inspection

1. Measure the free length of the front cushion spring.
2. Check the front fork pipe and bottom case for looseness or other damage.
3. Check the oil seal for scratches or other damage.
4. Check the front fork pipe sliding part for damage.

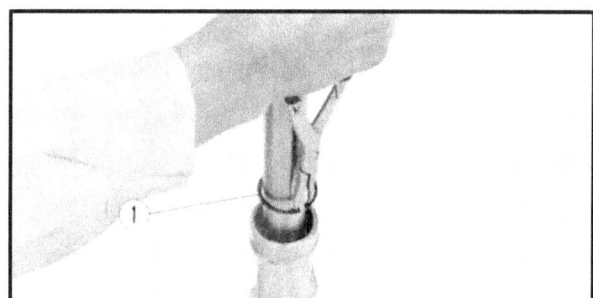

Fig. 4-51 ① Circlip

Reassembly

1. Install the front fork pipe with the damper unit into the fork bottom case.

NOTE:
Apply locking sealant to the 8 mm socket bolt.

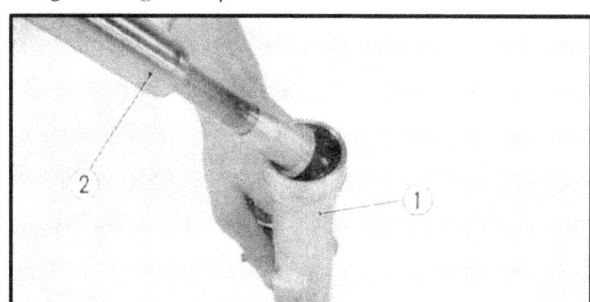

Fig. 4-52 ① Fork bottom case
         ② Front fork pipe

2. Apply a coat of ATF (automatic transmission fluid) around and inside the oil seal before installing it to the front fork pipe. Press-fit the seal using the front seal driver (Tool No. 07947-3330000).

NOTE:
1. **Be sure to properly install the circlip.**
2. **Replace the oil seal with a new one.**
3. Fill each front fork bottom case with **125 cc (4.2 ozs)** of high quality ATF.

NOTE:
When changing oil, add 105 cc (3.6 ozs).

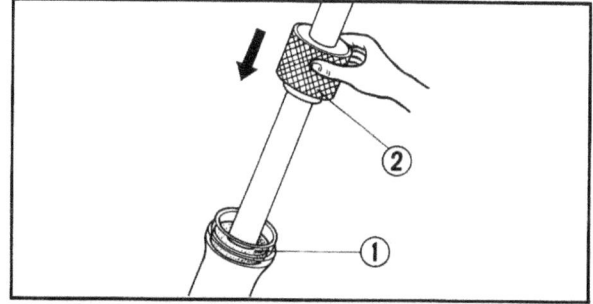

Fig. 4-53 ① Oil seal
         ② Front seal driver

7. REAR SUSPENSION

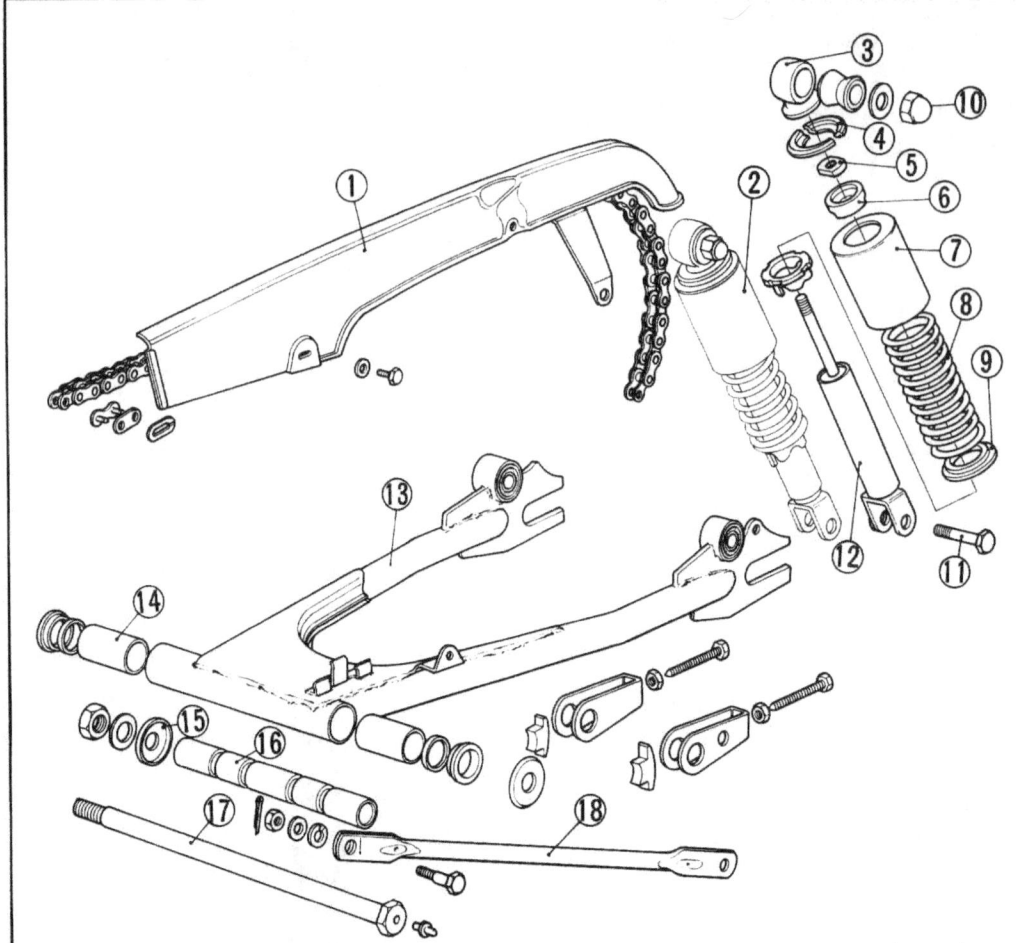

Fig. 4-54
① Drive chain case (2)
② Rear suspension (2)
③ Upper joint (2)
④ Spring seat stopper (4)
⑤ 9 mm lock nut (2)
⑥ Rear cushion stopper rubber (2)
⑦ Rear cushion upper case (2)
⑧ Rear cushion spring (2)
⑨ Spring under seat (2)
⑩ Rear cushion upper nut (2)
⑪ Hex bolt 10×32 (2)
⑫ Rear damper (2)
⑬ Rear fork
⑭ Rear fork pivot bush (2)
⑮ Rear fork dust-seal cap (2)
⑯ Rear fork center collar
⑰ Rear fork pivot bolt
⑱ Rear brake stopper arm

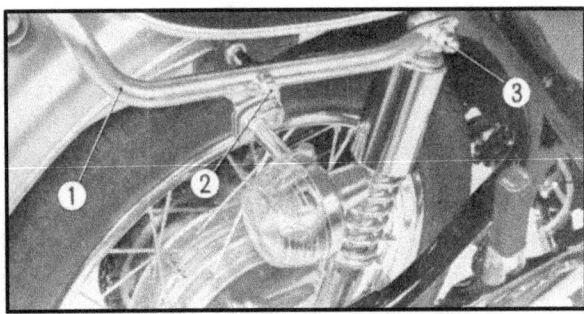

Fig. 4-55 ① Rear bumper
② 8 mm bolt
③ Rear cushion upper nut

Disassembly

Rear suspension

1. Remove the rear bumper by loosening the 8 mm bolts and rear cushion upper nuts.
2. Remove the rear suspension by removing 10 mm bolts.
3. Compress the rear suspension using service tool (Tool No. 07959-3290000) and remove the spring seat stoppers to remove the rear cushion spring.

Rear fork

4. Remove the rear wheel.
5. Loosen the self lock nut to pull out the rear fork pivot bolt. Remove the rear fork from the frame.

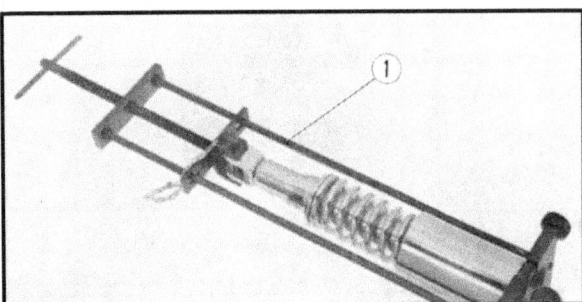

Fig. 4-56 ① Rear suspension service tool

IV. FRAME

Inspection

1. Measure the rear cushion spring free length.
2. Check the rear cushion damper for deformation or oil leakage.
3. Check the rear cushion stopper rubber for damage.
4. Measure the rear fork center collar-to-bushing clearance.
5. Check the rear fork swing arm for bending.

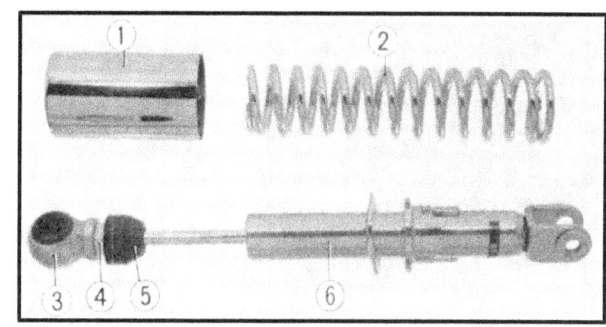

Fig. 4-57
① Upper case
② Rear cushion spring
③ Upper joint
④ Lock nut
⑤ Stopper rubber
⑥ Rear damper unit

Reassembly

1. Apply a coat of grease to the rear fork center collar before installing it to the rear fork.
2. Install the rear fork.
   Insert the rear fork pivot bolt from the left side.
3. Assemble the rear suspension.
   1) Compress the rear suspension with the service tool (Tool No. 07959-3290000) and pull the upper joint up to install the spring seat stoppers in place.
   2) Apply locking sealant to the upper joint before tightening.
4. Install the rear suspension to the frame.

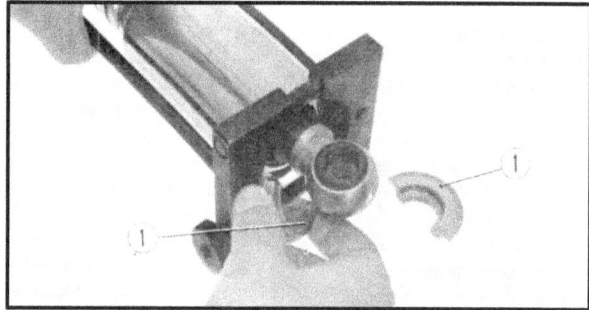

Fig. 4-58 ① Spring seat stoppers

8. FRAME BODY

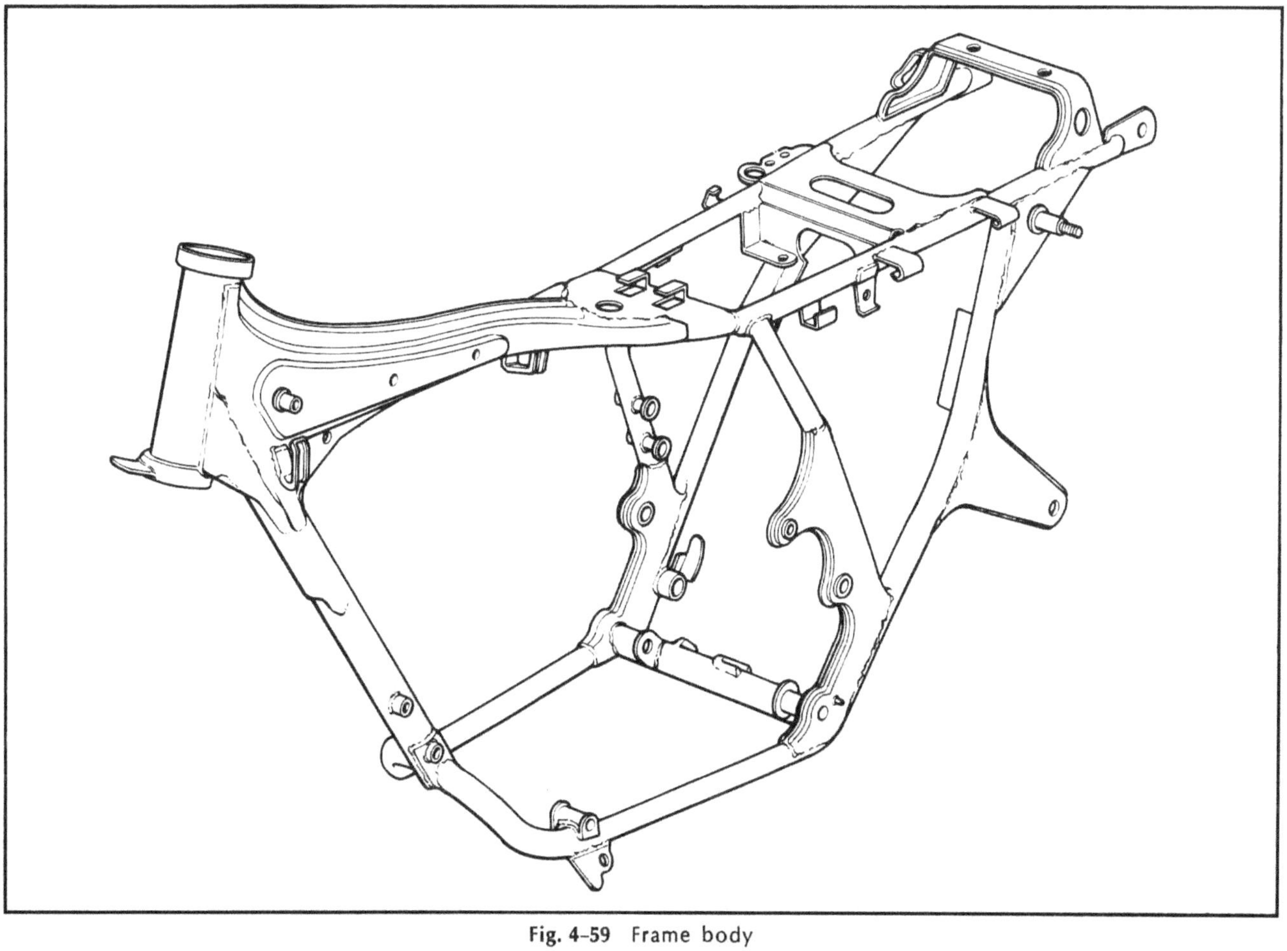

Fig. 4-59 Frame body

IV. FRAME

Fig. 4-60 ① ⊕ terminal
② ⊖ terminal

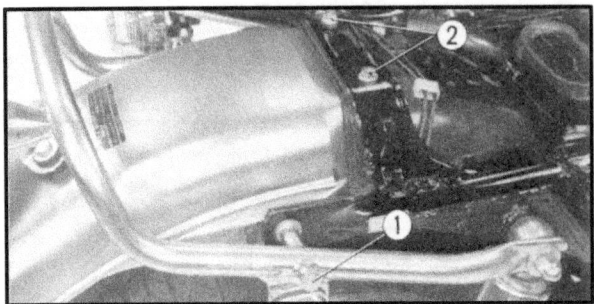

Fig. 4-61 ① 8 mm hex bolts
② 6 mm hex bolts

Fig. 4-62 ① 6 mm bolts
② Air cleaner case

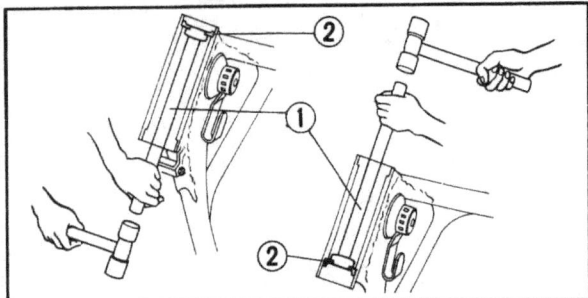

Fig. 4-63 ① Ball race remover
② Ball races

Fig. 4-64 ① Hole
② Fuel filler cap

Removal

1. Remove the fuel tank.
2. Remove the seat.
3. Remove the battery.
   Disconnect the ground cable at the negative terminal first and then the starter cable at the positive terminal of the battery.
4. Dismount the engine from the frame.
5. Remove the steering stem.
   Before removing the stem, remove the front wheel, front forks and steering handlebar.
6. Remove the rear fender.
   Disconnect the wire leads of the rear turn signals and tail/stop light.
   Loosen the 6 and 8 mm hex bolts that secure the rear fender.

7. Remove the air cleaner case and battery box.
   Disconnect each wiring at the connector and coupler.
   Remove the silicon rectifier, regulator and starter magnetic switch.
   Loosen the three hex bolts that secure the air cleaner case.
8. Disconnect the wire harness.

9. Remove the main and side stands.
10. Remove the top and bottom ball races from the steering head pipe using ball race remover (Tool No. 07953-3330000).

Inspection

1. Check the hole in the fuel filler cap for clogging.
2. Check the frame body for bending, cracking, deformation or other damage.

3. Check the steering head pipe for misalignment or deformation.
4. Check wire harness, coupler and connector for proper connection or other damage.

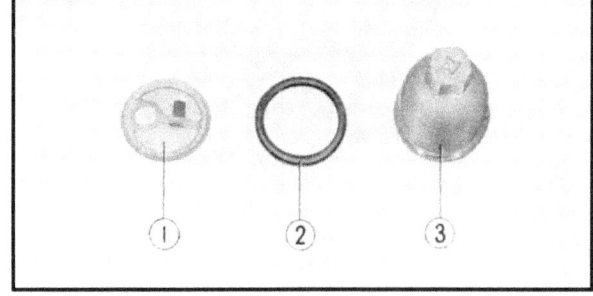

Fig. 4-65 ① Fuel strainer screen
② O-ring
③ Fuel strainer cup

5. Check the O-ring of the fuel valve drain and strainer cup for wear or other damage.
6. Check the fuel pipe for damage.

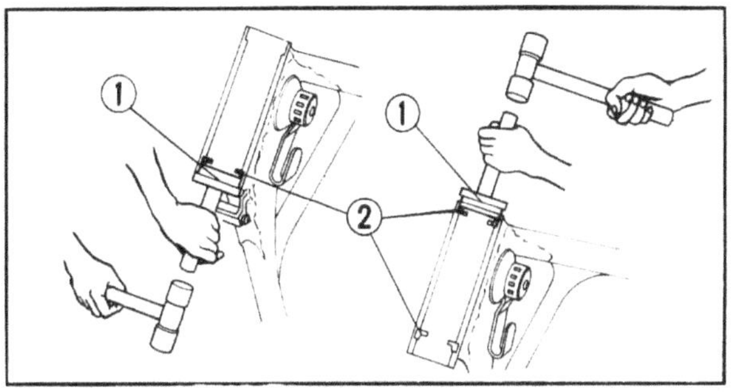

Installation

1. Drive the top and bottom ball races into the steering head pipe properly and evenly using the ball race driver attachment (Tool No. 07953-3330000) and driver handle (Tool No. 07949-6110000).

2. Connect the wire harness.
   Route the wirings and secure them with clips.

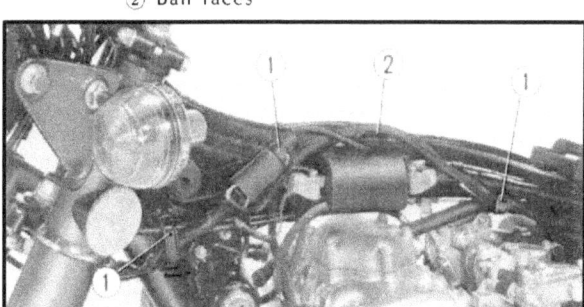

Fig. 4-66 ① Ball race remover
② Ball races

Fig. 4-67 ① Clips
② Wire harness

3. Install the air cleaner case and battery box.
   Remove any dust from the cleaner case and check the water drain hole for clogging before installation.

Fig. 4-68 ① Wire harness
② Starting motor cable

4. Install the battery box.
   Connect the starter cable to the positive terminal and connect the ground cable to the negative terminal of the battery.
   Route the battery overflow tube noting the battery caution mark.

Fig. 4-69 ① Battery over flow tube

IV. FRAME

Fig. 4-70 ① Main stand mounting bolts
② Battery over flow tube guide
③ Side stand spring

5. Install the main stand and side stand.

NOTE:
1. Do not overtighten the main stand mounting bolts. Be sure to install the battery overflow tube guide to the left side of the bolt.
2. Install the side stand spring as shown in Fig. 4-70.

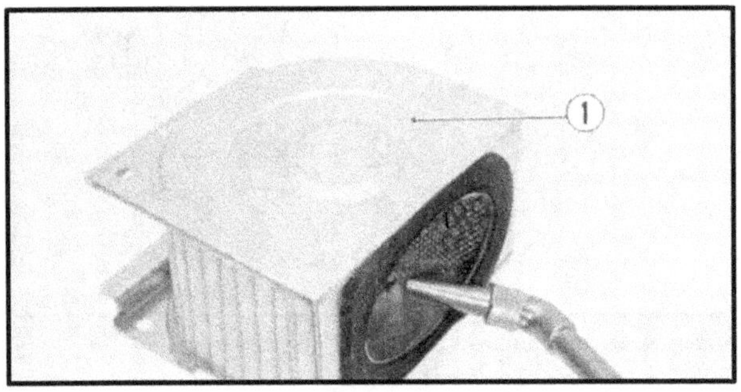

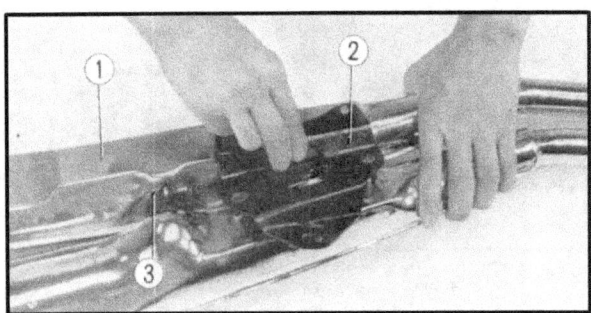

Fig. 4-71 ① Air cleaner

6. Clean the air cleaner.
   Lightly tap the cleaner element and apply a blast of compressed air from inside to remove dust.

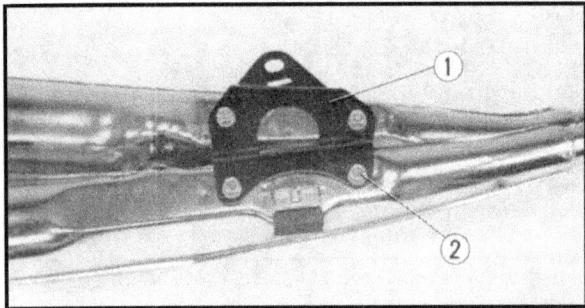

Fig. 4-72 ① Muffler
② Muffler bracket
③ Connecting tube

7. Install the mufflers.
   Join the upper and lower mufflers securely with the connecting tube and tighten the connecting pipe. Install the mufflers to the frame with the brackets and tighten the 8 mm nuts.

Fig. 4-73 ① Muffler bracket
② 8 mm nut

V. ELECTRICAL

1. GENERAL DESCRIPTION

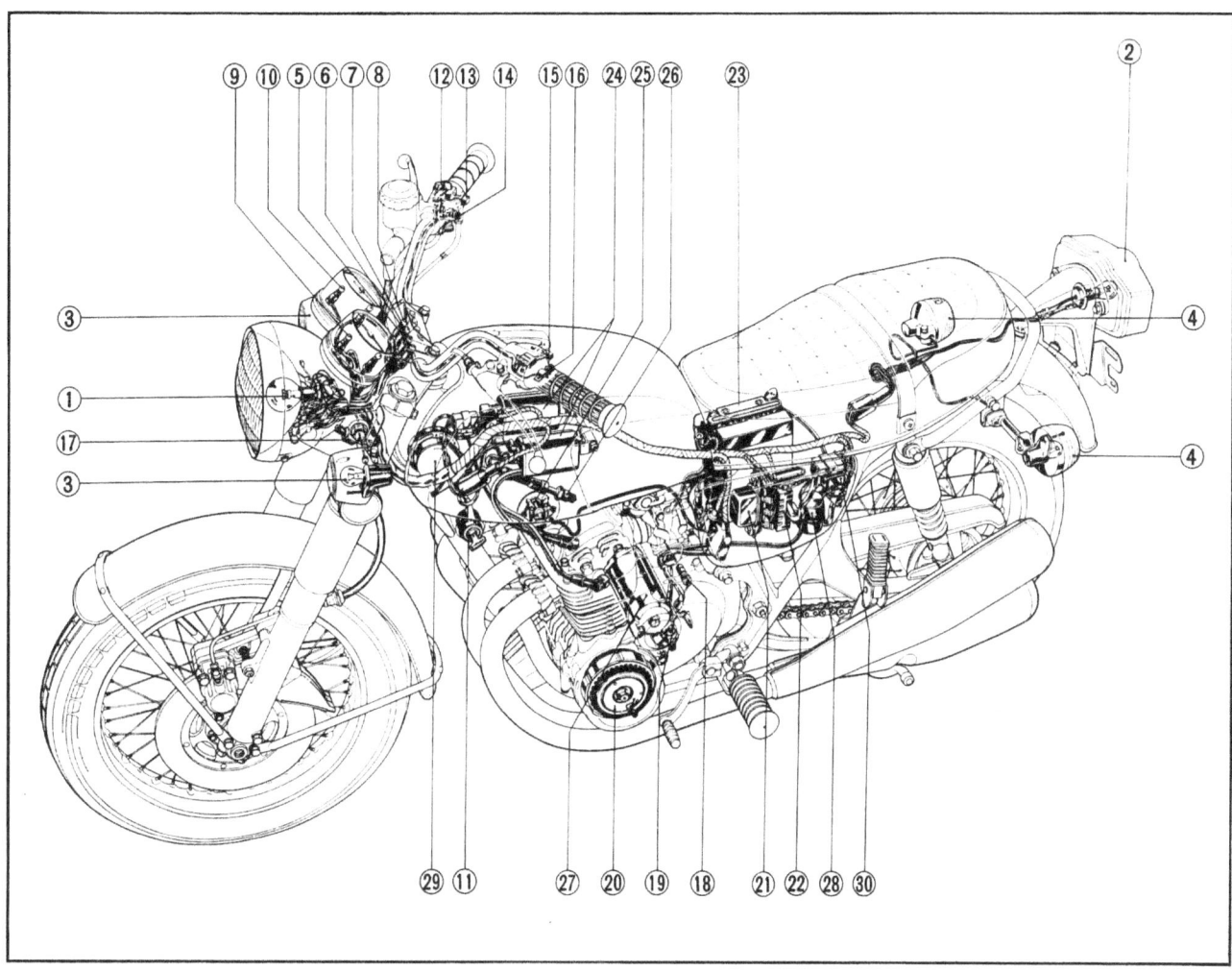

Fig. 5-1

LIGHTS
① Headlight
② Tail/stoplight
③ Front turn signal lights
④ Rear turn signal lights
⑤ Turn signal indicator lamp
⑥ Oil pressure warning lamp
⑦ Neutral indicator lamp
⑧ High beam indicator lamp
⑨ Speedometer lamp
⑩ Tachometer lamp

SWITCHES
⑪ Main switch
⑫ Emergency switch
⑬ Headlight control switch
⑭ Starter switch
⑮ Turn signal control switch
⑯ Horn button
⑰ Stop switch
⑱ Neutral switch
⑲ Oil pressure switch
CHARGING SYSTEM
⑳ A-C generator
㉑ Regulator

㉒ Silicon rectifier
㉓ Battery
IGNITION SYSTEM
㉔ Ignition coils
㉕ Contact breaker
㉖ Spark plugs
STARTING SYSTEM
㉗ Starting motor
㉘ Magnetic switch
ELECTRICAL EQUIPMENT
㉙ Horn
㉚ Winker relay

V. ELECTRICAL

2. IGNITION SYSTEM

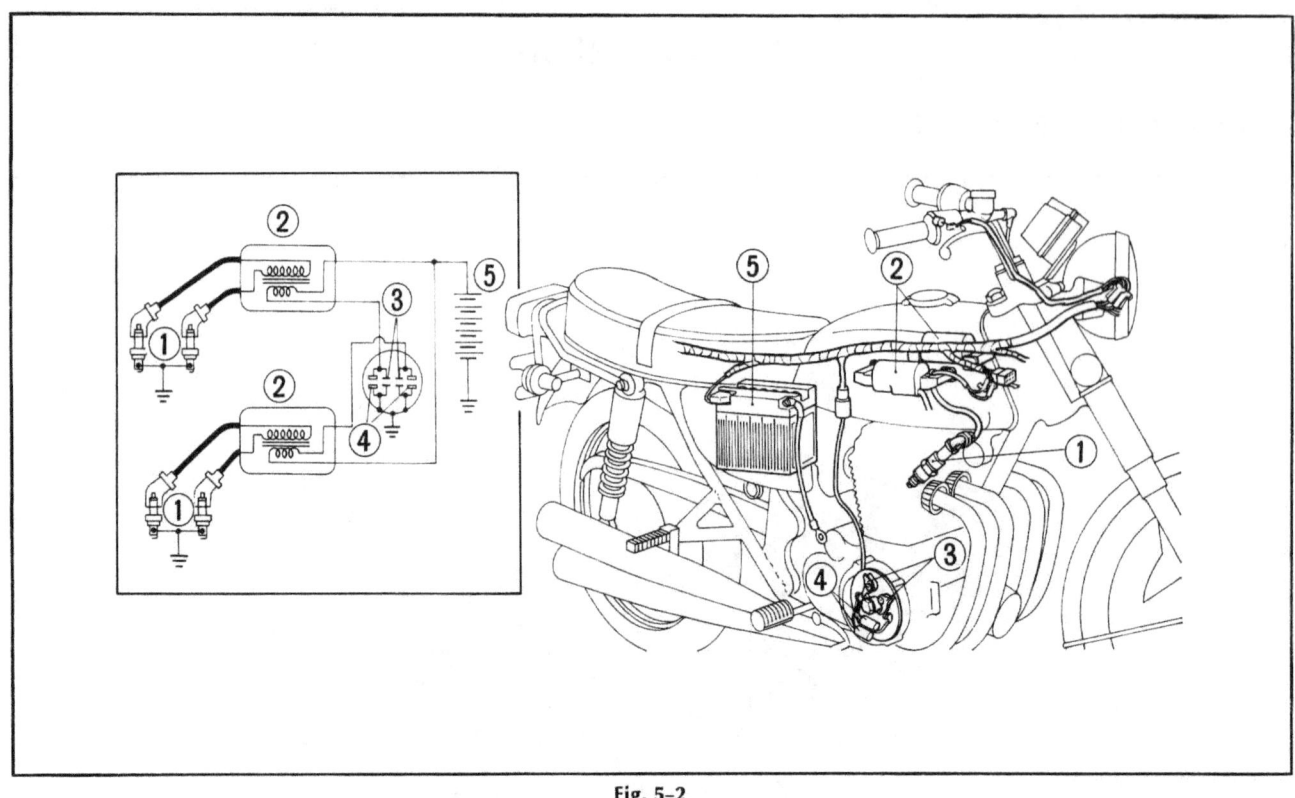

Fig. 5-2

① Spark plugs　② Ignition coils　③ Contact breakers　④ Capacitors　⑤ Battery

The ignition system fires the 4-cycle, 4-cylinder engine in a sequence of 1, 2, 4 and 3 of the cylinders at each 180° of the crankshaft rotation. The combustion strokes of all the cylinders are completed each time the crankshaft rotates two turns.

To the right end of the crankshaft are spark advancer and contact breaker housing which contains two contact breakers. The contact breakers are 180° out of phase and connect to two ignition coils that provide two high tension cords connecting four spark plugs as shown in the diagram above. Since no distributor is used, the system is simply constructed and facilitates servicing.

Ignition coil	
3 point spark gap opening	7 mm (0.27 in.), min.
Spark plug	
Type (standard)	D-8ESL (NGK), X-24ES (DENSO)
Plug gap	0.6–0.7 mm (0.024–0.028 in.)
Contact breaker	
Point gap	0.3–0.4 mm (0.012–0.016 in.)
Spring force	650–850 gr. (1.43–1.87 lbs)
Capacitor	
Capacity	0.22 μF ±10%
Insulation resistance	10 MΩ (1,000 V with a megger)
Spark advancer	
Start of advance (crankshaft rotation)	1,400–1,600 rpm
Full advance (crankshaft rotation)	2,300–2,500 rpm
Advance angle	23.5°–26.5°

Ignition coils

Inspection

1. Continuity test
   1) Primary coil
      Check for continuity between the two primary coil terminals with a radio tester.
      Right coil: yellow, black lead to white lead.
      Left coil : blue, black lead to white lead.
   2) Secondary coil
      Check the high tension cord terminal and primary side terminal on each cord for continuity. If there is no continuity, the coil has an open-circuit and must be replaced.

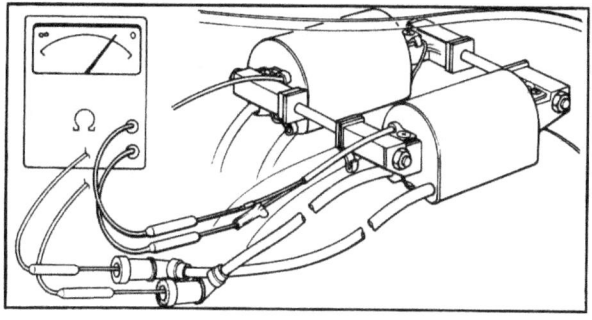

Fig. 5-3 Checking ignition coil for continuity

2. Performance test
   Even though continuity is ensured, an ignition coil may provide poor performance after long use. Check its performance as follows:
   1) Turn the service tester selector knob to "IGNITION TEST" and make connections of the tester following the tester manufacturers instructions.
   2) Connect the tester power supply cord to a fully charged battery.
      Measure the maximum distance where the spark jumps across the gap regularly, using a 3-point spark (B) as shown in Fig. 5-5. Connect the high tension cords in reverse for condition (A) in Fig. 5-5.

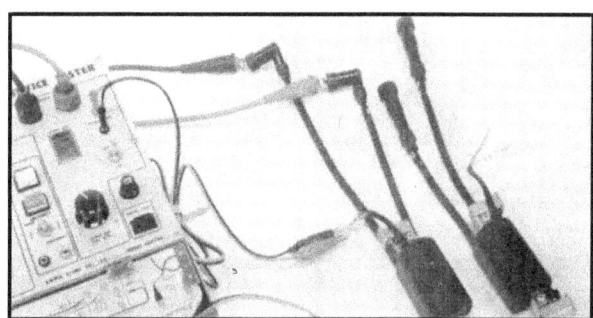

Fig. 5-4 Ignition coil performance test

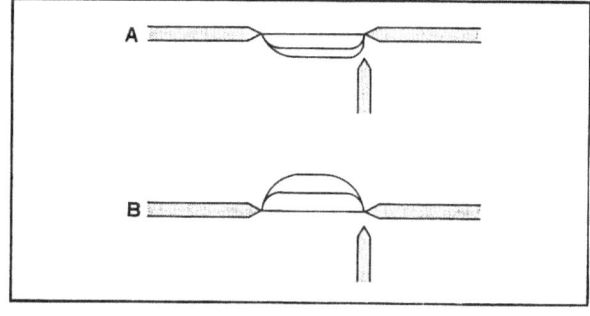

Fig. 5-5 3-point spark tester

Spark plugs

Inspection

1. Check the plug for worn or pitted electrodes, excessive gap, and damaged insulator.
   1) Clean dirty spark plug with a plug cleaner or wire brush.
   2) Measure the electrode gap with a thickness gauge, and adjust if necessary.
      Gap specification : **0.6~0.7 mm (0.024~0.028 in)**
   3) Replace the spark plug with a new one if the insulator or gasket is damaged or distorted.

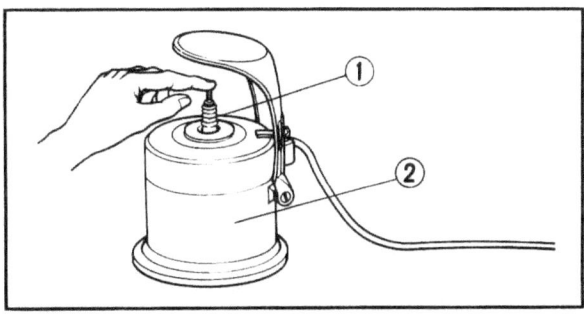

Fig. 5-6 ① Spark plug   ② Plug cleaner

V. ELECTRICAL

Fig. 5-7 ① Breaker point gap ③ "F" mark
② Matching mark

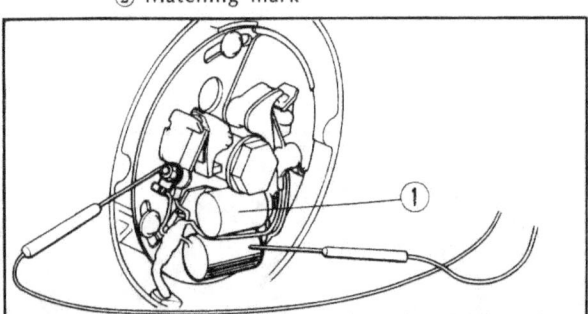

Fig. 5-8 ① Capacitors

Fig. 5-9 ① Spark advancer

Contact breakers and capacitors

1. Contact breakers
   For breaker point and ignition timing adjustment see section INSPECTION AND ADJUSTMENT.

2. Capacitors
   Measure the capacitance with a service tester.
   Capacitance specification : **0.22 μF ± 10%**

NOTE :
The point must remain open when measuring.

Spark advancer

Inspection

1. Wipe off any foreign matter from the friction surfaces and check for smooth operation.
2. Check the advancer pin for excessive wear.
3. Take the readings of the crankshaft rpm at initial and full advance angles with the timing light of the service tester.

MEMO

V. ELECTRICAL

3. CHARGING SYSTEM

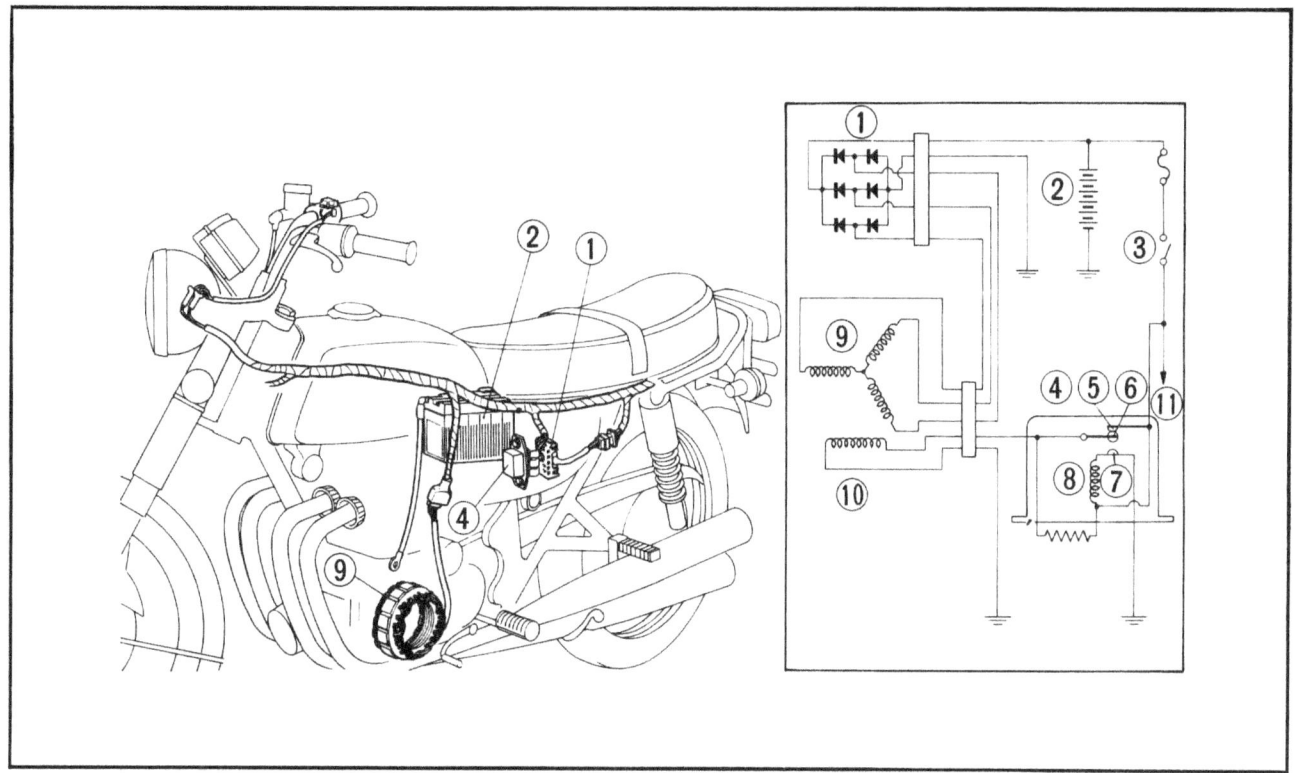

Fig. 5-10

① Silicon rectifier
② Battery
③ Main switch
④ Regulator
⑤ Upper contact
⑥ Moving contact
⑦ Lower contact
⑧ Relay coil
⑨ Stator coil
⑩ Field coil
⑪ Load

The charging system consists of a 3 phase AC generator, silicon diode rectifier, voltage regulator and storage battery. The 3 phase AC generator, a brushless exciting type, is capable of generating enough high voltage output to operate all electrical units of this machine. It features compact and light weight construction. The parts wear less to facilitate handling and servicing. A dual-contact type Tirrill regulator is used in the charging circuit.

1. Charging test

1) Use a fully charged battery for the test. (The specific gravity of the electrolyte in each cell must be **1.26~1.28 at 20 C°** or **68 F°**.)
2) Connect the negative probe of an ammeter to the positive terminal of the battery and the positive probe to the harness.
3) Connect the probes of a voltmeter to the battery terminals in similar polarity.
4) Run the engine under NIGHTTIME RIDING conditions (headlight on) and DAYTIME RIDING conditions (headlight off) and take the meter readings. If the readings are not within the charging characteristics specified on the next page, check the generator condition. If it is normal, check and adjust the regulator.

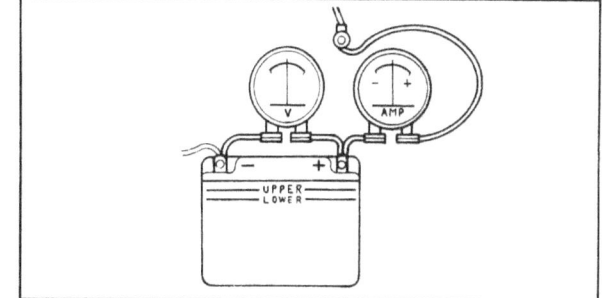

Fig. 5-11 Charging test

NOTE:
Remember the generator output may vary with temperature.

V. ELECTRICAL

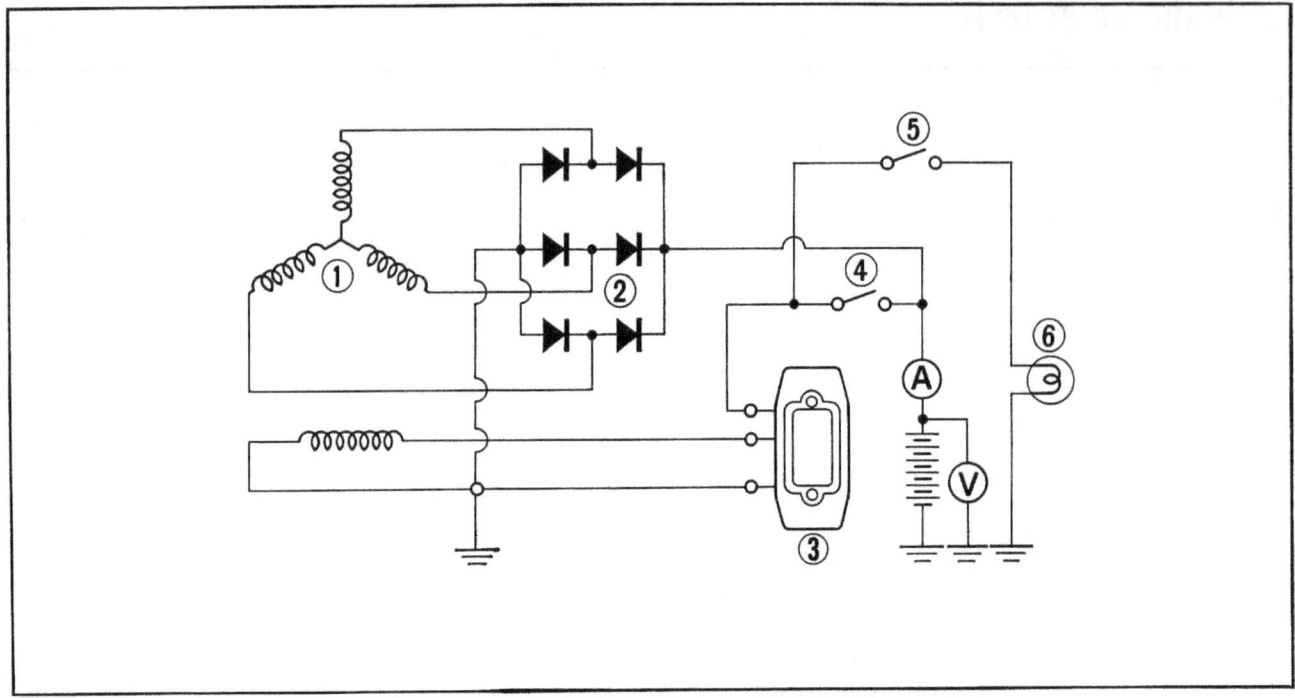

Fig. 5-12 Charging test circuit
① A-C generator   ③ Regulator   ⑤ Lighting switch
② Silicon rectifier   ④ Main switch   ⑥ Load

Charging characteristics

Engine (rpm) Charging current (Ampere)	1,000	2,000	3,000	4,000	5,000	6,000	7,000	8,000
NIGHTTIME RIDING	1.6	1.9	2.0	1.8	1.6	1.5	1.4	1.4
DAYTIME RIDING	—	—	4	2.6	2.0	1.6	1.4	1.4
Battery terminal voltage (Volt)	12.5	14.2	15	15	15	15	15	15

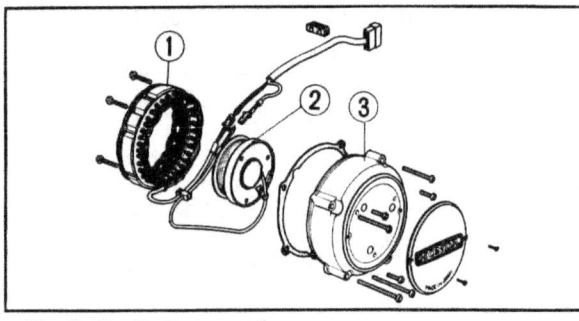

Fig. 5-13 ① Stator coil
② Field coil
③ Dynamo cover

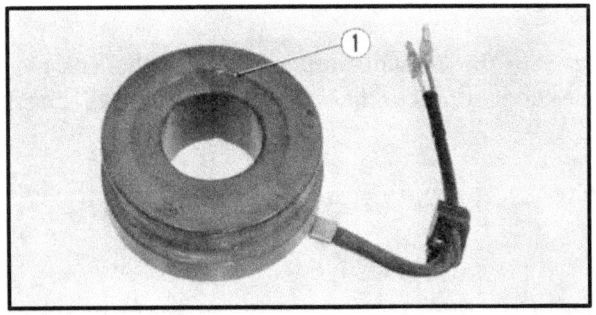

Fig. 5-14 ① Field coil

A-C generator

Rated current output	14.5 V	13 A
Rated charging speed	5,000 rpm	
Ground polarity	⊖	

Inspection

1. Checking field coil for continuity
   Check continuity between the two leads (white and green) with a radio tester.
   Resistance specification : **4.6~5.0 Ω**

V. ELECTRICAL

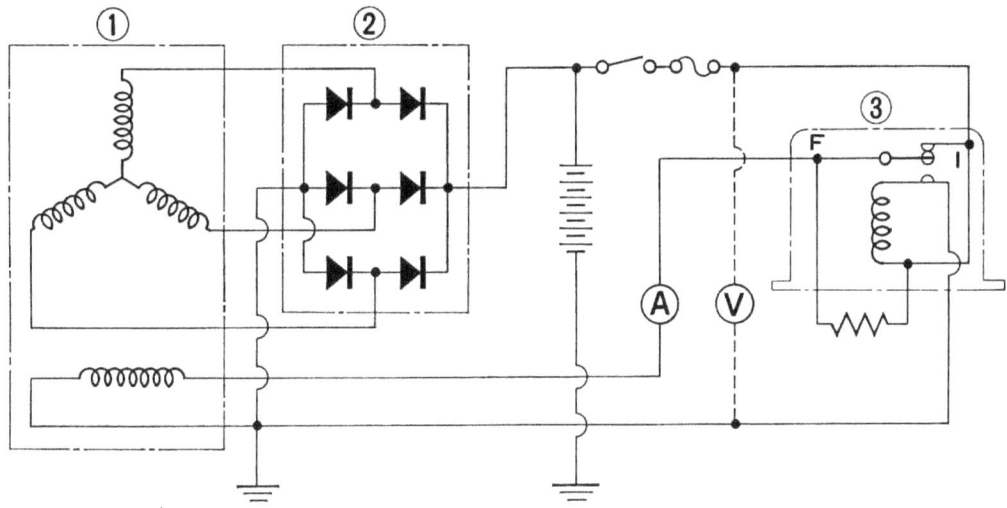

Fig. 5-15 ① A-C generator ② Silicon diode rectifier ③ Regulator

2. Checking resistance of the stator coil windings:
Using an ohmmeter set to its lowest scale range, measure the resistance between one yellow wire lead and each of the remaining two. Test all three leads in this manner.
Specification: 0.61–0.69 ohms resistance between leads

Silicon diode rectifier

Test each diode for forward and reverse continuity with an ohmmeter or test light. Touch one of the yellow wire coupling pins ③ with either of the test instrument leads, then touch the second test lead to pins ④ and ⑤ in turn. Note the continuity indication. Repeat this procedure at each of the two remaining yellow wire coupling pins ③ (**Fig. 5-18**).
Reverse the test instrument leads and repeat the above procedure.
The rectifier is in good condition if the test shows continuity in one direction only at all diodes. The rectifier is defective if:

a. There is continuity in both directions at any diode.
b. There is no continuity in either direction at any diode.

CAUTION:
Do not use an ohmmeter's megohm range (ohms × 1,000,000) for this test.

Do not operate the engine with the red/white rectifier lead disconnected.

When installing a battery, connect the battery terminal wires in correct polarity.

Disconnect the rectifier coupling plug when charging the battery from an external power source.

Failure to observe these precautions may result in diode damage.

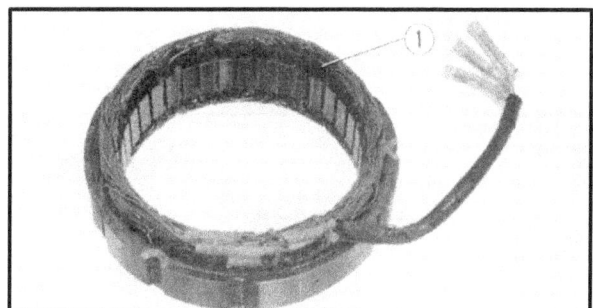

Fig. 5-16 ① Stator coil

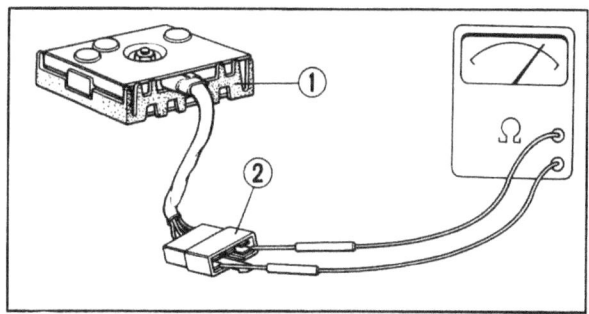

Fig. 5-17 ① Silicon diode rectifier
② Coupler

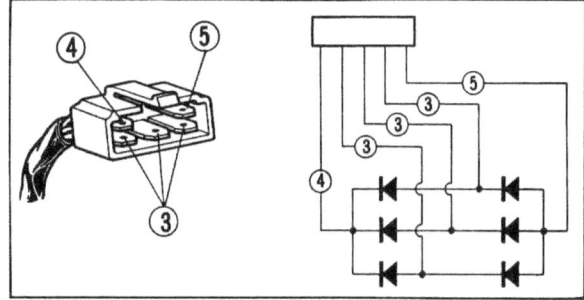

Fig. 5-18 ③ Yellow leads
④ Red/white lead
⑤ Green lead

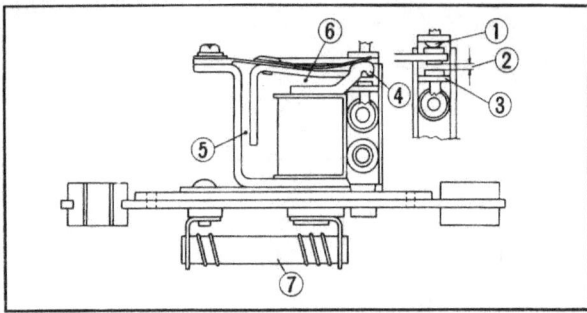

Fig. 5-19
① Upper contact point
② Point gap
③ Lower contact point
④ Charging rate adjustment arm
⑤ Angle gap
⑥ Armature gap
⑦ Resistor

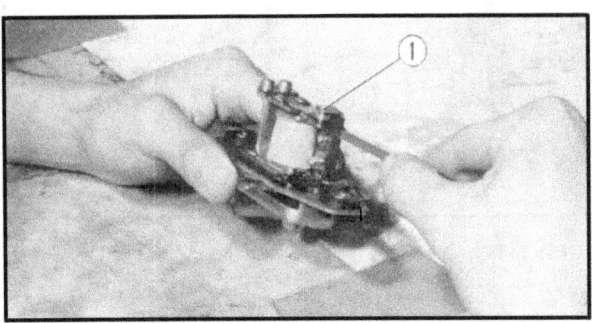

Fig. 5-20 ① Checking point gap with a feeler gauge

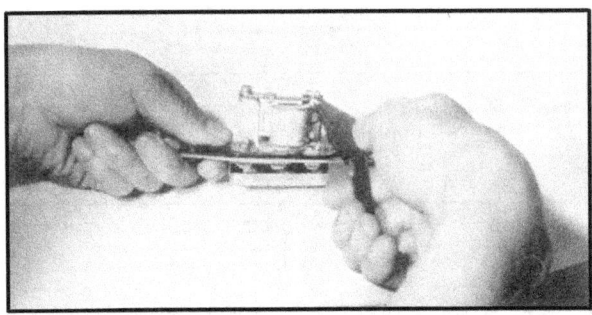

Fig. 5-21 Bending the adjusting arm to adjust the charging rate

Regulator
Intermittent opening of the regulator contact points during operation creates a resistance in the field circuit, reducing alternator output. The voltage level at which this occurs may be adjusted as necessary.

Testing
Test regulator with battery fully charged.
1. Connect a DC voltmeter from regulator ignition terminal (I) to ground. Remove the white lead from the field terminal (F), and connect an ammeter between the wire and the terminal.
2. With the engine idling, note the field current. If value exceeds Mode I limits shown in the table below, the regulator or alternator field coil is faulty.
3. Slowly increase engine speed until the ammeter needle deflects to half the Mode I value. Note the voltage reading when the ammeter needle deflects. Compare with Mode II in the table below.
4. Increase engine speed to 4000 rpm or more, and note the maximum voltage reading. Field current and voltage should agree with Mode III in the table below.

MODE	FIELD CURRENT	VOLTAGE
I (idle)	2.4-2.6 A	to 13.2 V
II	1.2-1.3 A	13.5-14.5 V
III	0-1.2 A	14.0-15.0 V

If field current does not decrease as voltage increases, the regulator is faulty.

If field current to voltage values are higher or lower than the limits in the table, adjustment is indicated.

If voltage exceeds 15.0 V at any speed, the system is overcharging.

Adjustment
1. **Armature gap: 0.6-1.0 mm (0.020-0.040 in.)**
   If adjustment is required, loosen the point base screw, and raise or lower the point assembly to obtain the correct armature gap.
2. **Angle gap: 0.6 mm (0.024 in.)**
   Adjustment of the armature gap simultaneously adjusts the angle gap.
3. **Point gap: 0.3 mm (0.012 in.)**
   If adjustment is required, carefully bend the lower point bracket to obtain the correct point gap.
4. **Adjusting arm**
   After checking armature gap and point gap, bend the adjusting arm up or down to obtain the correct voltage readings. Bend the adjusting arm up to increase the charging rate or down to decrease the charging rate.

V. ELECTRICAL

4. STARTING SYSTEM

The starting motor is located on the upper crankcase. It is a drip- and dust-proof type.
The torque developed by the motor is transmitted through reduction gears, driven gear, and overrunning clutch to the primary shaft.

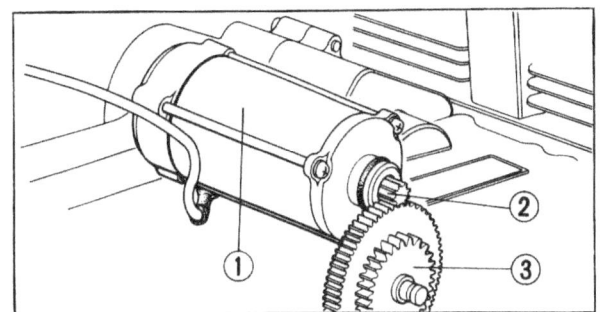

Fig. 5-22　① Starting motor
　　　　　② Starting motor shaft gear
　　　　　③ Starting motor reduction gear

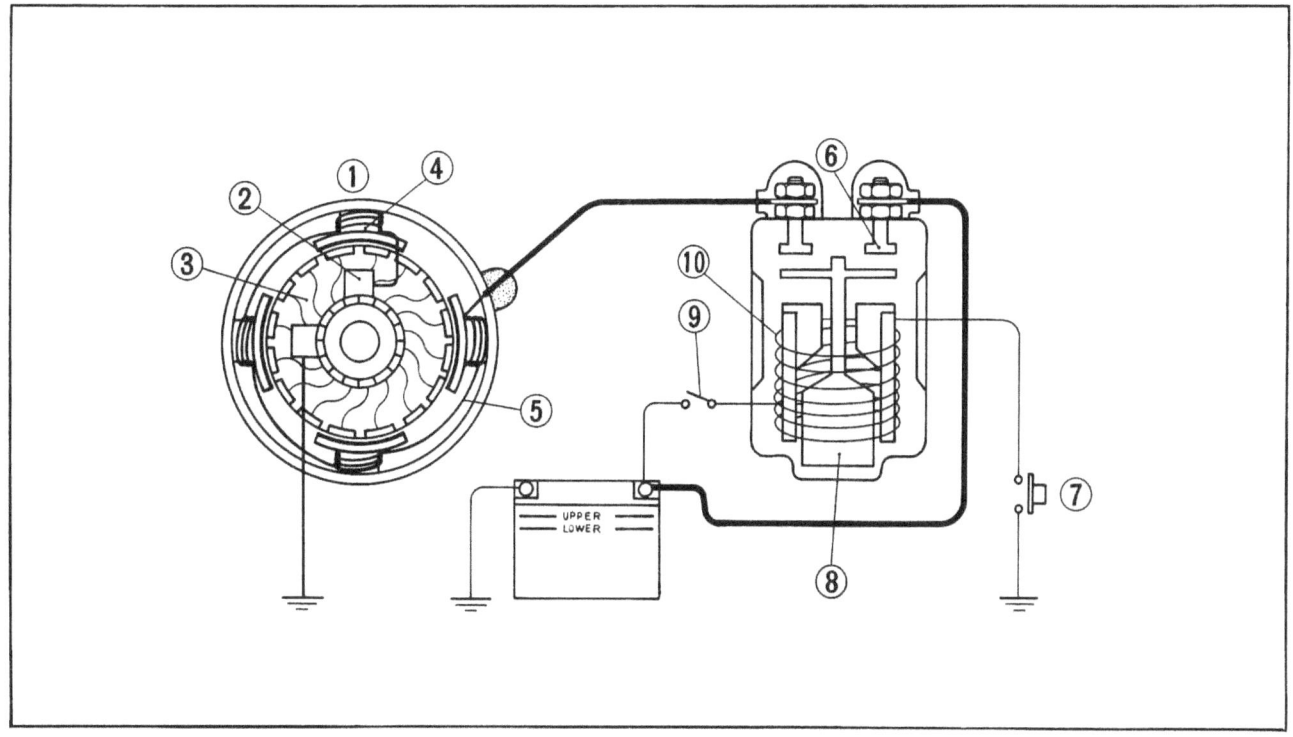

Fig. 5-23

① Starting motor　　④ Poles　　　　　　　⑦ Starter switch
② Brushes　　　　　⑤ Field coil　　　　　⑧ Plunger
③ Armature　　　　 ⑥ Magnetic switch　　 ⑨ Main switch

Starting motor

Specifications and characteristics
Rated output voltage : 12 V
Rated output　　　　: 0.6 kW
Rated operating time : 30 sec., (continuous)

	On-load	No-load	When locked
Voltage (V)	11	8	5
Amperage (A)	35	120	250
Torque (kg-cm) (lb-ft)	—	0.11 (0.795)	0.26 (1.880)
Speed (rpm)	1,100–22,000	3,200	—

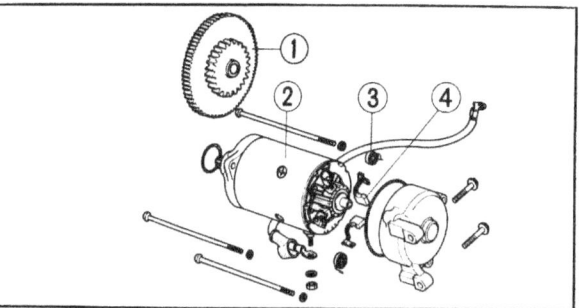

Fig. 5-24　① Starting motor reduction gear
　　　　　② Starting motor
　　　　　③ Brush spring
　　　　　④ Brush

V. ELECTRICAL

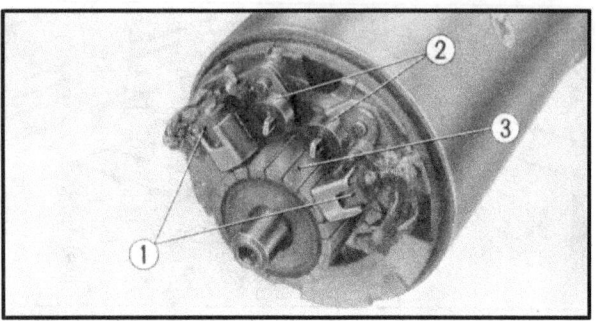

Fig. 5-25 ① Carbon brushes ③ Commutator
② Brush springs

Inspection

1. Checking carbon brushes
   Check the brushes and springs for condition. Excessively worn brushes that are not seating properly on commutator and a weakened brush spring may cause the starting motor inoperative. Replace the brush or spring if out of the specifications below.

	Standard value	Repair limit
Carbon brush length, mm (in.)	12~13 (0.47~0.51)	5.5 (0.22) max.
Brush spring tension, kg (lbs)	0.5~0.6 (1.1~1.3)	0.4 (0.8) max.

2. Cleaning commutator
   Check the condition of the commutator surface. Polish the surface with an emery cloth if dirty, and thoroughly wipe it clean before reassembly.

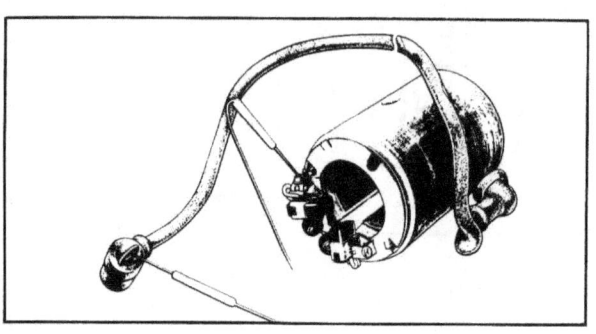

Fig. 5-26 Checking field coil for continuity

3. Checking field coil for continuity
   Check for continuity between the brushes connected to the field coil and starting motor cable. If there is no continuity, it is an indication that the field coil has an open circuit.

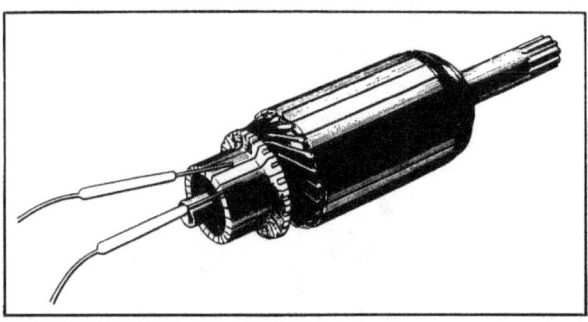

Fig. 5-27 Checking armature coil for continuity

4. Checking armature coil for continuity
   The armature coil with a short-circuit will result in a failure of the starting motor to operate properly. Check for continuity between the commutator surface and core. If there is any continuity, the stator coil is grounded.

V. ELECTRICAL

Starting magnetic switch

The starting motor draws approximately 100A of current when cranking the engine.
A large-capacity electromagnetic switch that is electrically remote-controlled by a separate switch (starter switch) is used for this reason.

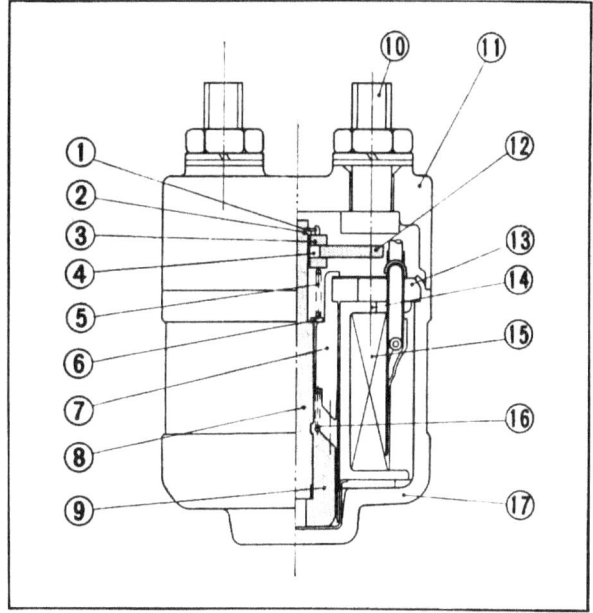

Fig. 5-28
① Stopper
② Stopper holder
③ Washer
④ Roller A
⑤ Contact spring
⑥ Flat washer
⑦ Plunger holder
⑧ Plunger shaft
⑨ Plunger
⑩ Contact bolt
⑪ Case
⑫ Contact plate
⑬ Yoke
⑭ Coil bobbin
⑮ Coil complete
⑯ Return spring
⑰ Body

Inspection

1. Checking primary coil for continuity
   It there is no continuity, the primary coil has an open-circuit. The coil is in good condition if a clicking sound is heard by applying a 12V battery across the two leads of the coil.

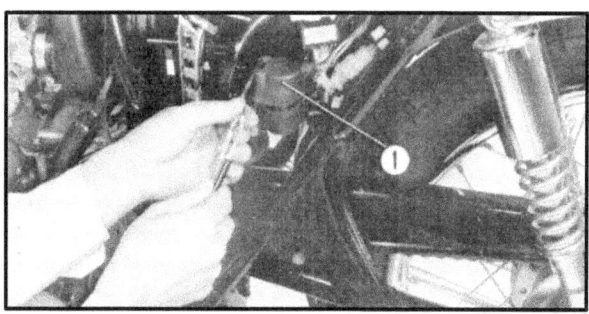

Fig. 5-29 ① Starting magnetic switch

2. After long use, the contact points of the magnetic switch will become pitted or burnt due to a large amount of current, and, in some cases, the current will not flow due to increased resistance.
   Check for continuity across the two leads of the primary coil by connecting a 12V battery with the switch turned on. If there is no continuity, it is an indication that the starting magnetic switch is faulty.

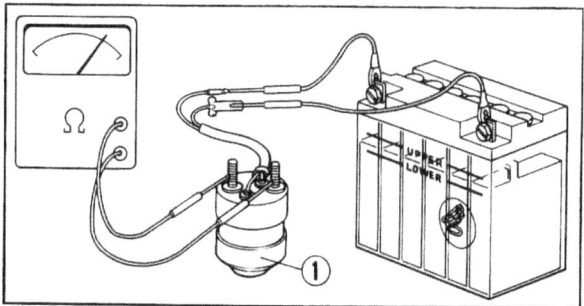

Fig. 5-30 ① Starting magnetic switch

V. ELECTRICAL

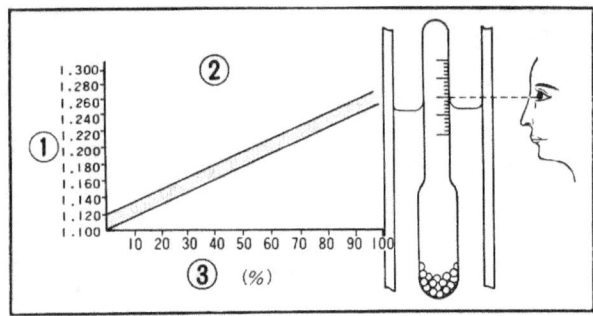

Fig. 5-31　① Specific gravity
　　　　　② Relation between specific gravity and residual charge
　　　　　③ Residual charge

Battery

Specifications

Type	12 N 12 A-4 A
Voltage	12 V
Capacity	12 AH

Measuring specific gravity of electrolyte.
Using a hydrometer, measure the specific gravity of the electrolyte in each cell. When the reading taken is below 1.200 at 20°C or 68°F, recharge the battery. When reading the hydrometer, hold the gauge barrel vertically as shown.

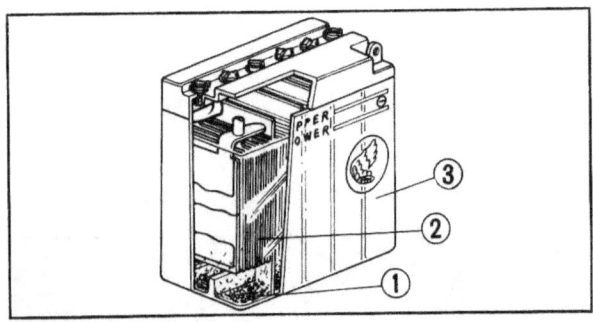

Fig. 5-32　① Sediment
　　　　　② Plates
　　　　　③ Battery case

Inspection

1. Check each battery cell for correct electrolyte level semi-monthly or monthly. If the level is low, add distilled water to the upper level.
2. When the electrolyte decreases rapidly, check the charging system.
3. Periodically check each cell for correct specific gravity. After adding distilled water, charge the battery by operating the engine, and then check the specific gravity.
4. Check the battery terminals for corrosion. Check for separated battery paste and sulfation. These defects are the symptoms of a run-down battery. Periodic inspection is always necessary, especially if the battery is stored for an extended period of time.

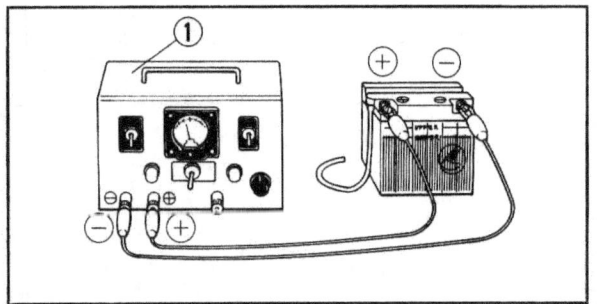

Fig. 5-33　① Battery charger

Charging battery

1. It is advisable that the battery be charged as slowly as possible since quick charging will shorten the battery service life. If the battery has to be charged quickly, the charging current should be held to 2.0A maximum.
2. Hydrogen gas is produced during charging operation. Keep away from fire.
3. After charging, clean the battery and lubricate the terminals.

V. ELECTRICAL

5. ELECTRICAL EQUIPMENT

Main switch

With the key at either ON or OFF, check the main switch for continuity. If there is continuity in the circuit (○—○), the switch is in good condition. If there is no continuity or if there is any continuity in other circuits shown below, the switch is faulty.

Cord color		BAT	IG	TL1	TL2
		Red	Black	Brown/white	Brown
Key Position	OFF				
	I	○—	—○	○—	—○
	II	○—			—○

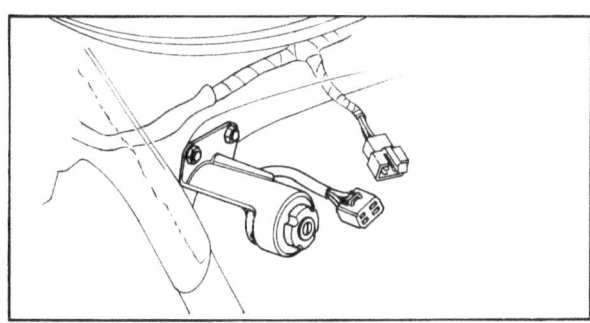

Fig. 5-34 Checking main switch

Front stop switch

Put the tester probes on the terminals of the front stop switch cords (black, green/yellow).
Operate the brake lever to check for continuity.
The stop light should come on when the brake lever is moved **5~10 mm (0.2~0.4 in.)** as measured at the tip of the lever.

NOTE:
Note that the lever play is 2~5 mm (0 08~0.2 in.) at the lever end.

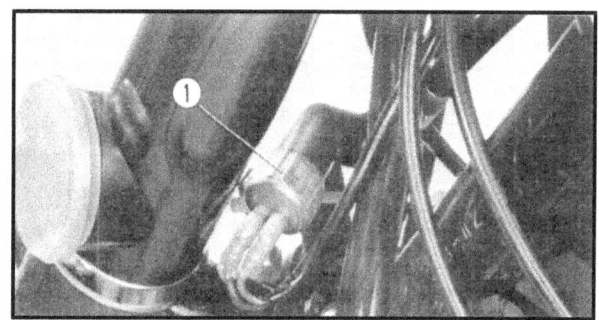

Fig. 5-35 ① Front stop switch

Rear stop switch

Put the tester probes on the terminals of the rear stop switch cords (green/yellow, black) to check for continuity. The rear stop light should come on when the rear brake pedal is depressed **20 mm (0.8 in.)** as measured at the tip of the pedal. Adjust by means of the adjusting nut if necessary.

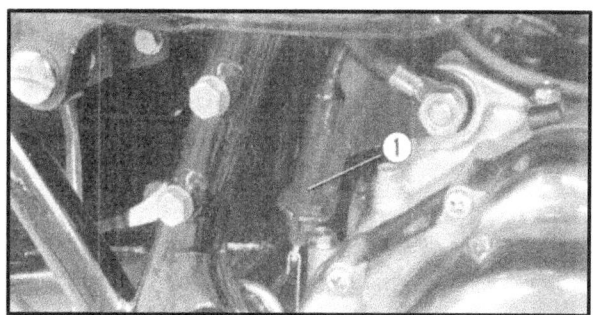

Fig. 5-36 ① Rear stop switch

Horn

Check for continuity between the horn cord terminals or check to make sure the horn sounds when it is connected to a fully charged 12 V battery.

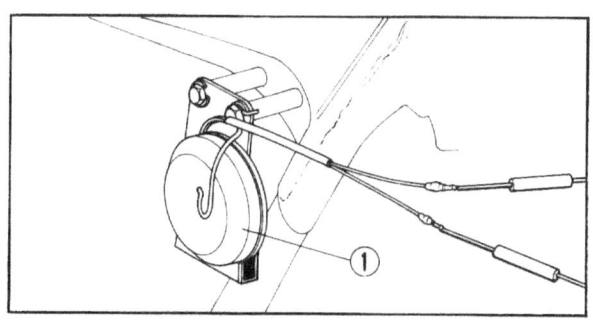

Fig. 5-37 ① Horn

V. ELECTRICAL

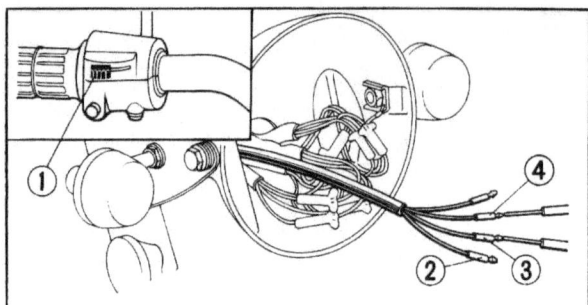

Fig. 5-38 ① Turn signal control switch
② Light blue cord
③ Gray cord
④ Orange cord

Turn signal control switch

Disconnect the cord of the turn signal control switch in the headlight case. Check for continuity between the terminals of the gray cord and orange cord (left turn signal) and between those of the gray cord and light blue cord (right turn signal). The switch is in good condition if there is continuity in the circuits (○—○) shown below:

Cord color Knob Position	Light blue	Gray	Orange
R	○——	——○	
OFF			
L		○——	——○

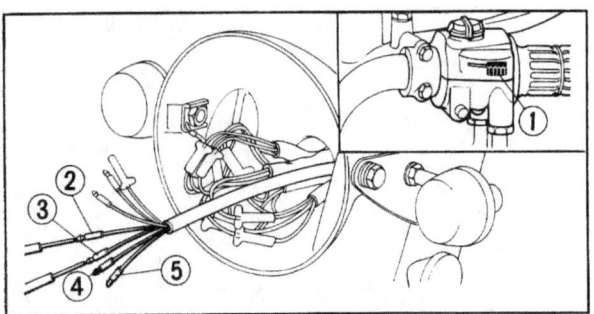

Fig. 5-39 ① Headlight control switch
② Black cord   ④ Brown, white cord
③ Blue cord   ⑤ White cord

Headlight control switch

Check for continuity between the respective terminals of the switch cords in the headlight case.
The switch is in good condition if there is continuity in the circuits (○—○) with the switch selector knob set in each position.
Any continuity in other circuits shown below is the symptom of a switch malfunction.

		IG	HB	TL	LB
Cord color		Black	Blue	Brown/white	White
ON	H	○——	——○——	——○	
	N	○——	——○——	——○——	——○
	L	○——	———————	——○——	——○

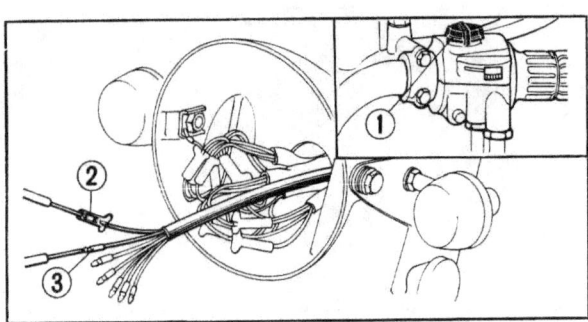

Fig. 5-40 ① Emergency switch
② Black cord   ③ White cord

Emergency switch and starter switch

Check for continuity between the respective terminals of the switch cords in the headlight case. The switch is normal if there is continuity as specified below (○—○) with the switch selector knob set in each position. Any continuity in other circuits shown below indicates switch malfunction.

Emergency switch

Cord color	Black	Black/white
RUN	○——	——○
OFF		

Starter switch

Cord color	Yellow/red	Body grounding
ON	○——	——○
OFF		

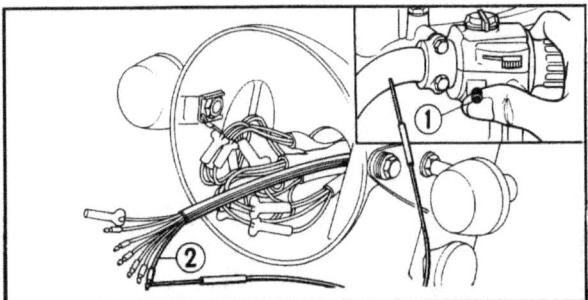

Fig. 5-41 ① Starter switch
② Yellow, red cord

Horn button

Check for continuity by contacting the tester lead probes on the terminal of the light green cord in the headlight case and on the handlebar with the horn button pushed. If there is continuity, the horn button is normal.

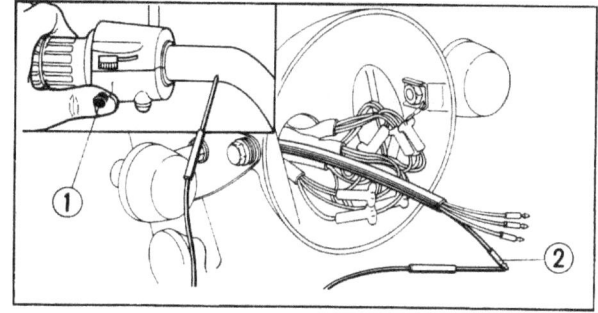

Fig. 5-42　① Horn button
　　　　　② Light green cord

Oil pressure control switch

The oil pump supplies lubricating oil to the engine under pressure of **4.5 kg/cm² (64 lb/in²)**. When the oil pressure drops below **0.3 kg/cm² (4.3 lb/in²)**, the oil pressure control switch operates and the warning lamp comes on, indicating the oil supply is insufficient. Check the oil pressure control switch located on the oil pump for continuity. The switch is normal if there is continuity. The oil pressure pilot lamp will come on when the main switch is turned on and should go out after the engine is started.

If the pilot lamp remains on with the engine started, and the pressure control switch is in good condition, the cause may be in the hydraulic system. Locate and correct the problem with the engine stopped.

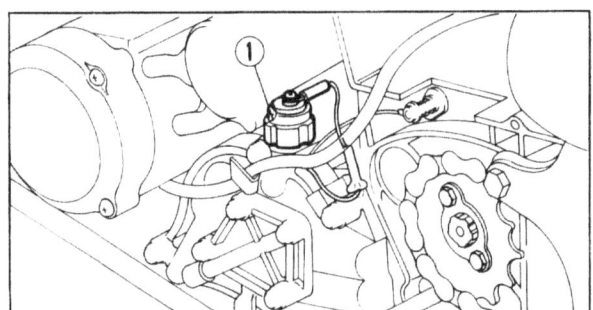

Fig. 5-43　① Oil pressure control switch

Neutral switch

The neutral switch is located on the left side of the crankcase. With the transmission in neutral, the neutral switch is grounded and the neutral pilot lamp comes on.

Place the transmission gears in neutral and remove the left crankcase cover. Check the neutral switch for continuity. The switch is normal if there is continuity.

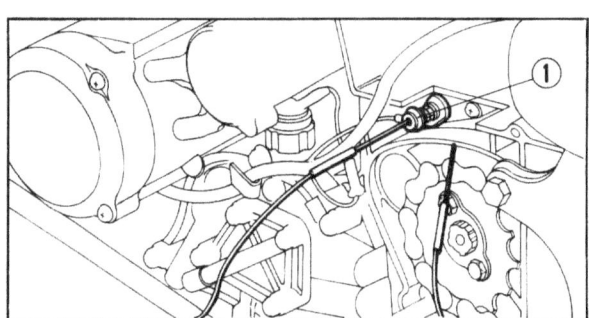

Fig. 5-44　① Neutral switch

VI. SERVICE DATA

1. CB350F SPECIAL TOOLS

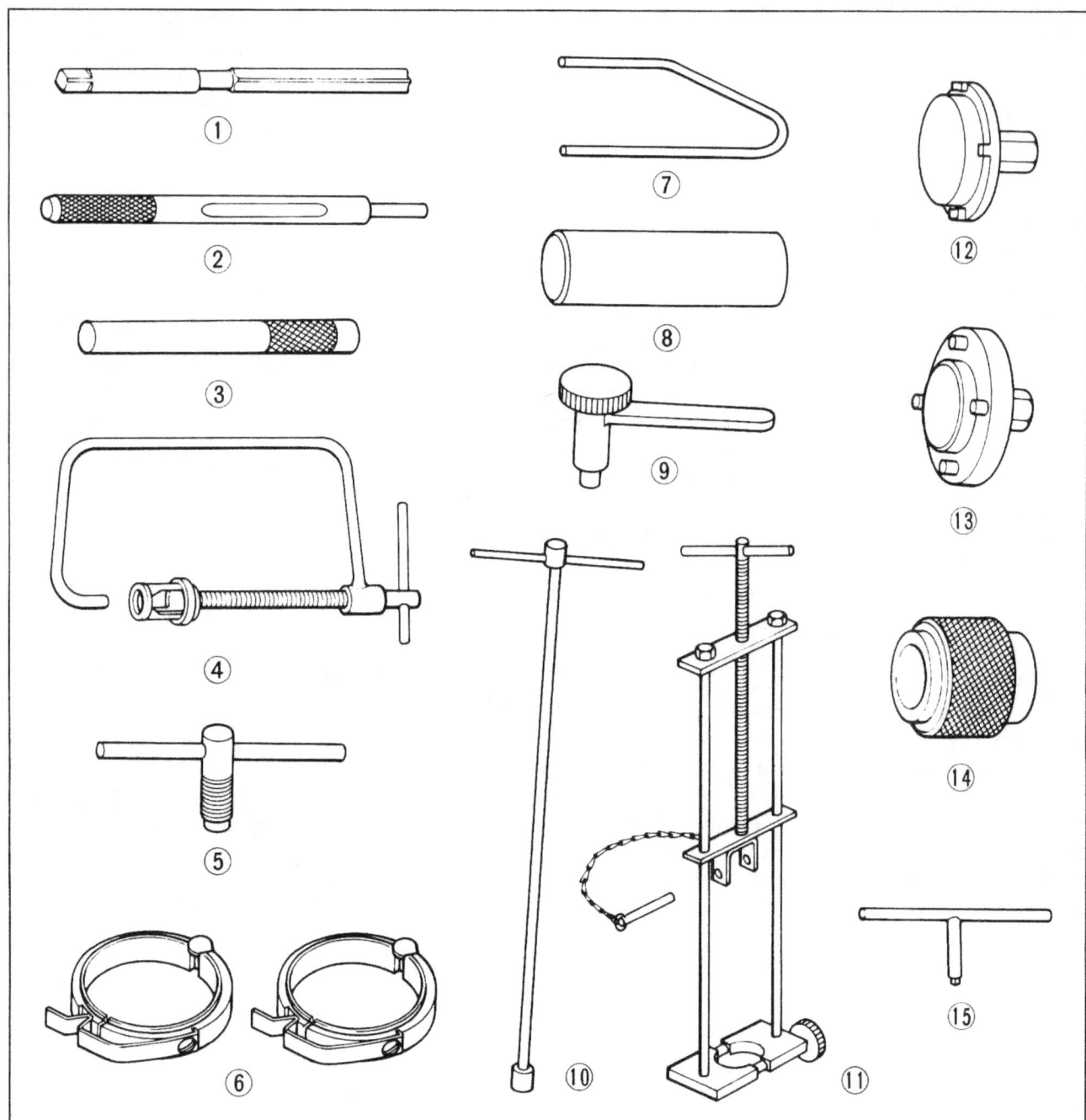

Ref. No.	Tool No.	Description
	07900-3330000	CB350F Special tool set
①	07984-2000000	Valve guide reamer
②	07942-3290100	Valve guide remover
③	07942-3290200	Valve guide driver
④	07957-3290000	Valve lifter
⑤	07933-3330000	Generator rotor puller
⑥	07955-3330000	Piston ring compressor (4PCS)
⑦	07958-3330000	Piston base (4PCS)
⑧	07945-3330100	Inner bearing driver
⑨	07908-0010000	Tappet wrench set
⑩	07906-3230000	Box wrench 12mm
⑪	07959-3290000	Rear suspension service tool
⑫	07910-3230101	Front wheel retainer wrench
⑬	07910-3290000	Rear wheel retainer wranch
⑭	07947-3330000	Front fork oil seal driver
⑮	07917-3230000	Hollow set wrench 6mm

VI. SERVICE DATA

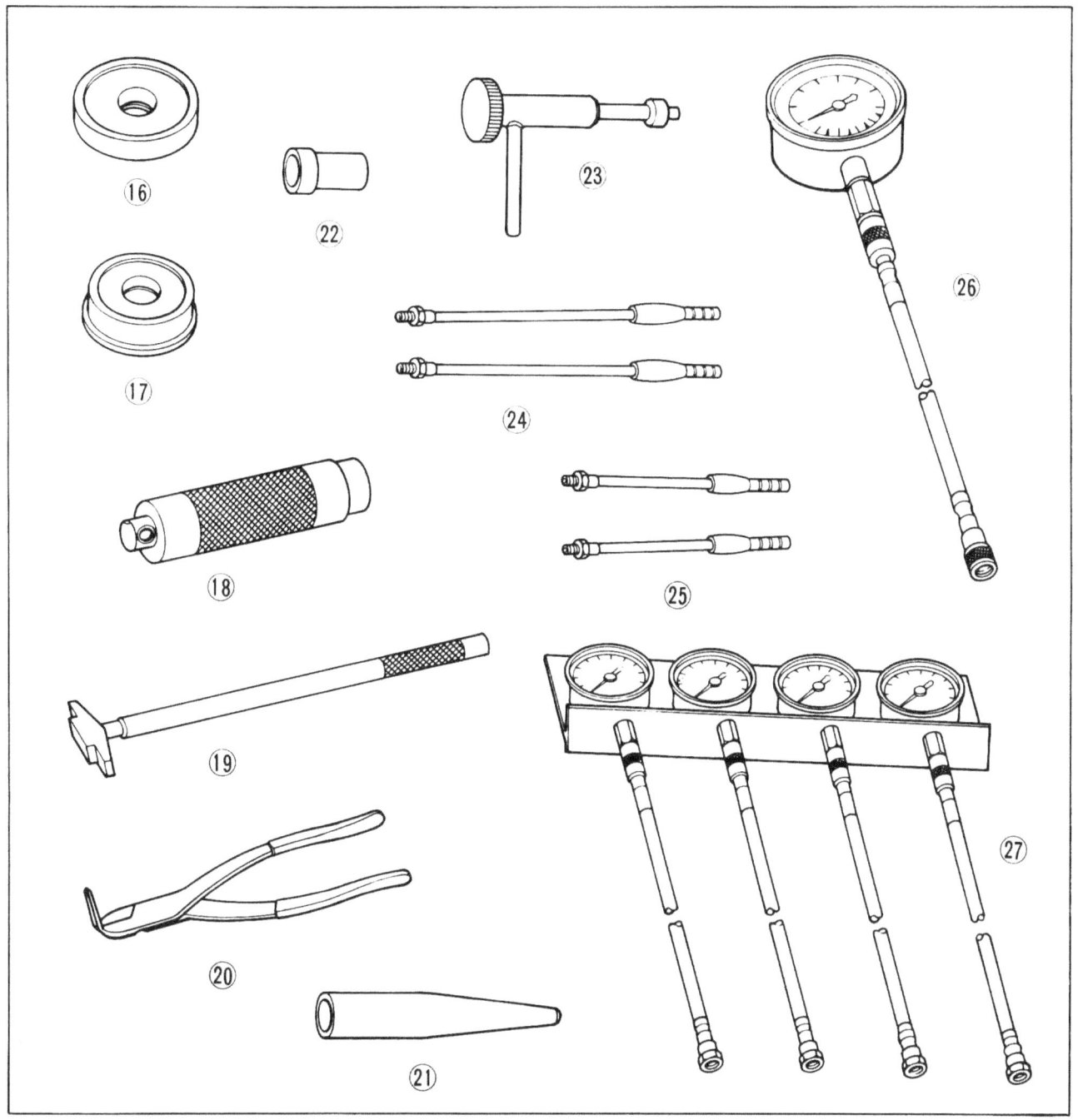

Ref. No.	Tool No.	Description
⑯	07945-3330300	Bearing driver
⑰	07945-3330200	Bearing driver attachment
⑱	07949-6110000	Driver handle
⑲	07953-3330000	Ball race remover
⑳	07914-3230000	Snap ring pliers
㉑	07974-3230200	Piston cup guide
㉒	07974-3230100	Piston guide
㉓	07908-3230200	Carburetor synchronization wrench
㉔	07510-3000100	Vacuum gauge attachment A
㉕	07510-3000200	Vacuum gauge attachment B
㉖	07504-3000200	Vacuum gauge
㉗	07504-3000100	Vacuum gauge set

73

2. MAINTENANCE SCHEDULE

MAINTENANCE SCHEDULE This maintenance schedule is based upon average riding conditions. Machines subjected to severe use, or ridden in unusually dusty areas, require more frequent servicing.	INITIAL SERVICE PERIOD 500 miles	REGULAR SERVICE PERIOD Perform at every indicated month or mileage interval, whichever occurs first.			
		1 month 500 miles	3 months 1,500 miles	6 months 3,000 miles	12 months 6,000 miles
Engine Oil—change.	●		○		
Oil Filter Element—replace.	●			○	
Oil Filter Screen—clean.					○
Spark Plug—clean and adjust gap.				○	
*Contact Points—check, and adjust gap.	●			○	
*Ignition Timing—check, and adjust if necessary.	●			○	
*Valve Tappet Clearance—check, and adjust if necessary.	●			○	
*Cam Chain Tension—adjust.	●			○	
Air Cleaner—clean.	(Clean more frequently if operated in dusty areas)			○	
Air Cleaner—replace.					○
Carburetors—check, and adjust if necessary.	●			○	
Throttle Operation—inspect cables, check, and adjust free play.	●			○	
Fuel valve Filter Screen—clean.				○	
Fuel Lines—check.				○	
*Clutch—check operation, and adjust if necessary.	●			○	
Drive Chain—check, lubricate, and adjust if necessary.	●	○			
Brake Fluid Level—check, and add fluid if necessary.	●			○	
*Brake Shoes/Pads—inspect, and replace if worn.				○	
Brake Control Linkage—check linkage, and adjust free play if necessary.	●			○	
*Wheel Rims and Spokes—check. Tighten spokes and true wheels, if necessary.	●			○	
Tires—inspect and check air pressure.	●		○		
Front Fork Oil—drain and refill.	●				○
Front and Rear Suspension—check operation.	●			○	
Rear Fork Bushing—grease.				○	
*Steering Head Bearings—adjust.					○
Battery—check electrolyte level, and add water if necessary.	●		○		
Lighting Equipment—check and adjust if necessary.	●	○			
All Nuts, Bolts, and Fasteners—check security and tighten if necessary.	●	○			

Items marked * should be serviced by an authorized Honda dealer, unless the owner has proper tools and is mechanically proficient. All other maintenance items are simple to perform and may be serviced by the owner.

VI. SERVICE DATA

3. TORQUE SPECIFICATIONS

ENGINE

Tightening point	Thread dia. (mm)	Torque kg-cm	Torque lbs-ft
Crankcase and crankcase covers	6, P1.0	70–110	5.1–8.0
Cylinder head	8, P1.25	200 (Apply oil to the nuts before tightening)	14.5
Carburetor insulator-to-cylinder head	6, P1.0	70–110	5.1–8.0
Cam sprocket	7, P1.0	160–200	11.6–14.5
AC generator rotor	10, P1.25	300–400	21.7–29.0
Primary drive gear	12, P1.25	300–400	21.7–29.0
Tappet adjusting nut	5, P0.5	70–110	5.1–8.0
Upper and lower crankcases	8, P1.25	220–260	15.2–18.9
Cylinder head cover	6, P1.0	70–110	5.1–8.0

FRAME

Tightening point	Thread dia. (mm)	Torque kg-cm	Torque lbs-ft
Steering stem nut	24, P1.0	800–1,200	57.9–86.9
Fork top bridge to front forks	8, P1.25	180–230	13.1–16.7
Handlebar holder	8, P1.25	180–230	13.1–16.7
Front fork bottom bridge to front forks	8, P1.25	180–230	13.1–16.7
Spokes — Front wheel	—	25–30	1.9–2.2
Spokes — Rear wheel	—	20–25	1.5–1.9
Rear fork pivot bolt	14, P1.5	550–700	39.8–50.7
Front wheel axle nut	12, P1.5	450–550	32.6–39.8
Front fork axle holder	8, P1.25	180–230	13.1–16.7
Engine hanger bolt	10, P1.25	300–400	21.7–29.0
Rear wheel axle nut	16, P1.5	800–1,000	57.9–72.4
Final driven sprocket	10, P1.25	300–400	21.7–29.0
Brake arm	6, P1.0	80–100	5.9–7.3
Front and rear brake torque links	8, P1.25	180–230	13.1–16.7
Rear suspension	10, P1.25	300–400	21.7–29.0
Step bar	12, P1.25	450–550	32.6–39.8
Gear change pedal and kick arm	6, P1.0	80–100	5.9–7.3
Seat band	6, P1.0	80–100	5.9–7.3

4. SERVICE DATA

ENGINE

Unit: mm (in.)

Item	Assembly standard	Service limit
Rocker arm-to-rocker arm shaft clearance	0.016–0.052 (0.0006–0.0020)	0.1 (0.0039)
Cam height of camshaft Intake Exhaust	28.185–28.225 (1.1096–1.1112) 28.184–28.224 (1.1096–1.1111)	28.0 (1.1024) 28.0 (1.1024)
Camshaft center journal runout	—	0.1 (0.0039)
Valve seat width	0.7 (0.03)	1.5 (0.06)
Valve stem O. D. Intake Exhaust	5.48–5.49 (0.2158–0.2161) 5.46–5.47 (0.2150–0.2154)	5.35 (0.2106) 5.35 (0.2106)
Valve-to-valve guide clearance Intake Exhaust	0.01–0.03 (0.0004–0.0012) 0.03–0.05 (0.0012–0.0020)	0.3 (0.0118) 0.3 (0.0118)
Valve spring preload Inner Outer	19.2/13.0–14.6 kg (0.7559/28.665–32.1930 lbs) 23.7/32.0–32.4 kg (0.9330/70.560–71.4420 lbs)	— —
Valve spring free length Inner Outer	29.0 (1.1417) 34.5 (1.3583)	27.0 (1.0630) 32.5 (1.2795)
Cylinder head flatness	—	0.3 (0.0118)
Cylinder I. D.	47.00–47.01 (1.8504–1.8508)	47.1 (1.8543)
Piston skirt O. D.	46.97–46.99 (1.8492–1.8500)	46.85 (1.8445)
Piston pin hole I. D.	13.002–13.008 (0.5119–0.5121)	13.05 (0.5138)
Piston pin O. D.	12.994–13.00 (0.5116–0.5118)	12.9 (0.5079)
Piston ring-to-piston ring groove clearance Top ring Second ring Oil ring	0.03–0.055 (0.0012–0.0022) 0.015–0.045 (0.0006–0.0018) 0.015 (0.0006)	0.15 (0.0059) 0.15 (0.0059) 0.15 (0.0059)
Piston ring end gap Top ring Second ring Oil ring	0.1–0.3 (0.0039–0.0118) 0.1–0.3 (0.0039–0.0118) 0.1–0.3 (0.0039–0.0118)	0.7 (0.0276) 0.7 (0.0276) 0.7 (0.0276)
Outer rotor O. D.-to-pump body clearance Main pump Auxiliary pump	0.06–0.12 (0.0024–0.0047) 0.15–0.20 (0.0059–0.0079)	0.35 (0.0138) 0.35 (0.0138)
Outer rotor-to-inner rotor clearance Main pump Auxiliary pump	0.15 (0.0059), max. 0.15 (0.0059), max.	0.3 (0.0118) 0.3 (0.0118)
Friction disc thickness	2.62–2.78 (0.1032–0.1095)	2.3 (0.0906)
Clutch plate surface warpage	0.1 (0.0039), max.	0.2 (0.0079)
Clutch spring preload	25.0/19.3–20.7 kg (0.9842/42.557~45.643 lbs)	—
Clutch spring free length	35.5 (1.3976)	34.0 (1.3386)

VI. SERVICE DATA

Unit: mm (in.)

Item	Assembly standard	Service limit
Clutch center-to-clutch plate B clearance	0.1–0.5 (0.004–0.02)	Beyond assembly standard
Gear shift fork finger width	5.93–6.00 (0.2335–0.2362)	5.5 (0.2165)
Gear shift guide shaft O. D.	12.957–12.984 (0.5101–0.5112)	12.9 (0.5079)
Gear shift fork I. D.	13.000–13.018 (0.5118–0.5125)	12.95 (0.5098)
Kick starter pinion-to-shaft clearance	0.04–0.082 (0.0016–0.0032)	0.1 (0.004)
Gear shift fork dowel-to-drum groove clearance	0.05–0.22 (0.0020–0.0087)	0.3 (0.0118)
Transmission gear backlash		
1st and 2nd	0.044–0.134 (0.0017–0.0053)	0.2 (0.0079)
3rd, 4th and 5th	0.046–0.142 (0.0018–0.0056)	0.2 (0.0079)
Transmission gear-to-shaft clearance		
C-1	0.04–0.074 (0.0016–0.0029)	0.2 (0.0079)
Other gears	0.04–0.081 (0.0016–0.0032)	0.2 (0.0079)
Cam chain tensioner slipper thickness (center)	4.0 (0.1575)	3.0 (0.118) max.
Cam chain guide thickness	6.1–6.3 (0.2402–0.2480)	5.0 (0.197)
Crankshaft runout (center)	0.03 (0.0012), max.	0.05 (0.0020)
Crankshaft journal clearance	0.018–0.048 (0.0007–0.0019)	0.08 (0.0032)
Connecting rod small end I. D.	13.012–13.033 (0.5123–0.5131)	13.10 (0.5158)
Connecting rod big end side clearance	0.02–0.07 (0.0008–0.0028)	0.15 (0.0059)
Connecting rod big end-to-crankshaft journal clearance	0.018–0.048 (0.0007–0.0019)	0.08 (0.0032)
Primary chain guide thickness (center)	6.0–6.3 (0.236–0.248)	5.0 (0.197)

FRAME

Unit: mm (in.)

Item	Assembly standard	Service limit
Brake disc face runout	0.3 (0.0118), max.	0.3 (0.0118). min.
Brake disc thickness	6.9–7.1 (0.2717–0.2795)	—
Wheel rim face runout	0.5 (0.0197), max.	2.0 (0.079)
Wheel bearing end play	0.07 (0.0028), max.	0.1 (0.0039)
Wheel bearing radial play	0.03 (0.0012), max.	0.05 (0.0020)
Front axle runout	0.01 (0.0004)	0.2 (0.0079)
Caliper cylinder I. D.	38.18–38.20 (1.5032–1.5039)	38.215 (1.5045)
Caliper piston O. D.	38.115–38.480 (1.5006–1.5150)	38.105 (1.5002)
Master cylinder I. D.	14.00–14.043 (0.5512–0.5529)	14.055 (0.5533)
Master cylinder piston O. D.	13.957–13.984 (0.5495–0.5505)	13.940 (0.5488)
Rear axle runout	0.01 (0.0004)	0.2 (0.0079)
Rear brake lining thickness	4.9–5.0 (0.1929–0.1969)	2.5 (0.0984)
Rear brake drum I. D.	160.0–160.3 (6.2992–6.3110)	161 (6.3386)
Front suspension spring preload	389.2/26.4 kg (15.3229/58.212 lbs)	—
Front suspension spring free length	426.5 (16.7917)	416 (16.378)
Rear suspension spring free length	195.8 (7.7087)	190 (7.480)
Rear fork pivot bushing-to-center collar clearance	0.1–0.3 (0.0039–0.0118)	0.5 (0.02)
Rear fork bushing I. D.	21.5–21.552 (0.8465–0.8485)	21.70 (0.8543)
Center collar O. D	21.427–21.460 (0.8436–0.8449)	21.35 (0.8406)
Front fork bottom case I. D.	33.000–33.039 (1.2992–1.3007)	33.18 (1.3063)
Front fork bottom piston O. D.	32.925–32.950 (1.2963–1.2973)	32.875 (1.2944)

5. TROUBLE SHOOTING

ENGINE

Trouble	Probable Cause	Remedies
Engine does not start	1. Excessive wear of piston ring or cylinder. 2. Seized valve in valve guide. 3. Seized piston. 4. Faulty valve timing. 5. Low or lack of compression pressure. • Pressure leak 5. Blown out cylinder head gasket. 6. Warped gasketting surface of the cylinder and cylinder head.	Replace. Replace. Replace. Adjust. Lap the valve to obtain good valve seating or replace. Replace. Repair or replace.
Poor engine idling	1. Incorrect tappet clearance. 2. Low or lack of compression pressure. 3. Excessive valve guide clearance.	Adjust to standard value. Repair. Replace valve and guide.
Loss of power	1. Valve sticking open. 2. Incorrect seating of valve. 3. Weak or broken valve spring. 4. Faulty valve timing. 5. Blown out cylinder head gasket. 6. Excessive wear of cylinder and piston. 7. Worn, weak or broken piston ring. 8. Loose spark plug.	Replace. Lap valve. Replace. Check valve timing and adjust if necessary. Replace. Replace. Replace. Retighten.
Overheating	1. Heavy carbon deposit on combustion chamber and piston head. 2. Lean fuel mixture. 3. Retarded ignition timing. 4. Low oil level, poor quality. 5. Extended operation in low gear.	Remove carbon. Adjust the carburetor. Adjust ignition timing. Add good grade oil.
Backfire	1. Incorrect seating of intake valve. 2. Faulty valve timing. 3. Incorrect ignition timing. 4. Excessive spark plug gap. 5. Improper fuel.	Check the valve seating. Adjust. Adjust. Adjust the gap to 0.6~0.7 mm (0.024~0.028 in.). Use recommended fuel.
White exhaust smoke	1. Excessive wear of cylinder and piston. 2. Overfilled engine oil. 3. Excessively high oil pressure. 4. Poor quality oil.	Replace the piston. Adjust the oil level. Check the breather. Replace with recommended oil.
Black exhaust smoke	1. Rich fuel mixture.	Adjust the carburetor.
Difficult gear shifting	1. Improper clutch disengagement. 2. Damaged gear or foreign object lodged in the gear. 3. Gear shift fork inoperative. 4. Incorrect operation of the gear shift drum stopper and change pedal. 5. Mainshaft and countershaft out of alignment. 6. High oil viscosity.	Adjust the clutch. Replace the defective parts. Repair or replace. Repair or replace. Repair or replace. Change the oil.
Excessive high gear noise	1. Excessive gear backlash. 2. Worn main and countershaft bearing.	Repair or replace. Repair or replace.

VI. SERVICE DATA

Trouble	Probable Cause	Remedies
Gear slip out	1. Worn fingers on gear shift fork. 2. Worn gear dog hole. 3. Worn spline.	Replace. Replace. Replace.
Clutch slippage	1. No play in the clutch lever. 2. Weak or no uniform clutch spring. 3. Worn or grazed friction disc.	Adjust the clutch. Replace the weak spring. Replace.
Poor clutch engagement	1. Excessive play of clutch lever. 2. Warped friction disc. 3. Warped pressure plate. 4. Bent main shaft.	Adjust clutch lever play. Replace. Replace. Replace.
Pedal does not return	1. Faulty return spring. 2. Unhook return spring.	Replace. Hook return spring.
Kick starter gear does not rotate	1. Excessive wear of kick starter pawl.	Replace.
Engine does not start	Carburetor 1. Choke fully open. 2. Carburetor air screw improperly set. 3. Air leaking into the cylinder head. 4. Clogged carburetor slow jet. 5. Clogged fuel valve or piping. 6. Clogged vent hole in the fuel tank cap. 7. No fuel in the tank.	Close choke. Adjust air screw. Retighten carburetor connecting tube. Check, clean and retighten. Disassemble and clean. Disassemble and clean. Fill tank with gasoline.
Poor engine idling	Carburetor 1. Clogged or loose carburetor slow jet. 2. Improper float level. 3. Incorrect air screw adjustment. 4. Carburetor linkage mulfunction. 5. Air leaks.	Check, clean and retighten. Adjust. Adjust. Adjust. Tighten all air passage connection.
Improper running of engine	Carburetor 1. Jet size too small. 2. Improper float level. 3. Clogged carburetor main jet. 4. Carburetor linkage mulfunction. 5. Air leaks.	Replace with larger size jet. Adjust. Clean and retighten. Adjust. Tighten all air passage connections.

CHASSIS

Trouble	Probable Cause	Remedies
Heavy steering	1. Steering stem excessively tightened. 2. Damaged steering stem steel balls. 3. Bent steering. 4. Low front tire pressure.	Loosen the steering stem nut. Replace. Replace. Add air to the specified pressure of 1.8 kg/cm² (26 psi).
Front and rear wheel wobble	1. Loose steering stem mounting bolt. 2. Worn front and rear wheel bearings. 3. Front or rear wheel runout or distorted. 4. Loose spoke. 5. Defective tire.	Retorque. Replace bearing. Repair or replace. Retorque. Replace
Soft suspension	1. Loss of spring tension. 2. Excessive load.	Replace.
Hard suspension	1. Ineffective front fork damper. 2. Ineffective rear damper.	Repair. Replace.
Suspension noise	1. Front case or rear damper rubbing. 2. Interference between cushion case and spring. 3. Faulty fork stopper rubber. 4. Insufficient front fork oil.	Inspect cushion spring and case. Repair or replace. Replace. Add ATF.
Defective brake	1. Front brake. • Insufficent brake fluid. • Air in the brake system. • Worn brake pad. • Worn piston. • Worn or distorted brake disc. • Brake lever out of adjustment. 2. Rear brake. • Worn brake lining. • Worn brake shoe or poor contacts. • Worn brake cam. • Wet brake from water or oil. • Worn brake shaft. • Brake pedal out of adjustment.	 Add brake fluid. Bleed brake system. Replace pad. Replace piston. Replace disc. Readjust. Replace. Replace. Replace. Clean. Replace. Readjust.

ELECTRICAL

Troubles	Probable Causes	Remedies
Engine does not Start	1. Battery	
	• Discharged.	Recharge or replace.
	• Poor contact of battery terminals.	Repair.
	2. Main switch	
	• Open or shorted circuit, disconnected connections.	Repair.
	• Poor contact between main switch wire and wire harness.	Repair.
	3. Ignition coil	
	• Improperly insulated high tension coil.	Replace.
	• Open or shorted circuit in ignition coil.	Replace.
	4. Contact breaker	
	• Open circuit in the primary coil.	Repair.
	• Dirty ground point with oil or dust.	Clean.
	• Point gap out of adjustment.	Readjust.
	• Improperly charged condenser.	Replace.
Starting motor does not operate	1. Defective battery.	Charge or replace.
	2. Poor contact of magnetic switch.	Repair or replace.
	3. Poor contact of starting motor carbon brush.	Repair or replace.
Horn inoperative, poor sound or too weak sound	1. Horn	
	• Cracked diaphragm.	Replace.
	2. Horn button.	
	• Poor grounding.	Repair.
	3. Wiring	
	• Poor contact.	Repair.
	4. Adjusting screw	
	• Out of adjustment.	Readjust.
Taillight and headlight inoperative	1. Fuse	
	• Blown fuse or burnt bulb filament	Replace.
	2. Bulb	
	• Burnt bulb filament.	Replace.
	3. Switch	
	• Poor contact of lighting switch.	Repair.
	4. Wiring	
Stop light inoperative	1. Bulb	
	• Burnt or broken bulb filament.	Replace.
	2. Front and tail stop light switch	
	• Malfunction of switch.	Readjust.
	3. Wiring	
	• Poor contact of leads.	Repair.
Winker lamp blinks too fast or too slow	1. Bulb	
	• Blinks unusually fast: improperly connected relay.	Replace.
	2. Wiring	
	• Blinks too fast: bulb with unsuitable wattage.	Replace.
	• Blinks too slow: burnt or broken bulb filament.	Replace.
	3. Defective relay	Replace.

VI. SERVICE DATA

Troubles	Probable Causes	Remedies
Winker lamp inoperative	1. Winker lamp switch • Poor contact of winker relay. • Open circuit in winker relay coil 2. Bulb • Bulb wattage is smaller than rated wattage. 3. Relay • Poor contact of winker relay. • Improperly connected lead.	 Replace. Replace. Replace. Replace. Replace.
No charging	1. Broken wire or shorted, loose connection. 2. Faulty coil due to short or grounding. 3. Faulty or shorted silicon diode. 4. Broken or shorted lead wire at regulator. 5. Regulator voltage at no load is too low.	Repair or replace. Replace. Replace. Repair or replace. Readjust.
Insufficient charging	1. Wiring • Broken wire, intermittent shorting or loose connection. 2. Generator • Shorting across layer in the field coil. (resistance indicated in continuity test) • Shorting across layer in stator coil. • Open circuit in one of the stator coil. • Faulty or shorted silicon diode. 3. Regulator • Voltage below specified value at no load. • Dirty or pitted points. • Coil or resistor internally shorted. 4. Battery • Low electrolyte level. • Defective battery plates.	 Repair. Replace. Replace. Replace. Replace. Readjust. Polish or replace. Replace. Add distilled water. Replace.
Excessive charging	1. Wiring P terminal circuit and F terminal circuit shorted resulting in split wound generator. 2. Battery Internal short. 3. Regulator • Excessive voltage at no load voltage. • Improper grounding. • Broken coil lead wire.	Repair. Replace. Repair. Provide proper ground. Repair or replace.
Unstable charging voltage	1. Wiring • Bare wire shorting intermittently under vibration or broken wire making partial contact. 2. Generator • Layer short (intermittent shorting). 3. Generator • Intermittent open circuit in the coil. • Improperly adjusted voltage. • Defective main switch. • Dirty points.	 Repair or replace. Repair or replace. Repair or replace. Readjust. Replace. Clean.

6. WIRING DIAGRAM

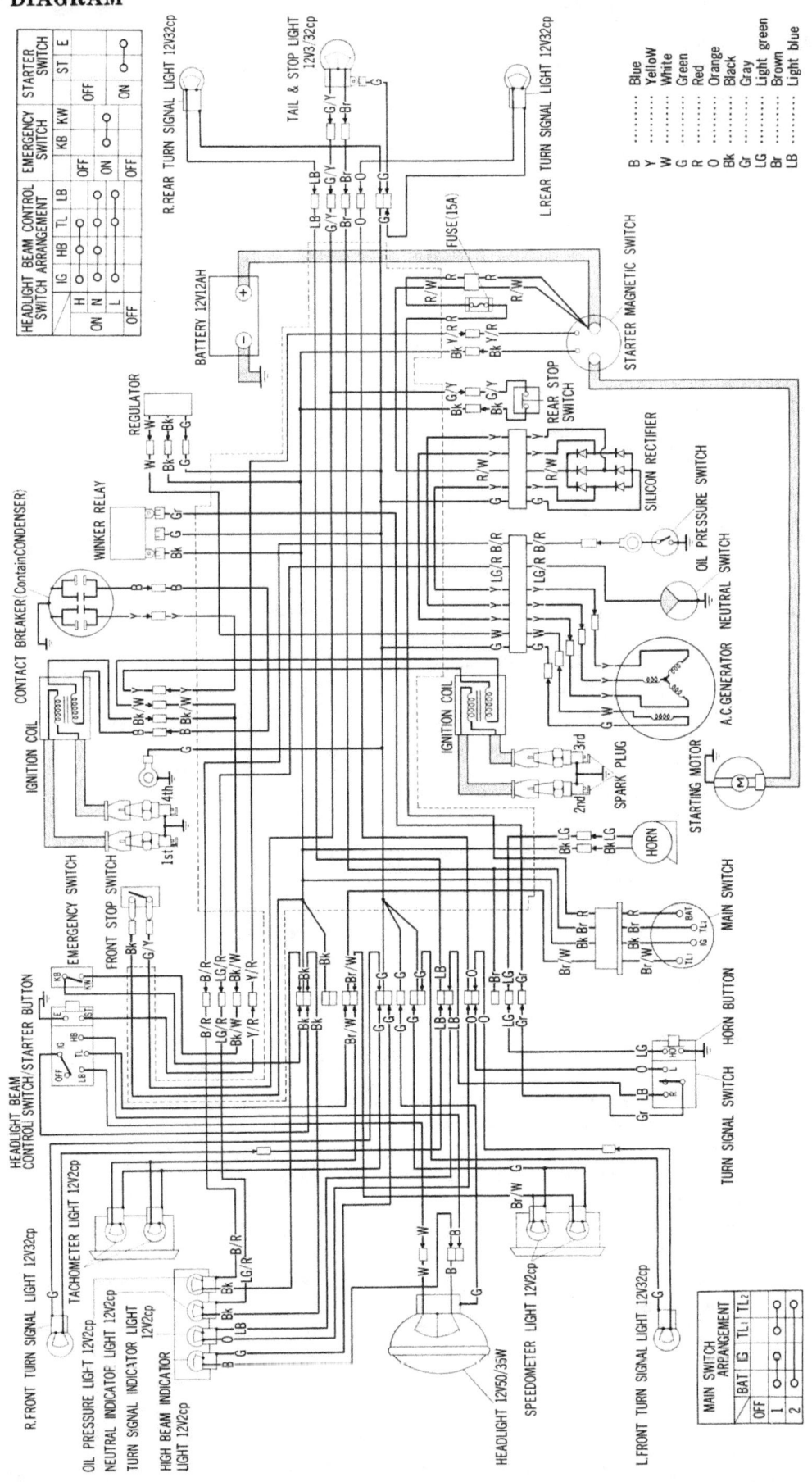

VI. SERVICE DATA

7. SPECIFICATIONS

	Item	Metric	English
Dimension	Overall length	2,060 mm	81.1 in.
	Overall width	780 mm	30.7 in.
	Overall height	1,090 mm	42.9 in.
	Wheel base	1,355 mm	53.3 in.
	Seat height	780 mm	30.7 in.
	Foot peg height	300 mm	11.8 in.
	Ground clearance	155 mm	6.1 in.
	Dry weight	170 kg	373 lbs.
Frame	Type	Semi-double cradle	
	F. suspension, travel	Telescopic fork, Travel 114.6 mm (4.5 in.)	
	R. suspension, travel	Swing arm, Travel 91.0 mm (3.6 in.)	
	F. tire size, pressure	3.00-18 (4PR), Air pressure 1.8 kg/cm² (26 psi)	
	R. tire size, pressure	3.50-18 (4PR), Air pressure 2.0 kg/cm² (28 psi)	
	F. brake, lining area	Disc brake, Lining swept areas 288 cm² (44.8 sq. in.)	
	R. brake, lining area	Internal expanding shoes, Lining swept areas 150 cm² (23 sq. in.)	
	Fuel capacity	12 lit.	3.2 U.S.gal. 2.6 Imp.gal.
	Fuel reserve capacity	2 lit.	0.5 U.S.gal. 0.4 Imp.gal.
	Caster angle	63°40'	
	Trail length	85 mm	3.3 in.
	Front fork oil capacity	125 cc (to fill if dry)	4.2 ozs.
	Front fork oil capacity	105 cc (refill after draining)	3.0 ozs.
Engine	Type	Air cooled, 4-stroke O.H.C. engine	
	Cylinder arrangement	Vertical four parallel	
	Bore and stroke	47.0×50.0 mm	1.850×1.969 in.
	Displacement	347 cc	21.1 cu·in.
	Compression ratio	9.3 : 1	
	Valve train	Chain driven over head camshaft	
	Oil capacity	3.5 lit.	3.7 U.S.qt. 3.1 Imp.qt.
	Lubrication system	Forced and wet sump	
	Cylinder head compression pressure	12 kg/cm² (170.7 psi)	
	Intake valve Opens	At 5° (before top dead center)	
	Intake valve Closes	At 35° (after bottom dead center)	
	Exhaust valve Opens	At 35° (before bottom dead center)	
	Exhaust valve Closes	At 5° (after top dead center)	
	Valve tappet clearance	IN·EX 0.05 mm	0.002 in.
	Idle speed	1,200 rpm	

VI. SERVICE DATA

	Item	Metric	English
Carburetor	Type	Piston valve	
	Setting mark	656 c	
	Main jet	#75	
	Slow jet	#35	
	Air screw opening	$^7/_8 \pm {}^3/_8$	
	Float height	21 mm	0.827 in.
Drive train	Clutch	Wet, multi-plate type	
	Transmission	5-speed, constant mesh	
	Primary reduction	3.423	
	Gear ratio I	2.733	
	Gear ratio II	1.850	
	Gear ratio III	1.416	
	Gear ratio VI	1.148	
	Gear ratio V	0.965	
	Final reduction	2.235	
	Gear shift pattern	Left foot operated return system	
Electrical	Ignition	Battery and ignition coil	
	Starting system	Starting motor and kick starter	
	Alternator	A-C generator 0.156 kW/5,000 rpm	
	Battery capacity	12 V-12 AH	
	Spark plug	NGK D8ESL ND X24ES	
	Headlight	Low/High beam 12 V-35 W/50 W	
	Tail/stoplight	Tail/Stop 12 V-3/32 cp (SAE TRADE NO. 1157)	
	Turn signal light	12 V-32 cp (SAE TRADE NO. 1073)	
	Speedometer light	12 V-2 cp (SAE TRADE NO. 57)	
	Tachometer light	12 V-2 cp (SAE TRADE NO. 57)	
	Neutral indicator light	12 V-2 cp (SAE TRADE NO. 57)	
	Turn signal indicator light	12 V-2 cp (SAE TRADE NO. 57)	
	High beam indicator light	12 V-2 cp (SAE TRADE NO. 57)	

CB 400 F SUPPLEMENT

I. TECHNICAL FEATURES

BLOW-BY GAS CIRCULATOR

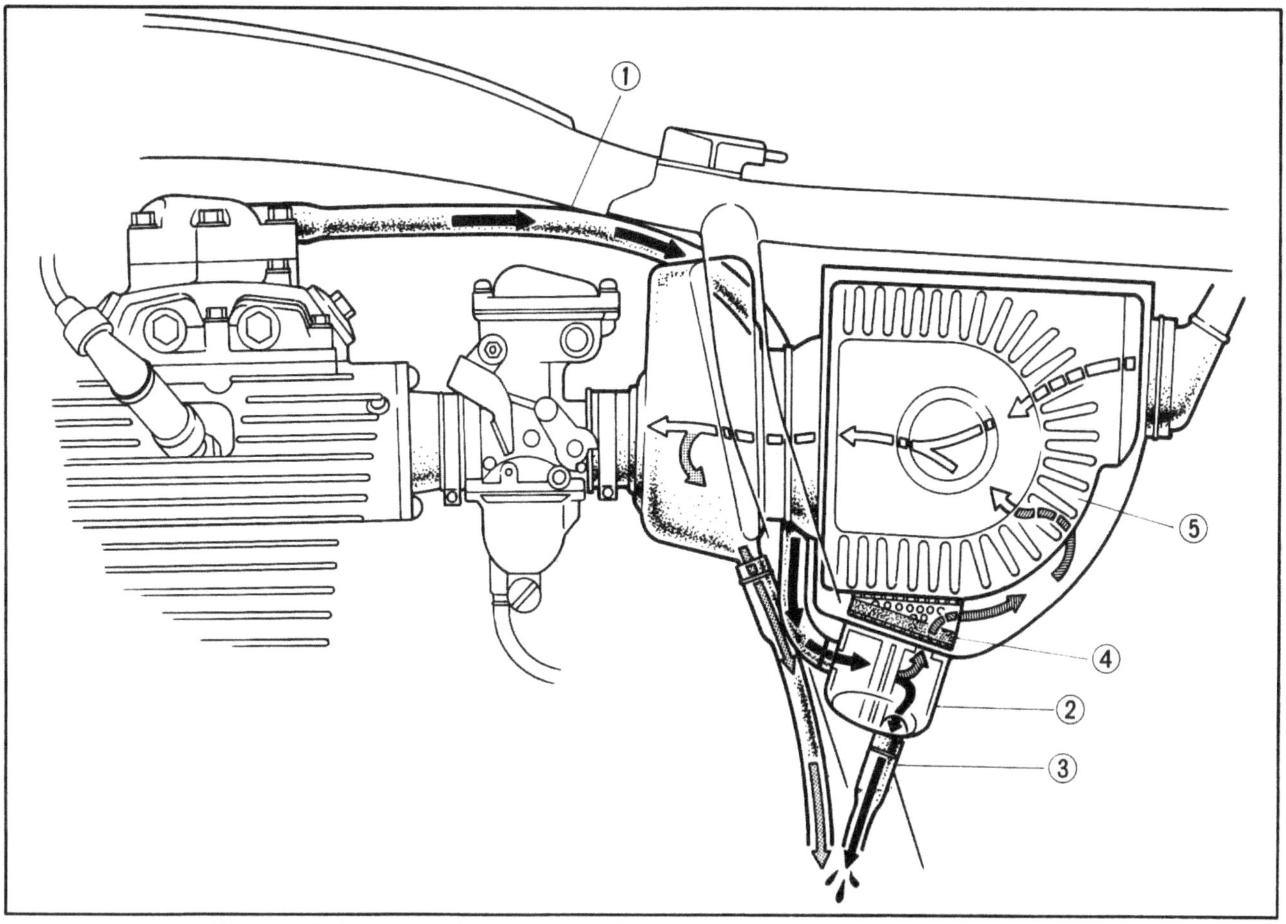

Fig. 1-1
① Breather tube
② Breather case
③ Oil drain tube
④ Breather element
⑤ Air cleaner element

The blow-by gas from inside the cylinder head through the breather tube enters the breather box. The oil is then separated by the breather element and the gas is led to the air cleaner. The gas enters the air cleaner and is filtered with the fresh air by the air cleaner element and is again led to the combustion chambers through the carburetors. Therefore, the blow-by gas is reduced by recombustion of the unburned gas.

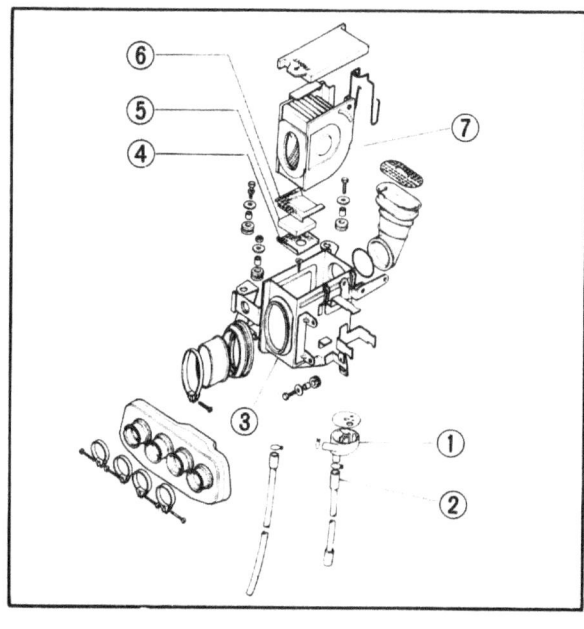

Fig. 1-2
① Breather box
② Oil drain tube
③ Air cleaner case
④ Lower element holder
⑤ Breather element
⑥ Upper element holder
⑦ Air cleaner element

II. INSPECTION AND ADJUSTMENT

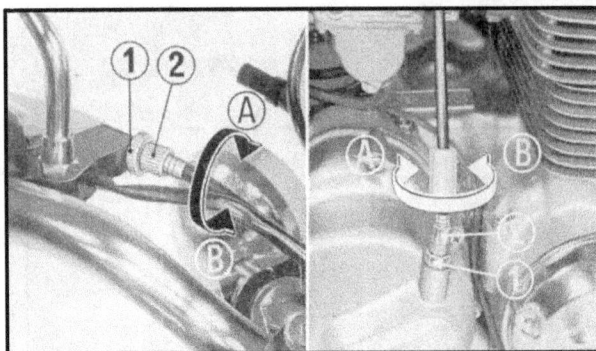

Fig. 2-1 ① Lock nut ② Clutch cable adjuster

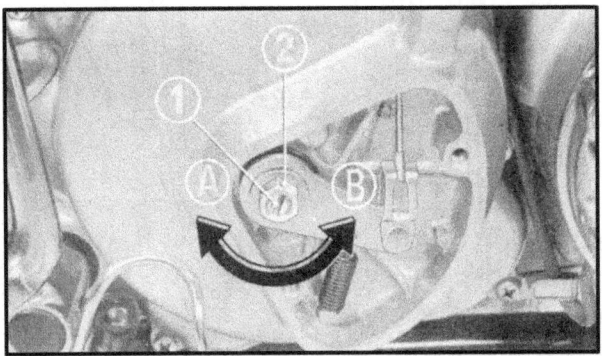

Fig. 2-2 ① Clutch adjusting screw
② Adjusting screw lock nut

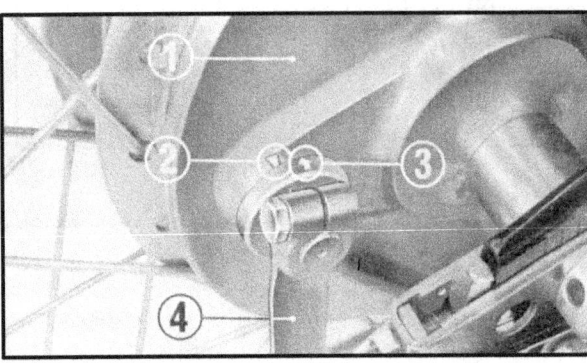

Fig. 2-3 ① Brake panel ③ Arrow
② Reference mark ④ Brake arm

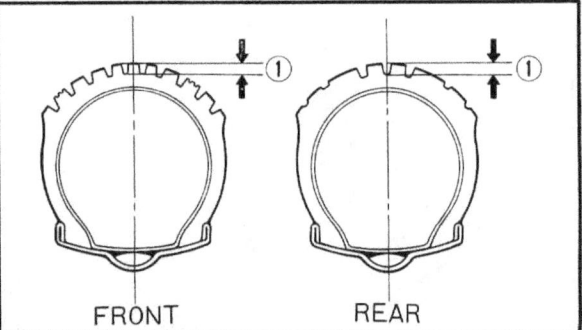

Fig. 2-4 ① Center tread depth

1. CLUTCH
1. Check the clutch lever for free play at its tip.
   Standard play: 10-20mm (0.4-0.8 in.)
2. Turn the clutch cable adjuster located at the clutch lever all the way in to (A) the clutch lever bracket.
3. Turn the clutch cable adjuster located at the clutch housing in direction A to loosen the clutch cable.
4. Remove the clutch cover. Loosen the clutch lifter adjusting screw lock nut (see Fig. 2-2), and turn the clutch adjusting screw clockwise (A) until a slight resistance is felt. From this position, turn the adjusting screw counterclockwise (B) 1/4~1/2 turn. Tighten the lock nut.
5. Turn the clutch cable adjuster, located at the clutch housing, in direction (A) so that there is approximately 3/4" of free play at the end of the clutch lever. Tighten the lock nut.
6. The remaining clutch lever free play is obtained by the clutch cable adjuster at the clutch lever.
7. After the adjustment has been made, check to see that the clutch is not slipping and is properly disengaging.
   After the engine starts, pull the clutch lever in and shift into gear. Make sure that the engine does not stall and the motorcycle does not creep. Gradually release the clutch lever and open the throttle, the motorcycle should start smoothly and gradually accelerate.

2. REAR BRAKE
Brake shoes
1. Check the distance between the arrow adjacent to the brake arm and reference mark on the brake panel on full brake application.
2. If the arrow aligns with the reference mark on full brake application, replace the brake shoes and check the brake drum for wear.

3. WHEEL
Tire tread wear
The tire should be replaced when the center tread depth is worn to the following limits.

Center tread depth:
   Front — 1.5mm (0.06-in.)
   Rear — 2.0mm (0.08-in.)

II. INSPECTION AND ADJUSTMENT

4. SPARK PLUG

1. Remove the spark plug cap from the spark plug. Unscrew the plug, using a spark plug wrench, and remove the spark plug from the cylinder head.
2. Check the spark plug for deposits, electrode erosion and a damaged gasket. A spark plug with burned electrodes, or damaged gasket should be replaced with a new one. A fouled spark plug can be cleaned with spark plug cleaner or a wire brush.
3. Using a feeler gauge, adjust the gap to the specification.
   Specified plug gap: 0.7-0.8 mm (0.028-0.032-in.)
   To adjust, bend the side electrode only.
4. Clean the plug seat in the cylinder head. Screw the plug into the thread hole in two steps: first, finger-tight, and then use a spark plug wrench to tighten the plug an additional 1/2 to 3/4 turns or until the sealing gasket is compressed.

5. FUEL FILTER

1. Place the fuel valve lever in "OFF" and disconnect the fuel tubes. Remove the fuel tank.
2. Loosen the fuel valve fixing nut and remove the fuel valve and fuel filter from the fuel tank.
3. Check the gasket to see if it is damaged. Replace with a new one, if it is damaged.
4. Wash the fuel filter in solvent and dry with compressed air. No damage can be tolerated. Replace the filter with a new one if it is clogged.
5. Install the fuel filter to the fuel valve with the fixing nut.
   Be sure to install the gasket into the groove of the fixing nut.
6. Install the fuel valve to the fuel tank with the fixing nut.
7. Install the fuel tank on the frame. Connect the tubes and secure with the clips.
8. Fill the tank with fuel. With the fuel valve lever at "ON", check for leaks past the tube joints or connections.

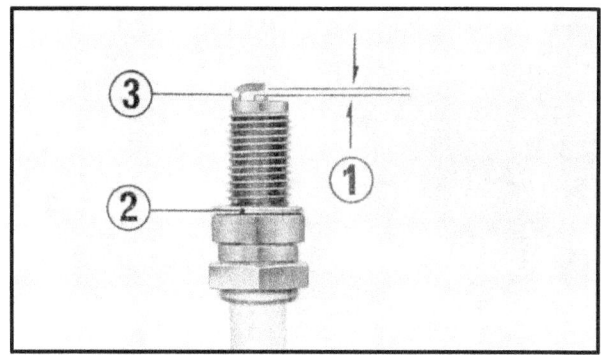

Fig. 2-5 ① Spark plug gap ③ Side electrode
         ② Gasket

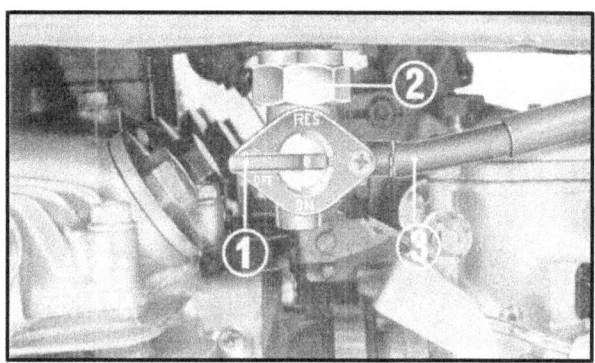

Fig. 2-6 ① Fuel valve lever ③ Fuel tube
         ② Fuel valve fixing nut

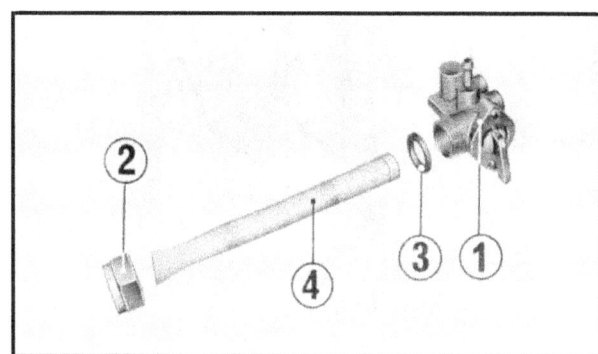

Fig. 2-7 ① Fuel valve ③ Gasket
         ② Fixing nut ④ Fuel filter

II. INSPECTION AND ADJUSTMENT

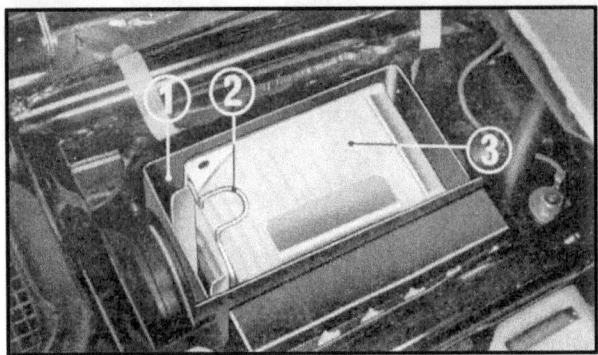

Fig. 2-8 ① Air cleaner case
② Retaining clip
③ Air cleaner element

6. AIR CLEANER

1. Raise the seat and remove the tool compartment with the air cleaner cover.
2. Lift the air cleaner element retaining clip out. Remove the air cleaner element.
3. Clean the air cleaner element by tapping it lightly to loosen dust. The remaining dust can be brushed from the outer element surface or blown away with compressed air from inside the element.

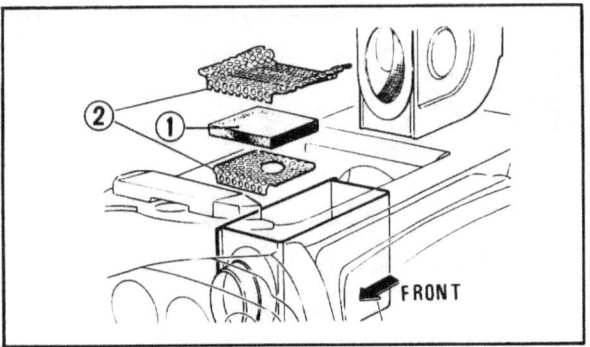

Fig. 2-9 ① Breather element   ② Element holder

4. Remove the element holders and breather element.
5. Wash the breather element in solvent. Squeeze out excess solvent and dry the element thoroughly.

WARNING:
- Gasoline or low flash point solvents are highly flammable and must not be used to clean the breather element.
- Do not use acid, alkali or organic solvent for washing the breather element.

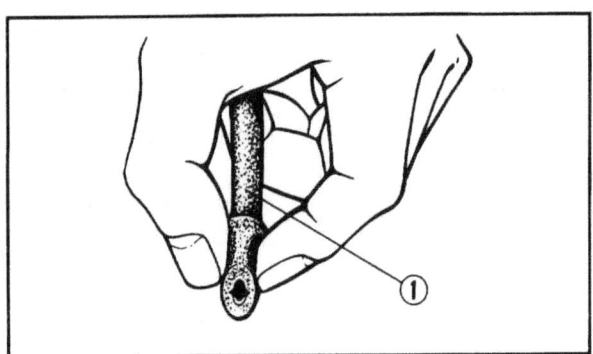

Fig. 2-10 ① Drain tube

6. Squeeze to open lower end of the drain tube, and remove any oil or water which has accumulated.
7. To reinstall the air cleaner, reverse the removal procedure.

Fig. 2-11 ① Checking front suspension

7. FRONT SUSPENSION

Checking

1. With the front brake applied, check the shock absorbers. This can be done by moving the shock absorbers up and down several times. Check for leaks, twist or bends, and replace if any parts worn or damaged beyond repair.
2. Check the front forks and handlebar mounting bolts for looseness.

Changing front fork oil

1. Remove the drain plugs from both forks. Grasp the handlebar and move it up and down several times to drain the remaining oil.
2. Replace the drain plugs. Place a block under the engine to raise the front wheel off the ground.

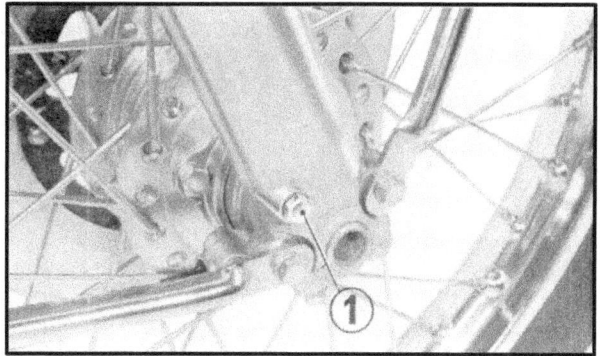

Fig. 2-12 ① Front fork drain plug

3. Remove the oil filler plugs and pour the specified amount of ATF (automatic transmission fluid) into the holes.
   Capacity: 145-150 cc (4.8-4.9 ozs.)
   NOTE:
   A specified amount of fluid will be required to fill one fork whenever disassembling.
   Specified amount: 160-165 cc (5.6-5.8 ozs.)
4. Replace the filler plugs and remove the block under the engine.

Fig. 2-13 ① Oil filler plug

8. REAR SUSPENSION

Inspection

1. Raise the rear wheel off the ground. Move the rear wheel in and out to check the rear fork bushings wear. If worn excessively beyond use, replace.
2. Check the suspension mountings for looseness.

Fig. 2-14 ① Rear fork   ② Rear shock absorber

Rear fork Bushing Lubrication

There is a lubrication point as shown in Fig. 2-15. It is recommended that lubrication be performed every 6 months or 3,000 miles, whichever occurs first. Use multipurpose grease, Type NLGI No. 2.

Fig. 2-15 ① Grease fitting

II. INSPECTION AND ADJUSTMENT

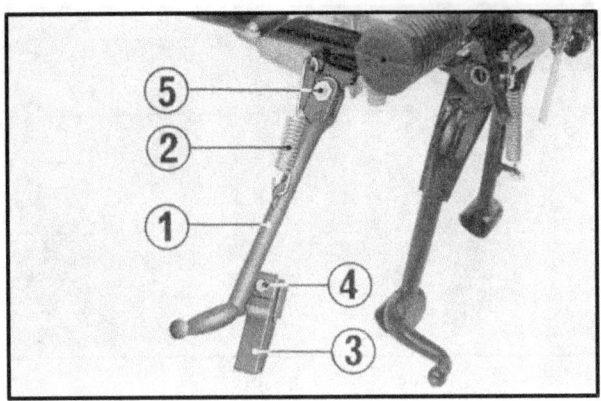

Fig. 2-16
① Side stand bar
② Spring
③ Rubber block
④ 6 mm bolt
⑤ Side stand pivot bolt

9. SIDE STAND

1. Check the entire stand assembly (side stand bar, bracket and rubber block) for installation, deformation or other excessive damage.
2. Check the spring for freedom from damage or other defects.

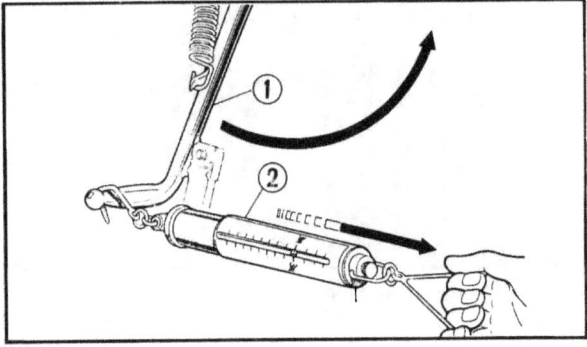

Fig. 2-17 ① Side stand bar ② Spring scale

3. Check the side stand for proper return operation:
   a. With the side stand applied, raise the stand off the ground using the main stand.
   b. Attach a spring scale to the lower end of the stand and measure the force the stand is returned to its original position.
   c. The stand condition is correct if the measurement falls within **2–3 kg (4.4–6.6 lbs.)**
      If the stand requires force exceeding the specified limit, this may be due to neglected lubrication, overtightened side stand pivot bolt, worn stand bar or bracket, or otherwise excessive tension. Repair as necessary.
4. Check the rubber block for deterioration or wear. When the rubber block wear is so excessive that it is worn down to the wear line, replace it with a new one.

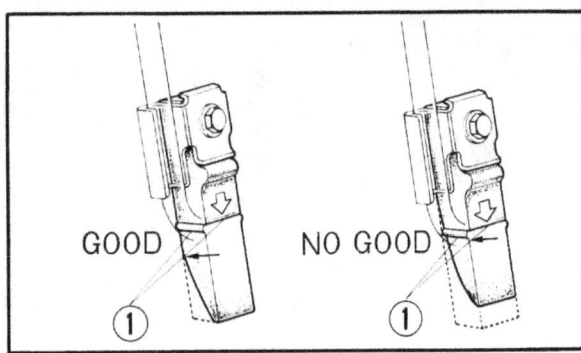

Fig. 2-18 ① Wear line

Rubber block replacement

1. Remove the 6 mm bolt; separate the rubber block from the bracket at the side stand.
2. After installing the collar, put a new rubber block in place in the bracket with the arrow mark out.

NOTE:
Use rubber block with the mark "OVER 260 lbs. ONLY"

3. Secure the rubber block with the 6 mm bolt.

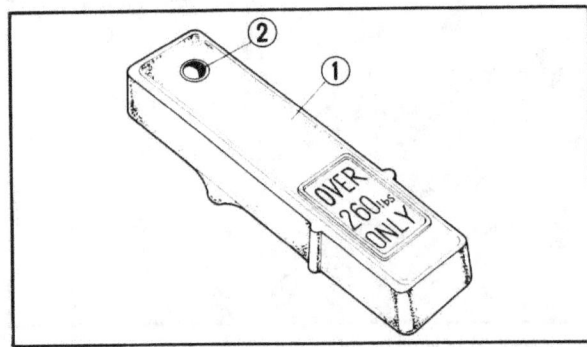

Fig. 2-19 ① Rubber block ② Collar

III. ENGINE

1. PISTON RINGS

Assembly

1. To install the oil ring, first place the spacer and then the rails in position. The spacer and rail gaps must be staggered **20-30 mm (0.8-1.2-in.)**.
2. Install the second and top rings in this order in the piston with their markings facing up.

NOTE:
a. Do not mix the top and second rings.
b. After installing all the piston rings, hand-rotate them and check to be sure they move smoothly without any binding.

3. The ring gaps must be staggered 120° and must not be in the direction of the piston pin boss or at a right angle to the pin.

NOTE:
For the gap of the three-piece type oil ring, use the gap of the spacer.

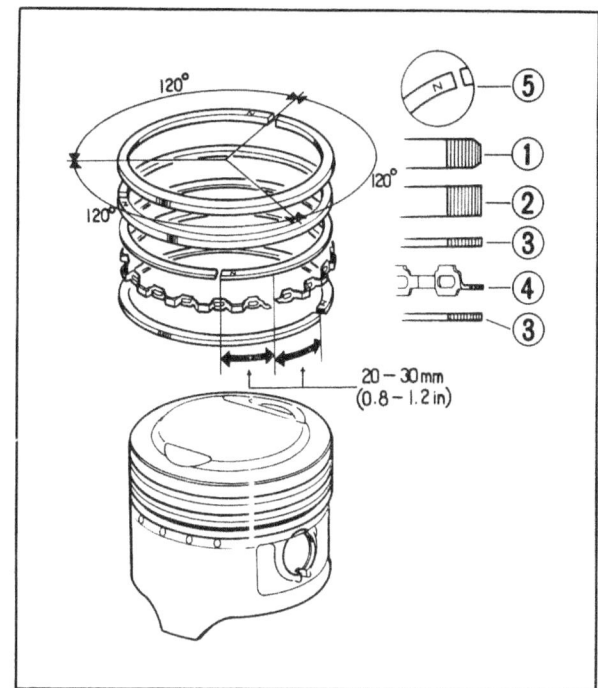

Fig. 3-1
① Top ring
② Second ring
③ Rail
④ Spacer
⑤ Piston ring marking

2. CLUTCH

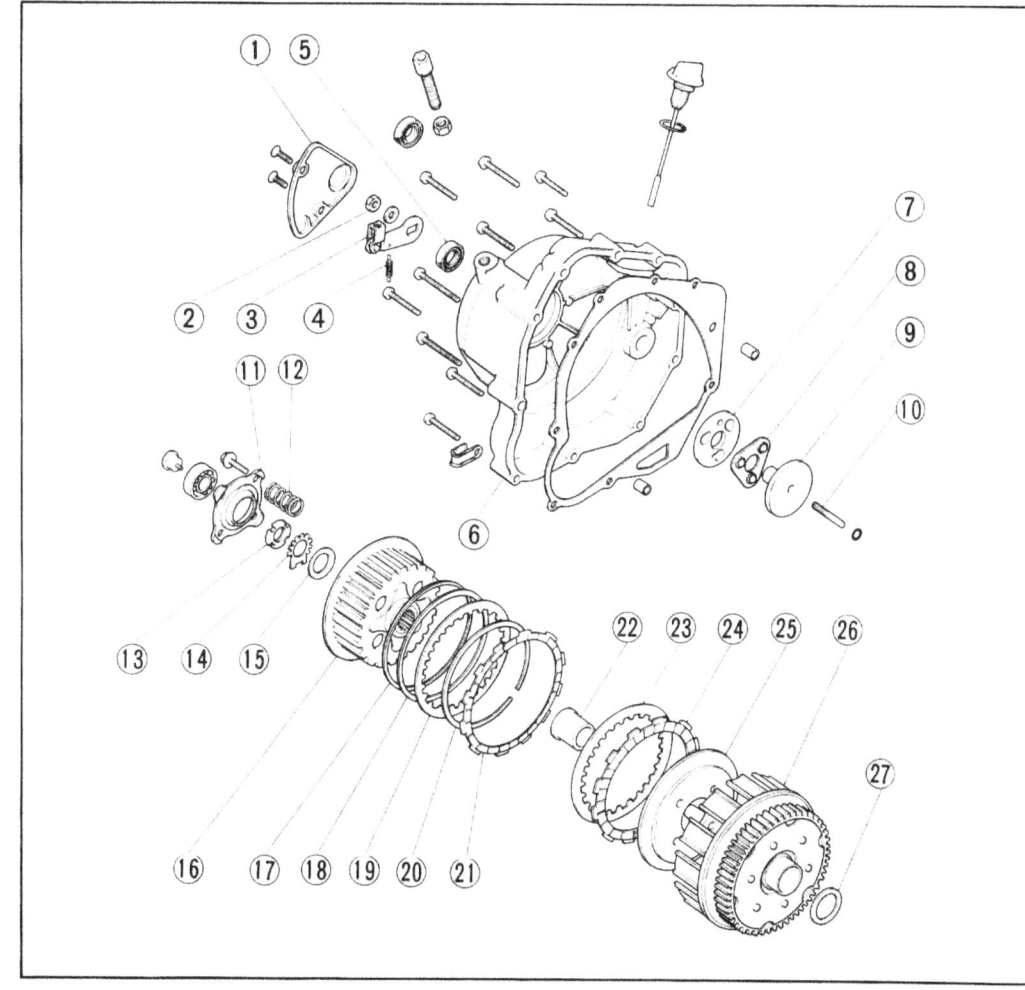

Fig. 3-2
① Clutch cover
② Lock nut
③ Clutch lifter lever
④ Clutch lever spring
⑤ Oil seal
⑥ Right crankcase cover
⑦ Clutch cam plate
⑧ Ball retainer
⑨ Clutch lifter
⑩ Clutch adjusting screw
⑪ Clutch lifter plate
⑫ Clutch spring
⑬ Lock nut
⑭ Lock washer
⑮ Lock washer
⑯ Clutch center
⑰ Disc spring seat
⑱ Clutch disc spring
⑲ Clutch plate B
⑳ Special set ring
㉑ Clutch friction disc
㉒ Collar
㉓ Clutch plate (6)
㉔ Clutch friction disc (6)
㉕ Clutch pressure plate
㉖ Clutch outer
㉗ Thrust washer

III. ENGINE

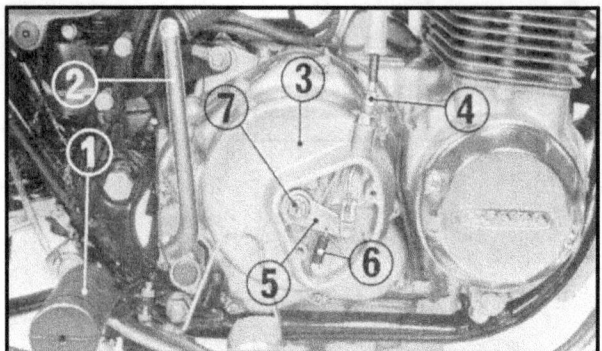

Fig. 3-3
① Foot peg
② Kick starter pedal
③ Right crankase cover
④ Clutch adjuster
⑤ Clutch lifter lever
⑥ Spring
⑦ Lock nut

Fig. 3-4
① 16mm lock nut
② Lock washer
③ Lock washer

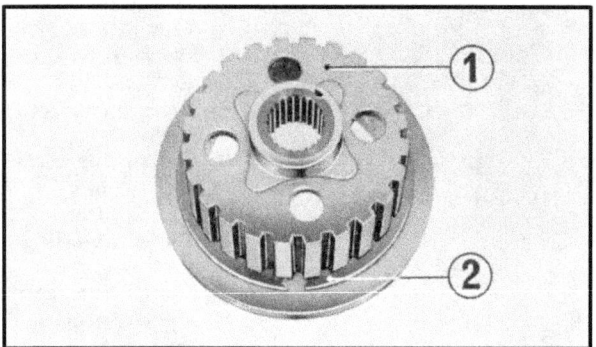

Fig. 3-5
① Clutch center
② 92mm special set ring

Fig. 3-6
① Snap ring
② Gearshift lever
③ Punch marks

Disassembly

1. Drain the engine throughly by removing the drain plug.
2. Remove the rear brake adjusting nut.
3. Remove the right foot peg and kick starter pedal.
4. Remove the clutch cover from the right crankcase cover.
5. Turn the clutch adjusters to loosen the clutch cable.
6. Disconnect the clutch cable from the clutch lifter lever.
7. Remove the right crankcase cover.
8. Loosen the clutch adjusting screw lock nut and remove the clutch lifter lever and spring.
9. Remove the clutch cam plate, ball retainer, clutch lifter and adjusting screw from the right crankcase cover.
10. Loosen the bolts and remove the clutch lifter plate and clutch springs.
11. Using the Lock Nut Wrench (Tool No. 07916-6390000), loosen the 16mm lock nut and remove the clutch assembly.

12. Remove the 92mm special set ring from the clutch center. Disassemble clutch plate B, clutch disc spring and disc spring seat.

3. GEARSHIFT MECHANISM

Gearshift pedal

Removal
1. Pry the snap ring off and loosen the gearshift lever locking bolt.
2. Remove the gearshift pedal assembly.

Installation
1. Install the gearshift pedal assembly with the punch mark on the gearshift lever lined up with that on the gearshift spindle.

2. Adjust the gearshift pedal position so that the pedal lever is parallel with the gearshift lever on the spindle.
Adjust by turning the adjuster after loosening the lock nuts. After adjustment, tighten the lock nuts firmly.

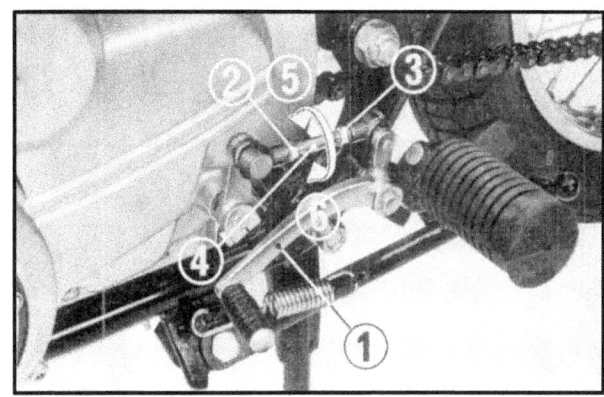

Fig. 3-7
① Gearshift pedal
② Lock nut (left hand thread)
③ Lock nut
④ Adjuster
⑤ To open
⑥ To close

4. CARBURETOR

Setting table

ITEM	
Setting number	054-A
Main jet	#75
Slow jet	#40
Jet needle setting	3rd. groove
Air screw opening	2±1/2
Float height (gauge)	21 mm (0.827-in.)

IV. FRAME

1. FRONT SUSPENSION

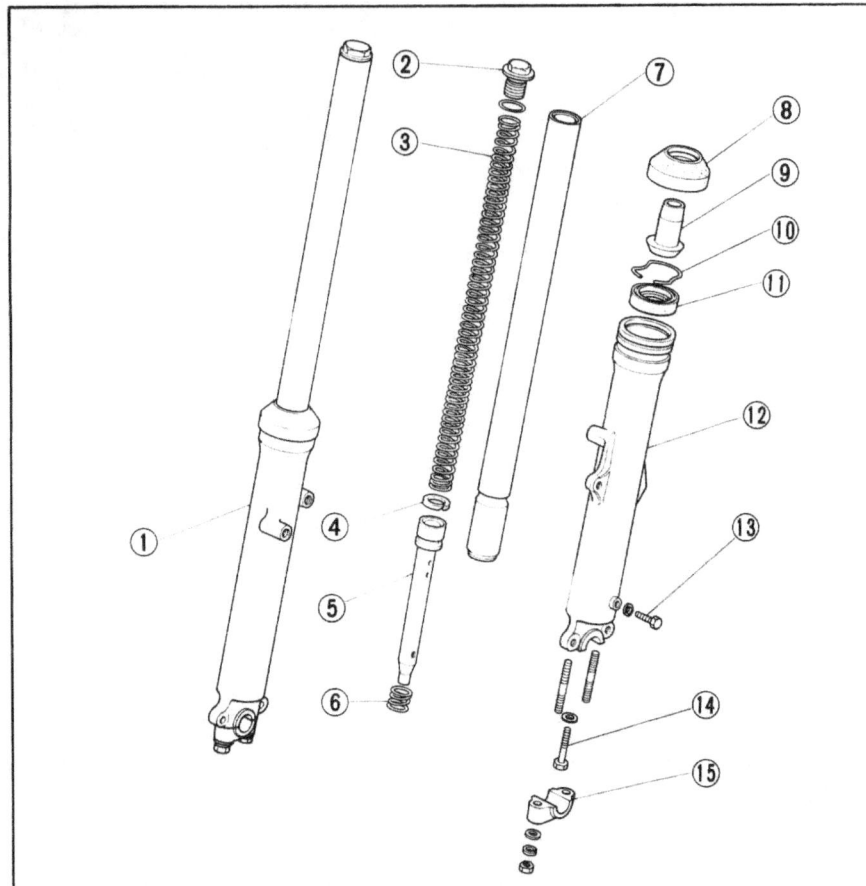

Fig. 4-1
① Right front shock absorber
② Fork bolt
③ Front shock absorber spring
④ Piston ring
⑤ Under seat pipe
⑥ Rebound spring
⑦ Front fork pipe
⑧ Bottom case cover
⑨ Oil lock piece
⑩ Oil seal stop
⑪ Oil seal
⑫ Bottom case
⑬ Drain bolt
⑭ Socket bolt
⑮ Front axle holder

Fig. 4-2 ① Front fork securing bolt
② Front fork bolt

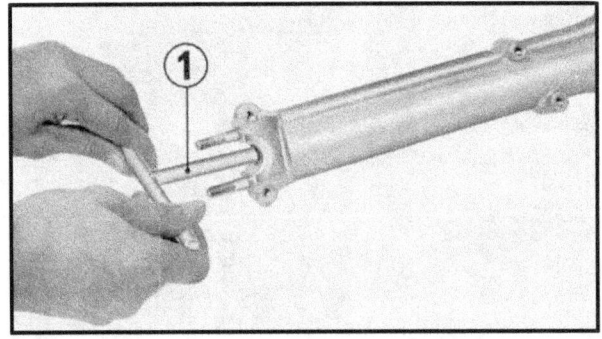

Fig. 4-3 ① Allen head wrench

Disassembly

1. Remove the front wheel.
2. Remove the caliper assembly from the left front fork.
3. With the front fork bolt loosened, loosen the bolts at the fork top bridge and steering stem, that secure the front fork. Pull the front fork toward the bottom.
4. Drain the front suspension oil.
5. Remove any rust on the front fork pipe, with an emery cloth.
6. Remove the socket bolt and separate the front fork pipe and oil lock piece from the bottom case. Use the Allen Head Wrench (Tool No. 07917-3230000) to remove the socket bolt.
   Protect the shock absorber with a rag when holding it on a vise.
   Remove the front fork bolt on top of the front fork pipe. Remove the front shock absorber spring, under seat pipe and rebound spring.

IV. FRAME

8. Remove the bottom case cover. Pry the oil seal stop off and remove the oil seal from the bottom case.

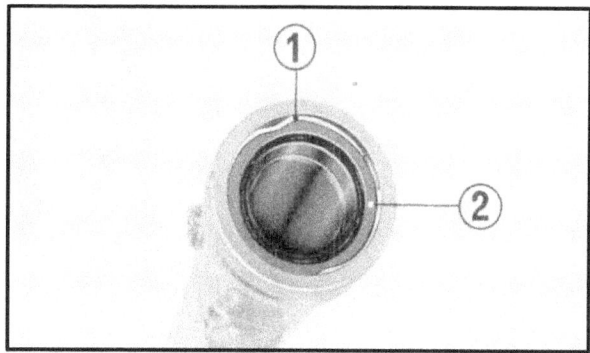

Fig. 4-4 ① Oil seal stop
② Oil seal

Inspection

1. Check the free length of the front shock absorber spring.
2. Check the front fork pipe for piston ring wear.
3. Check the bottom case and fork pipe for wear, cracks or other defects.
4. Check the oil seal for wear or damage.

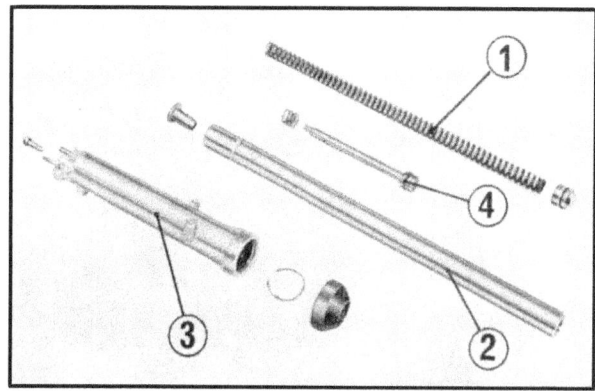

Fig. 4-5 ① Front shock absorber spring
② Front fork pipe
③ Bottom case
④ Piston ring

Assembly

1. Clean all parts in solvent before assembly.
2. Apply a coat of ATF (automatic transmission fluid) to the surface of the oil seal. Install the oil seal to the bottom case. Fit the oil seal using with the Fork Seal Driver (Tool No. 97947-3330000). Install the oil seal stop and bottom case cover.
3. Install the rebound spring and seat pipe into the front fork pipe.
4. After installing the oil lock piece, insert the front fork pipe to the bottom case and secure with the socket bolt.

NOTE:
Apply liquid sealant to the socket bolt threads.

5. Fill each front fork with 160-165 cc (5.6-5.8 ozs.) of ATF before installation.
6. Install the front fork assembly so that the chamfered edge on the fork pipe aligns with the upper surface of the fork top bridge as shown in Fig. 4-7.
7. After all parts have been installed, check the action of the front shock absorbers by grasping the handlebar and moving the front forks up and down. Check the front forks for leaks from the oil seal.

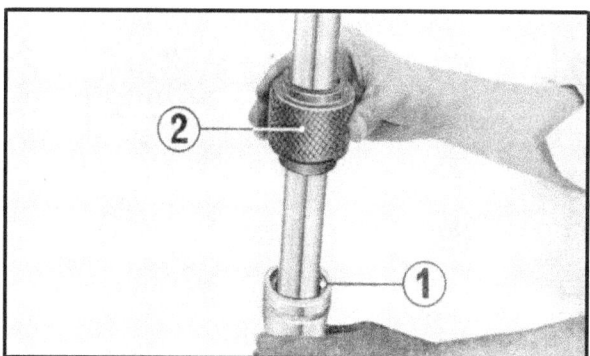

Fig. 4-6 ① Oil seal
② Fork seal driver

Fig. 4-7 Chamfered edge of front fork pipe

IV. FRAME

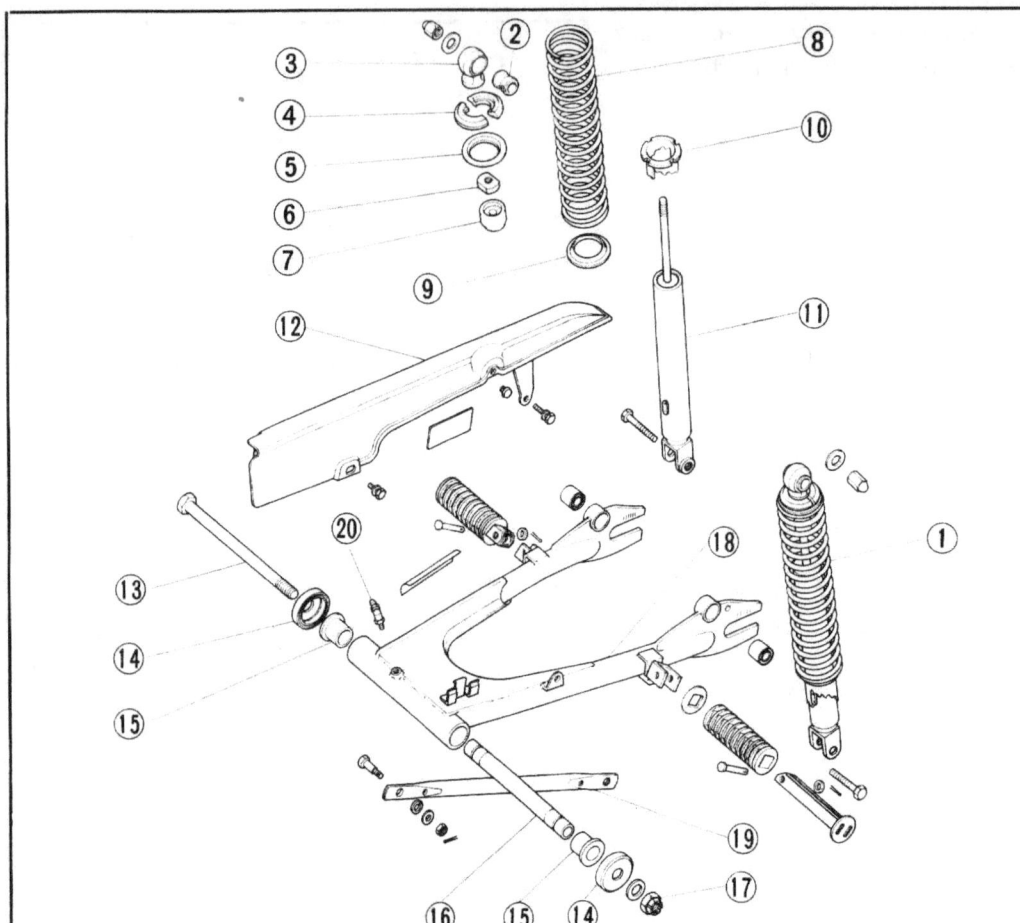

2. REAR SUSPENSION

Fig. 4-5
① Rear shock absorber assembly
② Joint rubber
③ Upper joint
④ Spring seat stop
⑤ Spring upper seat
⑥ Lock nut (10 mm)
⑦ Stop rubber
⑧ Rear shock absorber spring
⑨ Spring lower seat
⑩ Spring adjuster
⑪ Rear damper
⑫ Drive chain case
⑬ Rear fork pivot bolt
⑭ Dust seal cap
⑮ Rear fork pivot bushing
⑯ Rear fork center collar
⑰ Self-locking nut (14 mm)
⑱ Rear fork
⑲ Rear brake stop arm
⑳ Grease fitting

3. FRAME BODY

Fuel Valve

1. Place the fuel valve lever at "OFF" and disconnect the fuel tubes. Remove the fuel tank.
2. Loosen the fuel valve fixing nut and remove the fuel valve and fuel filter from the fuel tank.
3. Disassemble the fuel valve. Loosen the screws and remove the plate, washer, lever, spring, O-ring and valve from the fuel valve body.
4. Check the valve faces of the fuel valves for scores or other damage. Replace with a new valve assembly, if necessary.
5. Check the gasket for damage. Replace with a new one, if it is damaged too badly beyond use.
6. Wash the fuel filter in solvent and dry with compressed air. No damage can be tolerated. Replace the filter with a new one if it is clogged.
7. Install the fuel filter to the fuel valve with the fixing nut. Do not forget to install the gasket into the groove of the fixing nut.
8. Install the fuel valve to the fuel tank with the fixing nut.
9. Install the fuel tank on the frame. Connect the tubes and secure with the clips.
10. Fill the tank with fuel. With the fuel valve lever at "ON", check for leaks past the tube joints or connections.

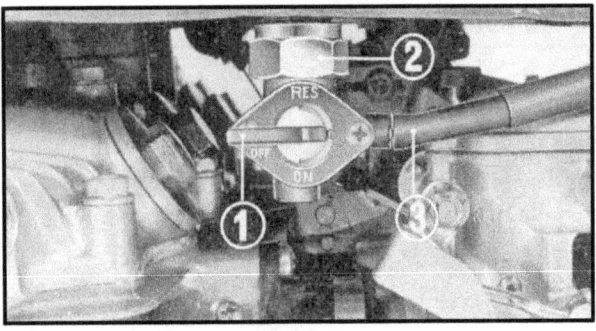

Fig. 4-9
① Fuel valve lever
② Fuel valve fixing nut
③ Fuel tube

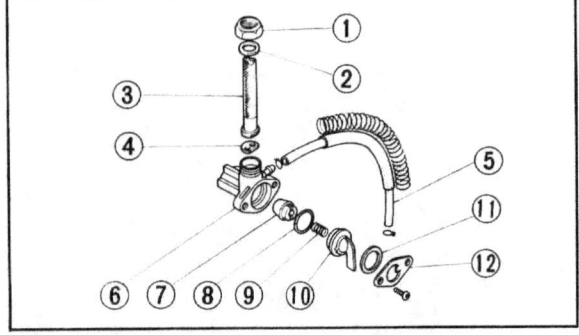

Fig. 4-10
① Nut
② Gasket
③ Fuel filter
④ Filter seat
⑤ Fuel tube
⑥ Fuel valve body
⑦ Valve
⑧ O-ring
⑨ Spring
⑩ Valve lever
⑪ Washer
⑫ Lever setting plate

Muffler

Removal

1. Loosen the two bolts that secure the muffler to the frame.

Fig. 4-11 ① Muffler
② Bolt

2. Loosen the eight joint nuts and remove the muffler assembly, exhaust pipe joints and joint collars.

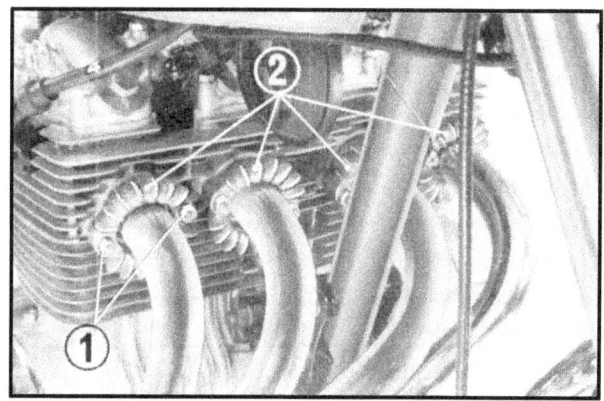

Fig. 4-12 ① Joint nut
② Exhaust pipe joint

3. Loosen the muffler band bolts and remove the two exhaust pipes and sealing gaskets from the muffler assembly.

Inspection

1. Check the exhaust pipe gaskets for damage.
2. Check the muffler sealing gaskets for damage.

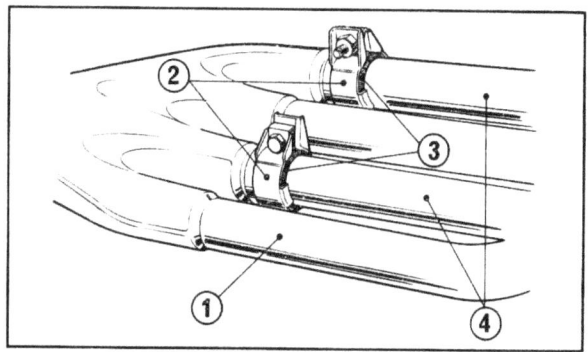

Fig. 4-13 ① Muffler assembly
② Band
③ Gasket
④ Exhaust pipe

Installation

1. Install the exhaust pipes to the muffler assembly through the sealing gaskets.
2. Tighten the muffler bands so that the bolts are at the upper part of the muffler.
3. Install the muffler assembly.

V. ELECTRICAL SYSTEM

1. CHARGING SYSTEM

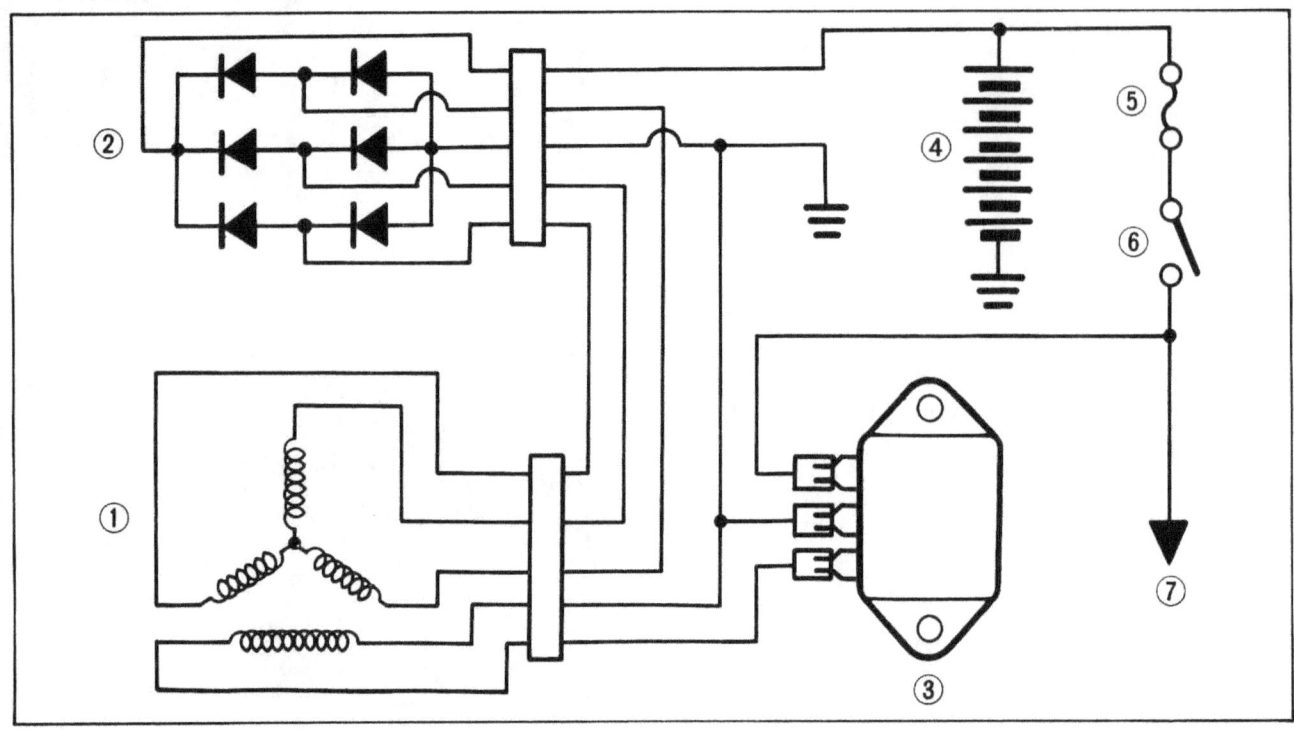

Fig. 5-1 ① AC generator ③ Pointless regulator ⑤ Fuse ⑦ Load
② Silicon diode rectifier ④ Battery ⑥ Main switch

2. STARTING SYSTEM

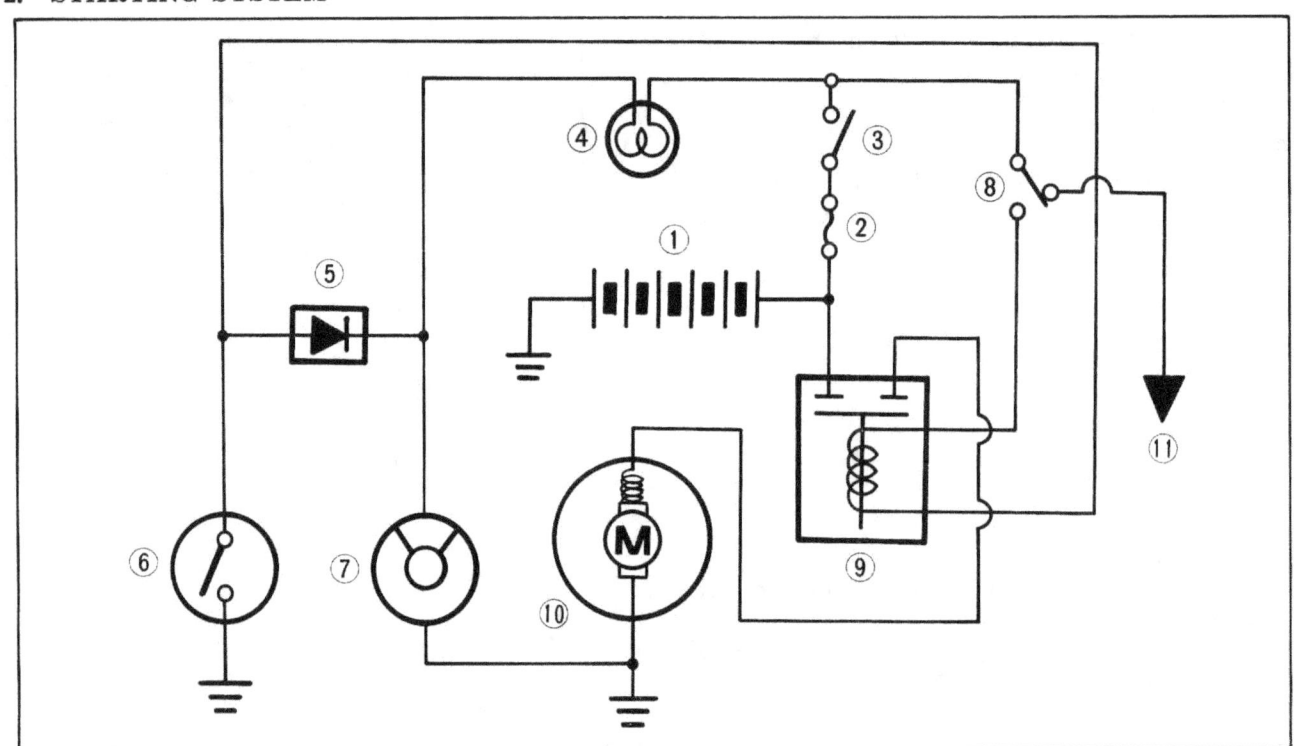

Fig. 5-2 ① Battery ④ Neutral pilot light ⑦ Neutral switch ⑩ Starting motor
② Fuse ⑤ Silicon diode ⑧ Starting switch ⑪ To lighting system
③ Main switch ⑥ Clutch switch ⑨ Starting magnetic switch

V. ELECTRICAL SYSTEM

Clutch switch

Check the continuity between the green and green/red leads of the switch in the headlight case. Continuity should exist only when the clutch is disengaged.

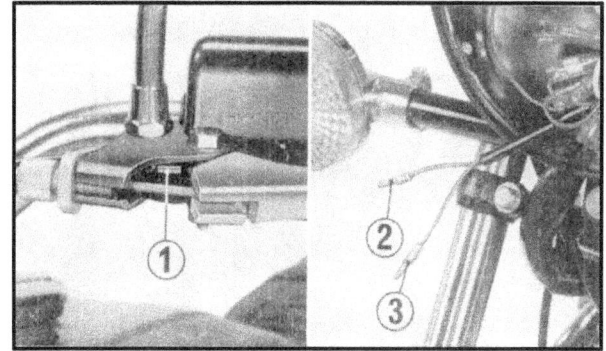

Fig. 5-3 ① Clutch switch
② Green lead
③ Green/red lead

Starting switch

Disconnect the terminals of the starting switch leads in the connector cover. Check for continuity between the circuits (o—o) as shown in the table below.

Terminal	ST1	ST2	HL
Wire color	Black	Yellow/red	Black/red
FREE	o		o
PUSH	o	o	

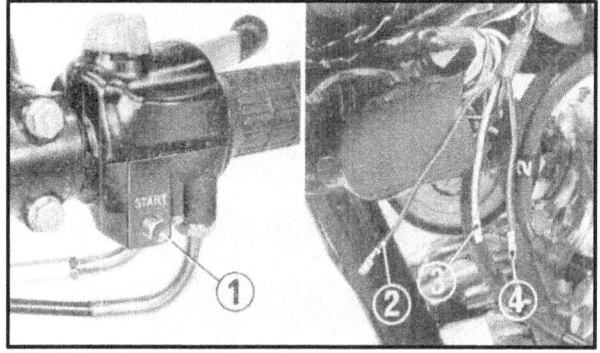

Fig. 5-9 ① Starting switch ③ Yellow/red lead
② Black lead ④ Black/red lead

Silicon diode

Check the diode for continuity with a radio tester in high-reading range. If current flows in only one direction (from cathode to anode), the diode is normal. Current flow in both directions or no current is a sign of a diode malfunction.

NOTE:
Do not use a megger. The high voltage generated in the megger will damage the diode.

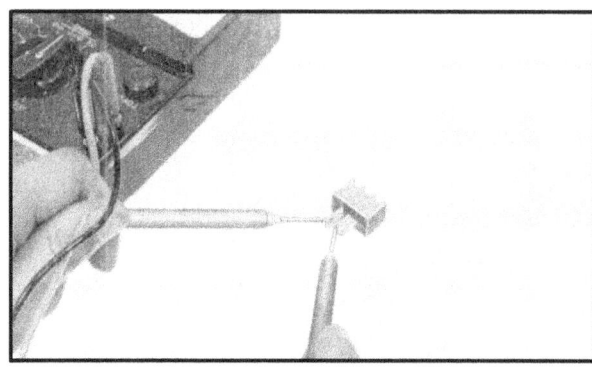

Fig. 5-5 Checking silicon diode

3. ELECTRICAL EQUIPMENT
Main switch

With the key in OFF, ON or PARK, check the main switch for continuity. The switch is normal if continuity exists in the circuit (o—o). Discard the switch if there is any continuity in other circuits shown below.

Terminal	BAT	IG	TL1	TL2	PA
Wire color	Red	Black	Brown	Brown/white	Brown
PARK	o			o	o
ON	o	o	o	o	o
OFF					
LOCK					

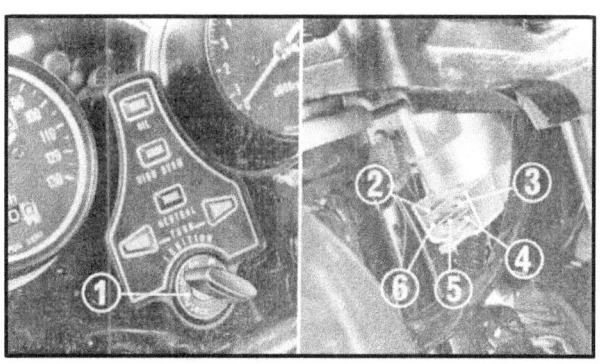

Fig. 5-6 ① Main switch ④ Brown
② Brown ⑤ Red
③ Brown/white ⑥ Black

V. ELECTRICAL SYSTEM

Fig. 5-7 ① Dimmer switch
② Turn signal control switch

Dimmer and turn signal control switch

Check for continuity between respective terminals of the switch leads in the connector cover. The switch is normal if there is continuity as specified below (o—o) with the switch selector knob in each position.

Terminal	W	L	R	P(F)	PL	PR
Wire color	Grey	Orange	Light blue	—	Light blue/white	Orange/white
L	o—————o			o————————————————o	
N				o—————o	o—————o
R	o———————————o		o—————o		

Terminal	HL	Hi	Lo	P(F)
Wire color	Black/Yellow	Blue	White	—
Hi	o—————o		
(N)	o—————o	o—————o	
Lo	o———————————o	o—————o	

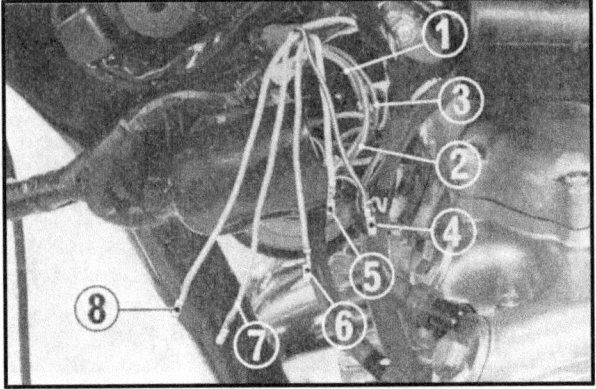

Fig. 5-8 ① Grey lead
② Orange lead
③ Light blue lead
④ Black/yellow lead
⑤ White lead
⑥ Blue lead
⑦ Orange/white lead
⑧ Light blue/white lead

Horn switch

Disconnect the terminal of the horn switch lead in the connector cover. Check the continuity between the gray lead and ground.
Continuity should exist only when the button is depressed.

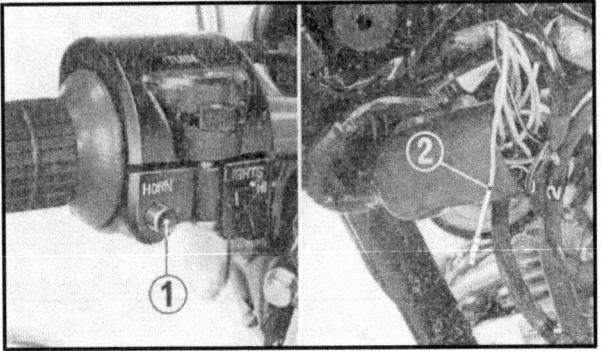

Fig. 5-9 ① Horn switch
② Gray lead

Engine stop switch

Check for continuity between the respective terminals of the switch leads in the connector cover. The switch is in good condition if there is continuity in the circuit (o—o) with the switch selector knob in each position.

Terminal	IG	RUN
Wire color	Black	Black/white
OFF		
RUN	o————————————o
OFF		

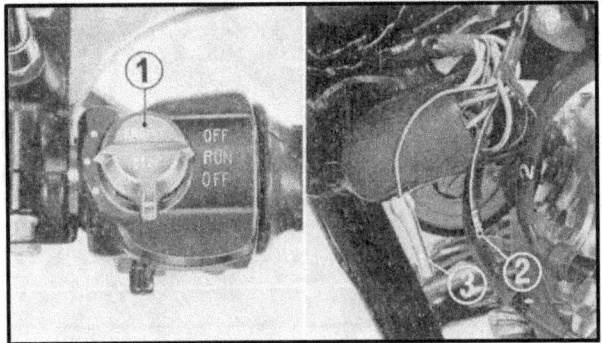

Fig. 5-10 ① Engine stop switch
② Black
③ Black white

VI. SERVICE DATA

1 CB 400 F SPECIAL TOOLS

○ = USED, × = NOT USED

No.	Tool No.	Description	CB 350 F Tool
	07900-3770000	CB 400 F special tool set	×
1	07902-2000000	Pin spanner (48 mm)	×
2	07906-3230000	Box wrench (12 mm)	○
3	07908-0010000	Tappet adjusting wrench	○
4	07910-3230101	Front wheel bearing retainer wrench	○
5	07910-3290000	Rear wheel bearing retainer wrench	○
6	07914-3230000	Snap ring pliers	○
7	07916-6390000	Lock nut wrench (16 mm)	×
8	07917-3230000	Allen head wrench (6 mm)	○
9	07933-3330000	Rotor puller	○
10	07942-3290200	Valve guide driver	○
11	07942-3290200	Valve guide driver	○
12	07945-3330100	Bearing driver attachment (inner)	○
13	07945-3330200	Bearing driver attachment (outer)	○
14	07945-3330300	Ball race driver attachment	○
15	07947-3330000	Fork seal driver	○
16	07949-6110000	Driver handle	○
17	07953-3330000	Ball race remover	○
18	07955-3770000	Piston ring compressor	×
19	07957-3290000	Valve spring compressor	○
20	07958-3330000	Piston base	○
21	07959-3290000	Shock absorber compressor	○
22	07984-2000000	Valve guide reamer (Intake)	○
23	07984-3770000	Valve guide reamer (Exhaust)	×
24	07921-0010000	Flare nut wrench	×
25	07922-2870000	Drive sprocket holder	×
26	07797-2920300	Special tool case	×
OPTIONAL			
27	07504-3000100	Vacuum gauge set	○
28	07908-3230200	Carburetor synchronization wrench set	○

2. MAINTENANCE SCHEDULE

This maintenance schedule is based upon average riding conditions. Machines subjected to severe use, or ridden in unusually dusty areas, require more frequent servicing.	INITIAL SERVICE PERIOD	REGULAR SERVICE PERIOD Perform at every indicated month or mileage interval, whichever occurs first.			
	500 miles	1 month / 500 miles	3 months / 1,500 miles	6 months / 3,000 miles	12 months / 6,000 miles
Engine Oil—Change	●		○		
Oil Filter Element—Replace	●			○	
Oil Filter Screen—Clean					○
Spark Plug—Clean and adjust gap or replace if necessary.				○	
*Contact Points and Ignition Timing—Clean, check, and adjust or replace if necessary.	●			○	
*Valve Tappet Clearance—Check, and adjust if necessary.	●			○	
*Cam Chain Tension—Adjust	●			○	
Paper Air Filter Element and Breather Element—Clean	(service more frequently if operated in dusty areas)			○	
Paper Air Filter Element—Replace					○
*Carburetor—Check, and adjust if necessary.	●			○	
Throttle Operation—Inspect cable. Check, and adjust free play.	●			○	
*Fuel Filter Screen—Clean				○	
Fuel Lines—Check				○	
*Clutch—Check operation, and adjust if necessary.	●			○	
Drive Chain—Check, lubricate, and adjust if necessary.	**●	○			
Brake Fluid Level—Check and add fluid if necessary.	●			○	
*Brake Shoes/Pads—Inspect, and replace if worn.				○	
Brake Control Linkage—Check linkage, and adjust free play if necessary.	●			○	
*Wheel Rims and Spokes—Check. Tighten spokes and true wheels, if necessary.	●			○	
Tires—Inspect and check air pressure.	●	○			
Front Fork Oil—Drain and refill.	***●				○
Front and Rear Suspension—Check operation.	●			○	
Rear Fork Bushing—Grease, check for excessive looseness.				○	
*Steering Head Bearings—Adjust.					○
*Side Stand—Check installation, operation, deformation, damage and wear.				○	
Battery—Check electrolyte level, and add water if necessary.	●		○		
Lighting Equipment—Check and adjust if necessary.	●	○			
All Nuts, Bolts, and Other Fasteners—Check security and tighten if necessary.	●	○			

Items marked * should be serviced by an authorized Honda dealer, unless the owner has proper tools and is mechanically proficient. Other maintenance items are simple to perform and may be serviced by the owner.
** Initial service period 200 miles.   *** Initial service period 1,500 miles.

3. TORQUE SPECIFICATIONS

ENGINE

Tightening point	Thread dia. (mm)	Torque	
		kg-cm	lbs-ft
Crankcase and crankcase covers	6, P1.0	70–110	5.1–8.0
Cylinder head	8, P1.25 (cap nut)	200–230 (Apply oil to the nuts before tightening)	14.5–16.7
Oil filter	20, P1.25	280–320	20.5–23.2
Carburetor insulator-to-cylinder head	6, P1.0	70–110	5.1–8.0
Cam sprocket	7, P1.0	160–200	11.6–14.5
AC generator rotor	10, P1.0	500–600	36.5–43.8
Primary drive gear	12, P1.25 (U.B.S. bolt)	500–600	36.5–43.8
Tappet adjusting nut	5, P0.5	70–110	5.1–8.0
Upper and lower crankcases	8, P1.25	220–260	15.2–18.9
Cylinder head cover	6, P1.0 (U.B.S. bolt)	120–150	8.5–12.1
Clutch outer	16, P1.5 (lock nut)	500–600	36.5–43.8
Connecting rod	8, P1.25	200–220	14.5–15.2

FRAME

Tightening point	Thread dia. (mm)	Torque	
		kg-cm	lbs-ft
Steering stem nut	24, P1.0	800–1,200	57.9–86.9
Fork top bridge to front forks	8, P1.25	180–230	13.1–16.7
Handlebar holder	8, P1.25	180–230	13.1–16.7
Front fork bottom bridge to front forks	8, P1.25	180–230	13.1–16.7
Spokes	—		
Front wheel	—	25–30	1.9–2.2
Rear wheel	—	20–25	1.5–1.9
Rear fork pivot bolt	14, P1.5 (self lock nut)	600–700	39.8–50.7
Front wheel axle nut	12, P1.5	450–550	32.6–39.8
Front fork axle holder	8, P1.25	180–230	13.1–16.7
Engine hanger bolt	10, P1.25 (U.B.S. nut)	300–400	21.7–29.0
Rear wheel axle nut	16, P1.5	800–1,000	57.9–72.4
Final driven sprocket	10. P1.25 (U.B.S. nut)	450–600	29.0–36.2
Brake arm stopper	6, P1.0 (U.B.S. nut)	110–150	8.0–10.3
Front and rear brake torque links	8, P1.25	180–230	13.1–16.7
Rear suspension	10, P1.25	300–400	21.7–29.0
Step bar	12, P1.25	450–550	32.6–39.8
Gear change pedal and kick arm	6, P1.0	80–100	5.9–7.3
Disc plate	8, P1.25 (U.B.S. nut)	270–330	20.6–23.9
Spark plug	12, P1.25	150–200	12.1–14.5
Headlight case	10, P1.25 (special bolt)	150–250	12.1–18.3

4. SERVICE DATA

ENGINE

Unit: mm (in.)

Item	Assembly standard	Service limit
Rocker arm-to-rocker arm shaft clearance	0.016–0.052 (0.0006–0.0020)	0.1 (0.0039)
Cam height of camshaft Intake	28.185–28.225 (1.1096–1.1112)	28.0 (1.1024)
Exhaust	28.184–28.224 (1.1096–1.1111)	28.0 (1.1024)
Camshaft center journal	—	0.1 (0.0039)
Valve seat width	0.7 (0.03)	1.5 (0.0039)
Valve stem O.D. Intake	5.48–5.49 (0.2158–0.2161)	5.35 (0.2106)
Exhaust	5.47–5.48 (0.2154–0.2158)	5.35 (0.2106)
Valve-to-valve guide clearance Intake	0.01–0.03 (0.0004–0.0012)	0.3 (0.0118)
Exhaust	0.01–0.03 (0.0004–0.0012)	0.3 (0.0118)
Valve spring preload Inner	19.2/13.0–14.6 kg (0.7559/28.665–32.1930 lbs)	—
Outer	23.7/32.0–32.4 kg (0.9330/70.560–71.4420 lbs)	—
Valve spring free length Inner	29.0 (1.1417)	27.0 (1.0630)
Outer	34.5 (1.3583)	32.5 (1.2795)
Cylinder head flatness	—	0.3 (0.0118)
Cylinder I.D.	51.00–51.01 (2.0079–2.0083)	51.1 (2.0118)
Piston skirt O.D.	50.97–50.99 (2.0067–2.0075)	50.85 (2.0020)
Piston pin hole I.D.	13.002–13.008 (0.5119–0.5121)	13.05 (0.5138)
Piston pin O.D.	12.994–13.00 (0.5116–0.5118)	12.9 (0.5079)
Piston ring-to-piston ring groove clearance Top ring	0.025–0.055 (0.0010–0.0022)	0.15 (0.0059)
Second ring	0.015–0.045 (0.0006–0.018)	0.15 (0.0059)
Piston ring end gap Top ring	0.15–0.35 (0.0059–0.0138)	0.7 (0.0276)
Second ring	0.15–0.35 (0.0059–0.0138)	0.7 (0.0276)
Oil ring	0.2–0.5 (0.0079–0.0197)	0.9 (0.0035)
Outer rotor O.D.-to-pump body clearance Main pump	0.06–0.12 (0.0024–0.0047)	0.35 (0.0138)
Auxiliary pump	0.15–0.20 (0.0059–0.0079)	0.35 (0.0138)
Outer rotor-to-inner rotor clearance Main pump	0.15 (0.0059), max.	0.3 (0.0118)
Auxiliary pump	0.15 (0.0059), max.	0.3 (0.0118)
Friction disc thickness	2.62–2.78 (0.1032–0.1095)	2.3 (0.0906)
Clutch plate surface warpage	0.1 (0.0039), max.	0.2 (0.0079)
Clutch spring free length	31.25 (1.2303)	29.75 (1.1712)
Clutch center-to-clutch plate B clearance	0.1–0.5 (0.004–0.02)	Beyond assembly standard
Gearshift fork finger width	5.93–6.00 (0.2335–0.2362)	5.5 (0.2165)

VI. SERVICE DATA

Unit: mm (in.)

Item	Assembly standard	Service limit
Gearshift guide shaft O.D.	12.957–12.984 (0.5101–0.5112)	12.9 (0.5079)
Gearshift fork I.D.	13.000–13.018 (0.5118–0.5125)	12.95 (0.5098)
Kick starter pinion-to-shaft clearance	0.04–0.082 (0.0016–0.0032)	0.1 (0.004)
Gearshift fork dowel-to-drum groove clearance	0.05–0.22 (0.0020–0.0087)	0.3 (0.0118)
Transmission gear backlash	—	0.2 (0.0079)

Transmission gear-to-shaft clearance
    C-1
    Other gears
	
	0.04–0.074 (0.0016–0.0029)
	0.04–0.081 (0.0016–0.0032)
		
		0.2 (0.0079)
		0.2 (0.0079)

Cam chain tensioner slipper thickness (center)	4.0 (0.1575)	3.0 (0.118) max.
Cam chain guide thickness	6.1–6.3 (0.2402–0.2480)	5.0 (0.197)
Crankshaft runout (center)	0.03 (0.0012), max.	0.05 (0.0020)
Crankshaft journal clearance	0.018–0.048 (0.0007–0.0019)	0.08 (0.0032)
Connecting rod small end I.D.	13.012–13.033 (0.5123–0.5131)	13.10 (0.5158)
Connecting rod big end side clearance	0.02–0.07 (0.0008–0.0028)	0.15 (0.0059)
Connecting rod big end-to-crankshaft journal clearance	0.018–0.048 (0.0007–0.0019)	0.08 (0.0032)
Primary chain guide thickness (center)	6.0–6.3 (0.236–0.248)	5.0 (0.197)

FRAME

Unit: mm (in.)

Item	Assembly standard	Service limit
Brake disc face runout	0.3 (0.0118), max.	0.3 (0.0118), min.
Brake disc thickness	6.9–7.1 (0.2717–0.2795)	—
Wheel rim face runout	0.5 (0.0197), max.	2.0 (0.079)
Wheel bearing end play	0.07 (0.0028) max.	0.1 (0.0039)
Wheel bearing radial play	0.03 (0.0012), max.	0.05 (0.0020)
Front axle runout	0.01 (0.0004)	0.2 (0.0079)
Caliper cylinder I. D.	38.18–38.20 (1.5032–1.5039)	38.215 (1.5045)
Caliper piston O. D.	38.115–38.480 (1.5006–1.5150)	38.105 (1.5002)
Master cylinder I. D.	14.00–14.043 (0.5512–0.5529)	14.055 (0.5533)
Master cylinder piston O. D.	13.957–13.984 (0.5495–0.5505)	13.940 (0.5488)
Rear axle runout	0.01 (0.0004)	0.2 (0.0079)
Rear brake lining thickness	4.9–5.0 (0.1929–0.1969)	2.5 (0.0984)
Rear brake drum I. D.	160.0–160.3 (6.2992–6.3110)	161 (6.3386)
Front suspension spring free length	478.6 (18.843)	450 (17.717)
Rear suspension spring free length	210.4 (8.284)	190 (7.480)
Rear fork pivot bushing-to-center collar clearance	0.1–0.3 (0.0039–0.0118)	0.5 (0.02)
Rear fork bushing I. D.	21.5–21.552 (0.8465–0.8485)	21.70 (0.8543)
Center collar O. D.	21.427–21.460 (0.8436–0.8449)	21.35 (0.8406)
Front fork bottom case I. D.	33.000–33.039 (1.2992–1.3007)	33.18 (1.3063)
Front fork Pipe O. D.	32.90–32.98 (1.2952–1.2984)	32.875 (1.2944)

VI. SERVICE DATA

5. WIRING DIAGRAM

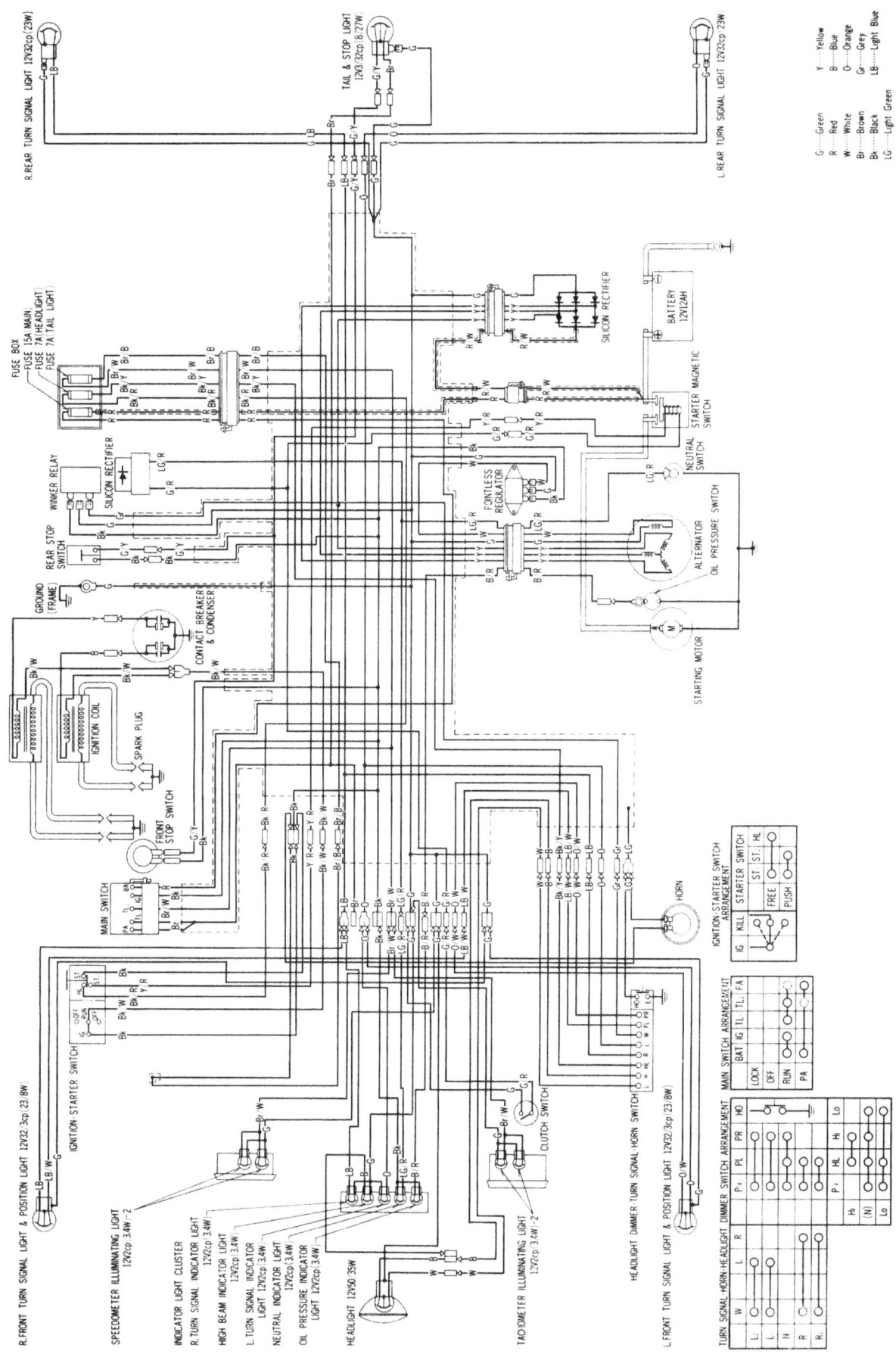

6. ROUTING

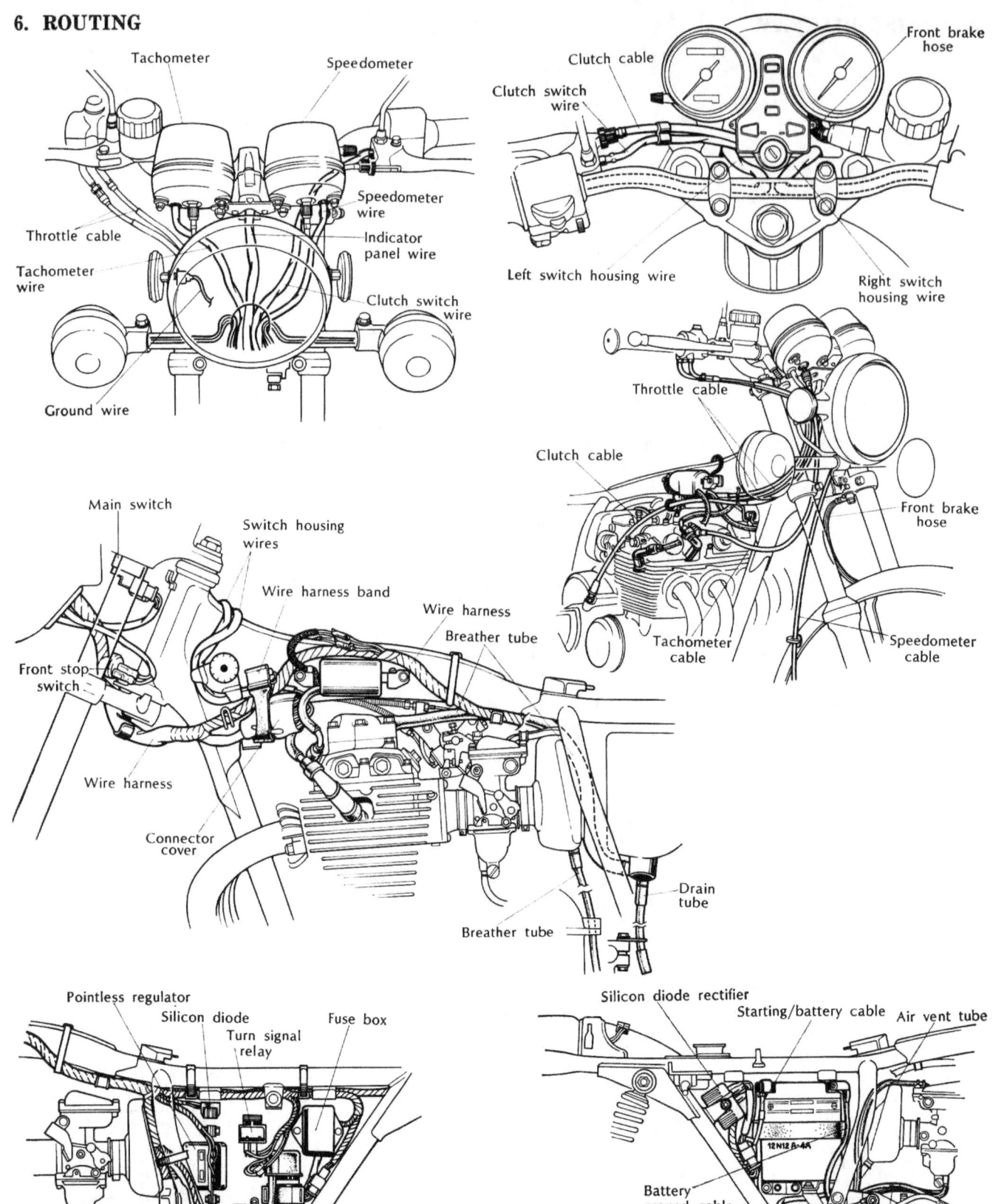

7. SPECIFICATION

	Item	Specification
Dimension	Overall length	2,040 mm (80.3 in.)
	Overall width	705 mm (27.8 in.)
	Overall height	1,040 mm (40.9 in.)
	Wheel base	1,355 mm (53.3 in.)
	Seat height	790 mm (31.1 in.)
	Foot peg height	330 mm (13.0 in.)
	Ground clearance	150 mm (5.9 in.)
	Dry weight	170 kg (375 lbs.)
Frame	Type	Semi-double cradle
	F. suspension, travel	Telescopic fork, Travel 114.5 mm (4.5 in.)
	R. suspension, travel	Swing arm, Travel 79.0 mm (3.1 in.)
	F. tire size, pressure	3.00S18 (4PR), Air pressure 1.8 kg/cm² (26 psi)
	R. tire size, pressure	3.50S18 (4PR), Air pressure 2.0/25 kg/cm² (28/36 psi)
	F. brake, lining area	Disc brake, Lining swept areas 38 cm² (5.9 sq. in)
	R. brake, lining area	Internal expanding shoes, Lining swept areas 70 cm² (10.9 sq. in.)
	Fuel capacity	14 lit. (3.7 U.S.gal. 3.1 Imp.gal.)
	Fuel reserve capacity	3 lit. (0.8 U.S.gal. 0.7 Imp.gal.)
	Caster angle	63°30′
	Trail length	85 mm (3.3 in.)
	Front fork oil capacity	160–165 cc (to fill if dry) (5.6–5.8 ozs.)
	Front fork oil capacity	145–150 cc (refill after draining) (4.8–4.9 ozs.)
Engine	Type	Air cooled, 4-stroke O.H.C. engine
	Cylinder arrangement	Vertical four parallel
	Bore and stroke	51.0 × 50.0 mm (2.008 × 1.969 in.)
	Displacement	408 cc (24.9 cu·in.)
	Compression ratio	9.4 : 1
	Valve train	Chain driven over head camshaft
	Oil capacity	3.5 lit. (3.7 U.S.qt. 3.1 Imp.qt.)
	Lubrication system	Forced and wet sump
	Cylinder head compression pressure	12 kg/cm² (170.7 psi)
	Intake valve — Opens	At 5° (before top dead center)
	Intake valve — Closes	At 35° (after bottom dead center)
	Exhaust valve — Opens	At 35° (before bottom dead center)
	Exhaust valve — Closes	At 5° (after top dead center)
	Valve tappet clearance	IN·EX 0.05 mm (0.002 in.)
	Idle speed	1,200 rpm

VI. SERVICE DATA

	Item	Specifications
Carburetor	Type	Piston valve
	Setting mark	054-A
	Main jet	#75
	Slow jet	#40
	Air screw opening	2±1/2
	Float height	21 mm (0.827 in.)
Drive train	Clutch	Wet, multi-plate type
	Transmission	6-speed constant mesh
	Primary reduction	3.423
	Gear ratio I	2.733
	Gear ratio II	1.800
	Gear ratio III	1.375
	Gear ratio IV	1.111
	Gear ratio V	0.965
	Gear ratio VI	0.866
	Final reduction	2.235
	Gear shift pattern	Left foot operated return system
Electrical	Ignition	Battery and ignition coil
	Starting system	Starting motor and kick starter
	Alternator	A-C generator 0.156 kW/5,000 rpm
	Battery capacity	12V-12AH
	Spark plug	NGK D8ESL, ND X24ES
	Headlight	Low/High beam 12V-35W/50W
	Tail/stoplight	Tail/Stop 12V-3/32 cp (SAE TRADE NO. 1157)
	Turn signal light	12V-32 cp (SAE TRADE NO. 1157/1073)
	Speedometer light	12V-2 cp (SAE TRADE NO. 57)
	Tachometer light	12V-2 cp (SAE TRADE NO. 57)
	Neutral indicator light	12V-2 cp (SAE TRADE NO. 57)
	Turn signal indicator light	12V-2 cp (SAE TRADE NO. 57)
	High beam indicator light	12V-2 cp (SAE TRADE NO. 57)
	Position light	12V-3 cp (SAE TRADE NO. 1757)

VII. CB400F '77 SUPPLEMENT

Engine No. CB400FE—2100001 and subsequent
Frame No. CB400F—2100001 and subsequent

1. MAINTENANCE SCHEDULE

MAINTENANCE SCHEDULE		INITIAL SERVICE PERIOD	REGULAR SERVICE PERIOD Perform at every indicated month or mileage interval whichever occurs first.			
	Month	—	1	3	6	12
	Mile	500	500	1,500	3,000	6,000
Engine Oil		R	R			
Engine Oil Filter Element		R			R	
Engine Oil Filter Screen						C
Spark Plugs					I	
*Contact Breaker Points		I			I	
*Ignition Timing		I			I	
*Valve Tappet Clearance		I			I	
*Cam Chain Tension		I			I	
Air Filter Elements		(Service more frequently if operated in dusty areas.)			C	R
Air Filter Breather Element					I	
*Carburetors		I			I	
Throttle Operation		I			I	
*Fuel Filter Screen					C	
Fuel Lines					I	
*Clutch		I			I	
Drive Chain		**I & L	I & L			
Brake Fluid Level		I			I	
*Brake Fluid		R (24 months or 12,000 miles)				
*Brake Shoes/Pads					I	
Brake Control Linkage		I			I	
*Wheel Rims and Spokes		I			I	
Tires		I			I	
Front Fork Oil		***R				R
Front and Rear Suspension		I			I	
Rear Fork Bushing					I & L	
*Steering Head Bearings						I
*Side Stand					I	
Battery		I		I		
Lighting Equipment		I			I	
Nuts, Bolts (Tighten)		I			I	

I—Inspect, clean, adjust or replace if necessary R—Replace C—Clean L—Lubricate
Items marked * should be serviced by an authorized HONDA dealer, unless the owner has proper tools and is mechanically proficient. Other maintenance items may be serviced by the owner. ** Initial service period 200 miles. *** Initial service period 1,500 miles.

2. SPECIFICATIONS

	Item	Specification
Dimension	Overall length	2,040 mm (80.3 in.)
	Overall width	780 mm (30.7 in.)
	Overall height	1,080 mm (42.5 in.)
	Wheel base	1,355 mm (53.3 in.)
	Ground clearance	150 mm (5.9 in.)
	Dry weight	170 kg (375 lbs.)
Frame	Type	Semi-double cradle
	F. suspension, travel	Telescopic fork, Travel 114.5 mm (4.5 in.)
	R. suspension, travel	Swing arm, Travel 79.0 mm (3.1 in.)
	F. tire size, pressure	3.00S18 (4PR), Air pressure 1.75 kg/cm² (25 psi)
	R. tire size, pressure	3.50S18 (4PR), Air pressure 2.0/2.5 kg/cm² (28/36 psi)
	F. brake, lining area	Disc brake, Lining swept area 564 cm² (57.4 sq.in)
	R. brake, lining area	Internal expanding shoes, Lining swept area 150 cm² (23.2 sq.in)
	Fuel capacity	13.5 lit. (3.5 U.S.gal. 3.0 Imp.gal.)
	Fuel reserve capacity	3.5 lit. (0.9 U.S.gal. 0.8 Imp.gal.)
	Caster angle	63°30′
	Trail length	85 mm (3.3 in.)
	Front fork oil capacity	160–165 cc (to fill if dry) (5.0–5.8 ozs.)
	Front fork oil capacity	145–150 cc (refill after draining) (4.8–4.9 ozs.)
Engine	Type	Air cooled, 4-stroke O.H.C. engine
	Cylinder arrangement	Vertical four parallel
	Bore and stroke	51.0 × 50.0 mm (2.008 × 1.969 in.)
	Displacement	408 cc (24.9 cu·in.)
	Compression ratio	9.4 : 1
	Valve train	Chain driven over head camshaft
	Oil capacity	3.5 lit. (3.7 U.S.qt. 3.1 Imp.qt.)
	Lubrication system	Forced and wet sump
	Cylinder head compression pressure	12 kg/cm² (170.7 psi.)
	Intake valve — Opens	At 5° (before top dead center)
	Intake valve — Closes	At 35° (after bottom dead center)
	Exhaust valve — Opens	At 35° (before bottom dead center)
	Exhaust valve — Closes	At 5° (after top dead center)
	Valve tappet clearance	IN·EX 0.05 mm (0.002 in.)
	Idle speed	1,200 rpm
Electrical	Ignition advance: "F" mark	10° BTDC
	Max. advance	33°–36° BTDC
	RPM from "F" to max. advance	1,400–2,500 rpm
	Dwell angle	190 ± 5°
	Condenser capacity	0.20–0.24 μF

VELOCEPRESS MANUALS – MOTORCYCLE BY MAKE

AJS 1932-1948 SINGLES & TWINS 250cc THRU 1000cc (BOOK OF)
AJS 1945-1960 SINGLES 350cc & 500cc MODELS 16 & 18 (BOOK OF)
AJS 1955-1965 SINGLES 350cc & 500cc (BOOK OF)
AJS 1957-1966 FACTORY WSM - ALL SINGLES & TWINS
ARIEL UP TO 1932 (BOOK OF)
ARIEL 1932-1939 PREWAR MODELS (BOOK OF)
ARIEL 1933-1951 (WORKSHOP MANUAL)
ARIEL 1939-1960 4 STROKE SINGLES (BOOK OF)
ARIEL 1958-1964 LEADER & ARROW FACTORY WSM & PARTS LIST
ARIEL 1958-1964 LEADER & ARROW (BOOK OF)
BMW R26 R27 (1956-1967) FACTORY WORKSHOP MANUAL
BMW R50 R50S R60 R69S (1955-1969) FACTORY WORKSHOP MANUAL
BRIDGESTONE 90 SERIES FACTORY WSM & PARTS CATALOGUE
BRIDGESTONE 175 SERIES FACTORY WSM & PARTS CATALOGUE
BRIDGESTONE 350 SERIES FACTORY WSM & PARTS CATALOGUES
BSA SERVICE SHEETS MASTER CATALOGUE ALL MODELS 1945-1967
BSA BANTAM D1 TO D7 1948-1966 FACTORY SERVICE SHEETS MANUAL
BSA BANTAM ALL MODELS FROM 1948 ONWARDS (BOOK OF)
BSA DANDY FACTORY WORKSHOP MANUAL (COMPILATION)
BSA SINGLES & V-TWINS UP TO 1927 (BOOK OF)
BSA SINGLES & V-TWINS UP TO 1930 (BOOK OF)
BSA SINGLES & V-TWINS UP TO 1935 (BOOK OF)
BSA SINGLES & V-TWINS 1936-1939 (BOOK OF)
BSA C10, C11 & C12 1945-1958 FACTORY SERVICE SHEETS MANUAL
BSA OHV & SV SINGLES 250-600cc 1945-1959 (BOOK OF)
BSA C15 & B40 1958-1967 FACTORY SERVICE SHEETS MANUAL
BSA OHV & SV SINGLES 250cc (ONLY) 1954-1970 (BOOK OF)
BSA B31, B32, B33 & B34 1945-60 FACTORY SERVICE SHEETS MANUAL
BSA OHV SINGLES 350 & 500cc 1955-1967 (BOOK OF)
BSA M20, M21 & M33 1945-1963 FACTORY SERVICE SHEETS MANUAL
BSA TWINS A7 & A10 1948-1962 FACTORY SERVICE SHEETS MANUAL
BSA TWINS A7 & A10 1948-1962 (BOOK OF)
BSA TWINS A50 & A65 1962-1965 FACTORY WORKSHOP MANUAL
BSA TWINS A50 & A65 1962-1969 (SECOND BOOK OF)
DOUGLAS 1929-1939 PREWAR ALL MODELS (BOOK OF)
DOUGLAS 1948-1957 POSTWAR ALL MODELS FACTORY SHOP MANUAL
DUCATI 160cc, 250cc & 350cc OHC WORKSHOP MANUAL
HONDA 50cc ALL MODELS UP TO 1970 INC MONKEY & TRAIL (BOOK OF)
HONDA 90cc ALL MODELS UP TO 1966 (BOOK OF)
HONDA TWINS & SINGLES 50cc THRU 305cc 1960-1966 (BOOK OF)
HONDA TWINS ALL MODELS 125cc THRU 450cc UP TO 1968 (BOOK OF)
HONDA C100 50cc SUPER CUB O.H.V. 1958 ONWARDS FACTORY WSM
HONDA C110 50cc SPORT CUB O.H.V. 1960 ONWARDS FACTORY WSM
HONDA 50-65-70-90cc O.H.C. SINGLES 1959-1983 FACTORY WSM
HONDA 100-125cc SINGLES CB/CD/CL/SL/TL 1970-1984 FACTORY WSM
HONDA 125-150cc TWINS C/CS/CB/CA 1959-1966 FACTORY WSM
HONDA 125-160-175-200cc TWINS 1965-1978 WORKSHOP MANUAL
HONDA 250-305cc TWINS C/CS/CB 1961-1968 FACTORY WSM
HOHDA 250-350cc TWINS CB/CL/SL 1968-1973 FACTORY WSM
HONDA 250-360cc TWINS CB/CL/CJ 1974-1977 FACTORY WSM
HONDA 350F & 400F 4-CYLINDER 1972-1977 FACTORY WSM
HONDA 450cc TWINS CB/CL 1965-1974 K0 TO K7 WORKSHOP MANUAL
HONDA 500cc & 550cc 4-CYL 1971-1978 FACTORY WORKSHOP MANUAL
HONDA 750cc SHOC 4-CYL 1969-1978 K0~K8 FACTORY WSM
INDIAN PONYBIKE, BOY RACER & PAPOOSE ILL PARTS LIST & SALES LIT
J.A.P. ENGINES 1927-1952 & MOTORCYCLES 1934-1952 (BOOK OF)
MATCHLESS 1931-1939 ALL MODELS 250cc THRU 990cc (BOOK OF)
MATCHLESS 1945-1956 350 & 500cc SINGLES (BOOK OF)
MATCHLESS 1955-1966 350 & 500cc SINGLES (BOOK OF)
MATCHLESS 1957-1966 FACTORY WSM - ALL SINGLES & TWINS
NEW IMPERIAL ALL SV & OHV FROM 1935 ONWARDS (BOOK OF)
NORTON 1932-1939 PREWAR MODELS (BOOK OF)
NORTON 1932-1947 (BOOK OF)
NORTON 1938-1956 (BOOK OF)
NORTON 1945-1963 MODELS 16H, Big4, ES2, 19 & 50 WSM'S & PARTS
NORTON 1955-1963 MODELS 19, 50 & ES2 (BOOK OF)
NORTON 1948-1970 DOMINATOR TWINS FACTORY WSM'S & PARTS
NORTON 1955-1965 DOMINATOR TWINS (BOOK OF)
NORTON 1960-1970 TWIN CYLINDER FACTORY WORKSHOP MANUAL
NORTON 1970-1975 COMMANDO 850 & 750cc FACTORY WSM
NORTON 1975-1978 MK 3 COMMANDO 850 cc FACTORY WSM
PANTHER 1932-1958 LIGHTWEIGHT MODELS 250 & 350cc (BOOK OF)
PANTHER 1938-1966 HEAVYWEIGHT MODELS 600 & 650cc (BOOK OF)
RALEIGH MOTORCYCLES 1919-1933 (BOOK OF)
ROYAL ENFIELD 1934-1946 SINGLES & V TWINS (BOOK OF)
ROYAL ENFIELD 1937-1953 SINGLES & V TWINS (BOOK OF)
ROYAL ENFIELD 1946-1962 SINGLES (BOOK OF)
ROYAL ENFIELD 1952-1963 700cc TWINS FACTORY WORKSHOP MANUAL
ROYAL ENFIELD 1958-1966 250cc & 350cc SINGLES (SECOND BOOK OF)
ROYAL ENFIELD 1962-1970 INTERCEPTOR WSM'S & PARTS (Compilation)
RUDGE 1933-1939 (BOOK OF)
SUNBEAM 1928-1939 (BOOK OF)
SUNBEAM 1946-1957 S7 & S8 (BOOK OF)
SUZUKI 50cc & 80cc UP TO 1966 (BOOK OF)
SUZUKI T10 1963-1967 FACTORY WORKSHOP MANUAL
SUZUKI T20 & T200 1965-1969 FACTORY WORKSHOP MANUAL
SUZUKI TWINS 1962 ONWARDS 125-500cc WORKSHOP MANUAL
TRIUMPH 1935-1949 SINGLES & TWINS (BOOK OF)
TRIUMPH 1937-1951 (WORKSHOP MANUAL)
TRIUMPH 1945-1955 FACTORY WORKSHOP MANUAL
TRIUMPH 1945-1959 TWINS (BOOK OF)
TRIUMPH 1956-1969 TWINS (BOOK OF)
TRIUMPH 1963-1970 UNIT CONSTRUCTION 650cc FACTORY WSM
TRIUMPH 1963-1974 UNIT CONSTRUCTION 350-500cc FACTORY WSM
TRIUMPH 1968-1974 TRIDENT T150 & T150V FACTORY WSM
VELOCETTE 1925-1970 ALL SINGLES & TWINS (BOOK OF)
VELOCETTE 1933-1952 MOV-MAC-MSS RIGID FRAME FACTORY WSM
VELOCETTE 1954-1971 MSS-VENOM-THRUXTON-VIPER FACTORY WSM
VILLIERS ENGINE UP TO 1959 INC. 3 WHEELERS (BOOK OF)
VILLIERS ENGINE UP TO 1969 (BOOK OF)
VINCENT 1935-1955 (WORKSHOP MANUAL)
YAMAHA 1961-1967 YA5 & YA6 (WORKSHOP MANUAL & ILL PARTS LIST)
YAMAHA 1971-1972 JT18 & JT2 (WORKSHOP MANUAL & ILL PARTS LIST)

VELOCEPRESS TECHNICAL BOOKS – MOTORCYCLE

1930'S BRITISH MOTORCYCLE CARBS & ELEC COMPONENTS (BOOK OF)
1930'S BRITISH MOTORCYCLE ENGINES (OVERHAUL & MAINTENANCE)
1930'S BRITISH MOTORCYCLE GEARBOXES & CLUTCHES (BOOK OF)
CATALOG OF BRITISH MOTORCYCLES (1951 MODELS)
LUCAS ELECTRONICS BRITISH M/CYCLES REPAIR & PARTS (1950-1977)
MOTORCYCLE ENGINEERING (P.E. Irving)
MOTORCYCLE ROAD TESTS 1949-1953 (Motor Cycle Magazine UK)
SPEED AND HOW TO OBTAIN IT (Motor Cycle Magazine UK)
TUNING FOR SPEED (P.E. Irving)
WIPAC (COMBO) MANUAL NUMBER 3 + M/CYCLE & SCOOTER MANUAL

VELOCEPRESS MANUALS – SCOOTERS BY MAKE

BSA SUNBEAM SCOOTER WORKSHOP MANUAL 1959-1965
BSA SUNBEAM SCOOTER 1959-1965 (BOOK OF)
LAMBRETTA 1947-1957 ALL 125 & 150cc MODELS (BOOK OF)
LAMBRETTA 1957-1970 LI & TV MODELS (SECOND BOOK OF)
NSU PRIMA 1956-1964 ALL MODELS (BOOK OF)
TRIUMPH TIGRESS SCOOTER WORKSHOP MANUAL 1959-1965
TRIUMPH TIGRESS SCOOTER (BOOK OF)
VESPA 1951-1961 (BOOK OF)
VESPA 1955-1963 125 & 150cc & GS MODELS (SECOND BOOK OF)
VESPA 1955-1968 GS & SS (BOOK OF)
VESPA 1963-1972 90, 125 & 150cc (THIRD BOOK OF)

VELOCEPRESS MANUALS – MOPEDS & MOTORIZED BICYCLES

CYCLEMOTOR (BOOK OF)
NSU QUICKLY 1953-1963 ALL MODELS (BOOK OF)
PUCH MAXI N & S MAINTENANCE & REPAIR (3 MANUAL COMPILATION)
RALEIGH MOPEDS 1960-1969 (BOOK OF)

VELOCEPRESS MANUALS - THREE WHEELER'S

BOND MINICAR THREE WHEELER 1948-1967 (BOOK OF)
BMW ISETTA FACTORY WORKSHOP MANUAL
BSA THREE WHEELER (BOOK OF)
RELIANT REGAL THREE WHEELER 1952-1973 (BOOK OF)
VINTAGE MORGAN THREE WHEELER (BOOK OF)

VELOCEPRESS MANUALS – AUTOMOBILE BY MAKE

ALFA ROMEO GIULIA WORKSHOP MANUAL 1300 TO 2000cc 1962-1975
ALFA ROMEO GIULIA TECH MANUAL CARBURETED CARS FROM 1962
ALFA ROMEO GIULIA TECH MANUAL FUEL INJECTED CARS FROM 1969
ALFA ROMEO GIULIETTA & GIULIA 750 & 101 SERIES 1955-1965 WSM
AUSTIN-HEALEY SPRITE & MG MIDGET WORKSHOP MANUAL 1958-1971
BMW 600 LIMOUSINE FACTORY WORKSHOP MANUAL
BMW 600 LIMOUSINE OWNERS HAND BOOK & SERVICE MANUAL
BMW 2000 & 2002 1966-1976 WORKSHOP MANUAL
CORVAIR 1960-1969 WORKSHOP MANUAL
CORVETTE V8 1955-1962 WORKSHOP MANUAL
FERRARI HANDBOOK ROAD & RACE CARS (SERVICE/SPECS) 1948-1958
FERRARI 250/GT SERVICE & MAINTENANCE MANUAL 1956-1965
FIAT 500 FACTORY WORKSHOP MANUAL 1957-1973
FIAT 600, 600D & MULTIPLA FACTORY WORKSHOP MANUAL 1955-1969
JAGUAR E-TYPE 3.8 & 4.2 SERIES 1 & 2 WORKSHOP MANUAL
JAGUAR MK 7, 8, 9 & XK120, 140, 150 WORKSHOP MANUAL 1948-1961
METROPOLITAN FACTORY WORKSHOP MANUAL
MGA & MGB OWNERS HANDBOOK & WORKSHOP MANUAL
MG MIDGET TC, TD, TF & TF1500 WORKSHOP MANUAL
PORSCHE 356 1948-1965 WORKSHOP MANUAL
PORSCHE 911 2.0, 2.2, 2.4 LITRE 1964-1973 WORKSHOP MANUAL
PORSCHE 911 2.7, 3.0, 3.2 LITRE 1973-1989 WORKSHOP MANUAL
PORSCHE 912 WORKSHOP MANUAL
PORSCHE 914/4 & 914/6 1.7, 1.8, 2.0 LITRE 1970-1976 WSM
TRIUMPH TR2, TR3, TR4 1953-1965 WORKSHOP MANUAL
VOLKSWAGEN TRANSPORTER, TRUCKS & WAGONS 1950-1979 WSM
VOLVO 1944-1968 ALL MODELS WORKSHOP MANUAL

VELOCEPRESS TECHNICAL BOOKS - AUTOMOBILE

HOW TO BUILD A FIBERGLASS CAR
HOW TO BUILD A RACING CAR
HOW TO RESTORE THE MODEL 'A' FORD
MASERATI OWNER'S HANDBOOK
PERFORMANCE TUNING THE SUNBEAM TIGER
SOUPING THE VOLKSWAGEN
SOLEX CARBURETORS (EMPHASIS ON UK & EU AUTOMOBILES)
SU CARBURETORS (EMPHASIS ON UK AUTOMOBILES)
WEBER CARBURETORS (EMPHASIS ON ALFA & FIAT)

VELOCEPRESS BOOKS & GUIDES - AUTOMOBILE

COMPLETE CATALOG OF JAPANESE MOTOR VEHICLES
FERRARI 308 SERIES BUYER'S AND OWNER'S GUIDE
FERRARI BROCHURES AND SALES LITERATURE 1968-1989
FERRARI SERIAL NUMBERS PART I - ODD NUMBERS TO 21399
FERRARI SERIAL NUMBERS PART II - EVEN NUMBERS TO 1050
HENRY'S FABULOUS MODEL "A" FORD
MASERATI BROCHURES AND SALES LITERATURE

VELOCEPRESS BOOKS – RACING

CARRERA PANAMERICANA - MEXICAN ROAD RACE (BOOK OF)
DIALED IN - THE JAN OPPERMAN STORY
VEDA ORR'S NEW REVISED HOT ROD PICTORIAL

www.VelocePress.com

Please check our website:

www.VelocePress.com

for a complete
up-to-date list of
available titles

www.ingramcontent.com/pod-product-compliance
Lightning Source LLC
Chambersburg PA
CBHW080747300426
44114CB00019B/2667